# Brilliant Microsoft® Windows 8 for the Over 50s

Joli Ballew

PEARSON

Harlow, England • London • New York • Boston • San Francisco • Toronto • Sydney • Auckland • Singapore • Hong Kong
Tokyo • Seoul • Taipei • New Delhi • Cape Town • São Paulo • Mexico City • Madrid • Amsterdam • Munich • Paris • Milan

**PEARSON EDUCATION LIMITED**
Edinburgh Gate
Harlow CM20 2JE
United Kingdom
Tel: +44 (0)1279 623623
Web: www.pearson.com/uk

---

**First published 2013** (print and electronic)



ISBN: 978-0-273-78429-6 (print)
978-0-273-78430-2 (PDF)

*British Library Cataloguing-in-Publication Data*
A catalogue record for the print edition is available from the British Library

*Library of Congress Cataloging-in-Publication Data*
A catalog record for the print edition is available from the Library of Congress



10 9 8 7 6 5 4 3 2 1
16 15 14 13 12

Print edition typeset in 11/14pt Arial MT Std Condensed by 30
Print edition printed and bound by L.E.G.O. S.p.A., Italy

NOTE THAT ANY PAGE CROSS-REFERENCES REFER TO THE PRINT EDITION

# Brilliant guides

## What you need to know and how to do it

When you're working on your computer and come up against a problem that you're unsure how to solve, or want to accomplish something in an application that you aren't sure how to do, where do you look? Manuals and traditional training guides are usually too big and unwieldy and are intended to be used as end-to-end training resources, making it hard to get to the info you need right away without having to wade through pages of background information that you just don't need at that moment – and helplines are rarely that helpful!

*Brilliant* guides have been developed to allow you to find the info you need easily and without fuss and guide you through the task using a highly visual, step-by-step approach – providing exactly what you need to know when you need it!

*Brilliant* guides provide the quick easy-to-access information that you need, using a table of contents and troubleshooting guide to help you find exactly what you need to know, and then presenting each task in a visual manner. Numbered steps guide you through each task or problem, using numerous screenshots to illustrate each step. Added features include 'See also...' boxes that point you to related tasks and information in the book, while 'Did you know?...' sections alert you to relevant expert tips, tricks and advice to further expand your skills and knowledge.

In addition to covering all major office PC applications, and related computing subjects, the *Brilliant* series also contains titles that will help you in every aspect of your working life, such as writing the perfect CV, answering the toughest interview questions and moving on in your career.

*Brilliant* guides are the light at the end of the tunnel when you are faced with any minor or major task.

# Author's acknowledgements

I'd like to thank everyone at Pearson UK for, once again, trusting me with a *Brilliant* title, as well as my agent Neil Salkind of The Salkind Literary Agency and Studio B for inviting me to take it on. I'd also like to thank Robert Cottee and Steve Temblett for their help managing the project, Melanie Carter for her editorial guidance and all members of the production team who copy-edited, proof-read and produced the finished work. I know the amount of work that goes into producing a book after the writing is done and appreciate their efforts.

# Publisher's acknowledgements

We are grateful to the following for permission to reproduce copyright material:

Amazon screenshot © 2010 Amazon.com Inc. and its affiliates. All rights reserved; Facebook screenshot courtesy of Facebook, Inc.; Twitter screenshots courtesy of Twitter, Inc.

In some instances we have been unable to trace the owners of copyright material, and we would appreciate any information that would enable us to do so.

## About the author

Joli Ballew is the author of close to 50 books, many with Pearson. She is a Professor at Brookhaven Community College in Dallas, Texas and is also the Microsoft IT Academy Coordinator there. In her spare time she enjoys working out at the gym, visiting her favourite pub (Chase Place) and taking care of her pets. More than anything, she loves spending time with her new granddaughter Allison.

## Dedication

For Dad, who, at 92, still hangs on, tries hard and is always in a good mood.

# Contents

# Introduction

i

Welcome to *Brilliant Windows 8 for the Over 50s*, a visual quick reference that will help you get the most you can from Windows 8. In this book you'll learn how to use Windows 8, or transition to it, with the least amount of effort possible!

## Find what you need to know – when you need it

You don't have to read this book in any particular order. We've designed the book so that you can jump in, get the information you need and jump out. To find the information that you need, just look up the task in the table of contents or Troubleshooting guide, and turn to the page listed. Read the task introduction, follow the step-by-step instructions along with the illustration, and you're done.

## How this book works

Each task is presented with step-by-step instructions in one column and screen illustrations in the other. This arrangement lets you focus on a single task without having to turn the pages too often.

### What you'll do

## Step-by-step instructions

This book provides concise step-by-step instructions that show you how to accomplish a task. Each set of instructions includes illustrations that directly correspond to the easy-to-read steps. Eye-catching text features provide additional helpful information in bite-sized chunks to help you work more efficiently or to teach you more in-depth information. The 'For your information' features provide tips and techniques to help you work smarter, while the 'See also' cross-references lead you to other parts of the book containing related information about the task. Essential information is highlighted in 'Important' boxes that will ensure you don't miss any vital suggestions and advice.

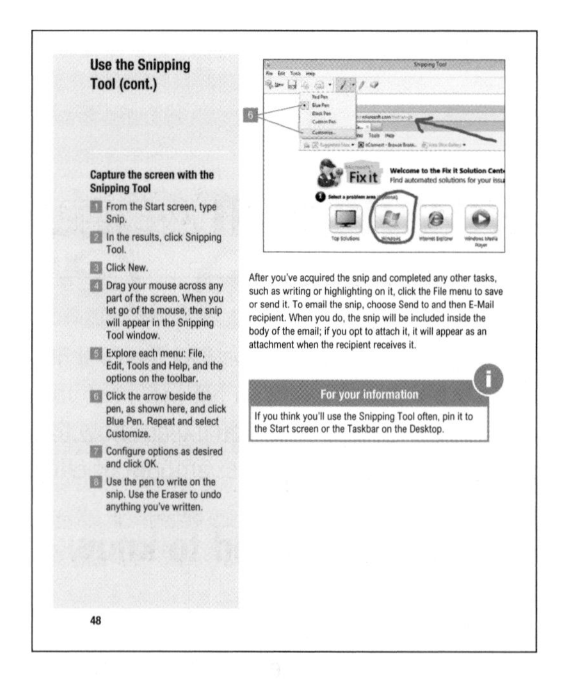
**Use the Snipping Tool (cont.)**

**Capture the screen with the Snipping Tool**

1. From the Start screen, type Snip.
2. In the results, click Snipping Tool.
3. Click New.
4. Drag your mouse across any part of the screen. When you let go of the mouse, the snip will appear in the Snipping Tool window.
5. Explore each menu: File, Edit, Tools and Help, and the options on the toolbar.
6. Click the arrow beside the pen, as shown here, and click Blue Pen. Repeat and select Customize.
7. Configure options as desired and click OK.
8. Use the pen to write on the snip. Use the Eraser to undo anything you've written.

After you've acquired the snip and completed any other tasks, such as writing or highlighting on it, click the File menu to save or send it. To email the snip, choose Send to and then E-Mail recipient. When you do, the snip will be included inside the body of the email; if you opt to attach it, it will appear as an attachment when the recipient receives it.

**For your information**

If you think you'll use the Snipping Tool often, pin it to the Start screen or the Taskbar on the Desktop.

48

## Troubleshooting guide

This book offers quick and easy ways to diagnose and solve common problems that you might encounter, using the Troubleshooting guide. The problems are grouped into categories that are presented alphabetically.

**Troubleshooting guide**



## Spelling

We have used UK spelling conventions throughout this book. You may therefore notice some inconsistencies between the text and the software on your computer, which is likely to have been developed in the US. We have, however, adopted US spelling for the words 'disk' and 'program', as these are commonly accepted throughout the world.

# 1

# Get to know Windows 8

## Introduction

You've made the move to Windows 8 – congratulations! It doesn't matter how you got here, what kind of device you have, or if you upgraded an old system or purchased a new one. You have some version of Windows 8 and you're ready to use it.

First things first, though. You have to turn on your new computer, laptop or tablet and work through the setup process. Part of this process involves naming your computer; logging in with an existing Microsoft account or creating one, or creating a local account; joining a network if applicable; and configuring a few settings. With that done, you have to bypass the Lock screen and log in. These are the first two things you'll learn how to do in this book. If you've already done this, you can skip past the first section.

Once you have access to Windows 8, the main thing you'll notice after bypassing the Lock screen is that it looks much different from any other Windows-based computer you've used. Windows 8 opens at a Start screen, not the Desktop. This new Start screen can be somewhat daunting at first glance – that may have been what prompted you to buy this book. Don't worry, though, the Start screen is just a new-fangled way to access and use your computer. You'll use the Start screen to get to the familiar Desktop (complete with the Recycle Bin and Taskbar), access a web browser so you can surf the Internet, and open all your installed programs. And yes, you'll use this screen to access and use the new 'apps' and to get more apps online, too.

### What you'll do

To make sure you aren't confused about apps before we even get started, note that it's highly likely you've used apps before and have some basic understanding of them already. Most smartphones, including the Windows phone, iPhone and android phones, come with apps. So does the Apple iPad, Galaxy Tab, Motorola Xoom and others. These apps help you do things and get information quickly, and are less cumbersome and easier to use than more complicated applications (referred to now as the *Desktop apps*). Apps such as those you'll find on the Start screen are the future of technology, so it's important to jump on board with them now rather than later.

## Set up Windows 8 and log in

The first time you turn on your Windows 8 device you will be prompted to make choices regarding how you'd like to set it up. Most of the decisions you'll make are simple, such as what colour you'd like the Start screen to be. Other decisions require information you'll have to look up, such as the name and password of your local network if you have one.

The only difficult decision is to decide whether you want to use a Microsoft account or create a local one. Because you must have a Microsoft account to use the Microsoft Store to get apps, movies, music and video, we suggest you go that route, but there are lots of others reasons why a Microsoft account is a better option. So that you are fully informed, though, here are the differences:

- **Microsoft Account** – a global account you use to log in to your Windows 8 computer or any other Internet-enabled Windows 8 computer. When you use this kind of account, Windows 8 will automatically configure certain apps with personalised information and your preferences and settings will be available to you no matter what computer you log on to. This means, among other things, that if you change your Start screen's colour to purple on your desktop computer at home, the next time you log on to your laptop, tablet or a child's computer with that same account, your Start screen will be purple there, too.
- **Local Account** – a personal account you use to log on to your Windows 8 computer that is associated only with that computer. Your account settings and preferences can't 'follow' you from one Windows 8 computer to another like a Microsoft Account can. You won't be able to make purchases from the Store without a Microsoft account either.

After you've decided whether or not to use a Microsoft account, you can turn on and set up your Windows 8 device. During the process you'll be prompted to input the following information:

- **Background Color** Use the slider to select the background colour of the Start screen.

### Did you know?

You can change almost anything about your current Windows 8 configuration from the PC Settings hub. You'll learn how to use this hub in various places throughout the book. However, you can always use the familiar Control Panel if you prefer.

## Set up Windows 8 and log in (cont.)

### Log in to Windows 8

1. If you have a touch screen, touch the screen or use your finger to swipe upwards from the bottom. If you have a mouse or keyboard, do any of the following:
   - **a** Swipe upwards with the mouse.
   - **b** Tap any keyboard key.
   - **c** Click with the mouse anywhere on the screen.
2. Type your password and tap Enter on the keyboard, or type your password and tap or click the right-facing arrow.
3. The Start screen appears.

- **Computer Name** Type a name for your computer, which must be unique if you have a personal network.
- **Network** Type the name, passcode and other attributes of your home network if applicable. To get the most from Windows 8 you really need an always-on Internet connection.
- **Settings** Select the default options. You can always change the settings later.
- **Microsoft Account or Local User Account** Choose how to log in to your computer. We suggest a Microsoft account. You can always change your mind later, though.
- **Password** Type the password you'll enter to unlock your computer. If you input a Microsoft account during setup, input the password already associated with that account.
- **Password Hint** Type a few words to remind you of what your password is, should you ever forget it.

**Important**

There are many different types of devices that can run Windows 8, including tablets, netbooks, laptops and desktop computers. Some tablets offer a touch screen only and not a physical keyboard. Desktop computers, laptops and high-end tablets may offer keyboard, mouse *and* touch.

Once setup is complete, and any time your computer goes to sleep or you shut it down and start it back up, the Lock screen appears. The Lock screen offers the time, the date, information about your current network connection and other information. 'Behind' the Lock screen is the option to input your password and log on to the computer. Thus, the log-in process requires two steps: bypassing the Lock screen and entering your password.

## Explore the Start screen and its apps

1

Once you gain access to the Start screen, your device is ready to use. Take a look and make a mental note of what you see. You will probably see two dozen or so colourful rectangles and squares. These are called tiles. Read the names of each of these tiles and try to imagine what its related app might offer. You may conclude that you'll click the Mail tile for email, the Photos tile to access your photos, and the Calendar tile to manage events and appointments. You'd be right.

Beyond offering access to apps, tiles for apps can serve other purposes. Some tiles offer up-to-date information for the app they represent, for instance. As an example, Mail, once configured, can show up-to-date information about new email you've received on the tile itself, and the tile for the Store can offer information about available app updates in the same manner. The information you'll see on these tiles is dynamic and changes as the information it represents does. This makes it easy to see if anything new has arrived or arisen since you last used the app. When an app shows this kind of information on its tile, it's called a live tile. The four tiles you see here are all live tiles.

Your user name appears in the top right corner of the Start screen (not shown here). You can click here to sign out or lock the computer. You can also opt to change your account picture, which opens the PC Settings hub. You'll learn about this later. You can position your cursor at the bottom of the screen and look for a scroll bar (shown here), or right-click the screen to see additional options as well.

# Explore the Start screen and its apps (cont.)

## Explore the Start screen

1. Access the Start screen. If you've somehow moved away from it, press the Windows key on the keyboard (or a Windows button on a tablet).
2. Look at each tile and imagine what its app might offer.
3. Click your user name in the top right corner. Note the options.

**Important**

If you purchased a simple tablet and it's running Windows 8 RT, you won't have access to everything that the full operating system offers. This pared-down operating system was created for such devices and does not offer every Windows 8 feature.

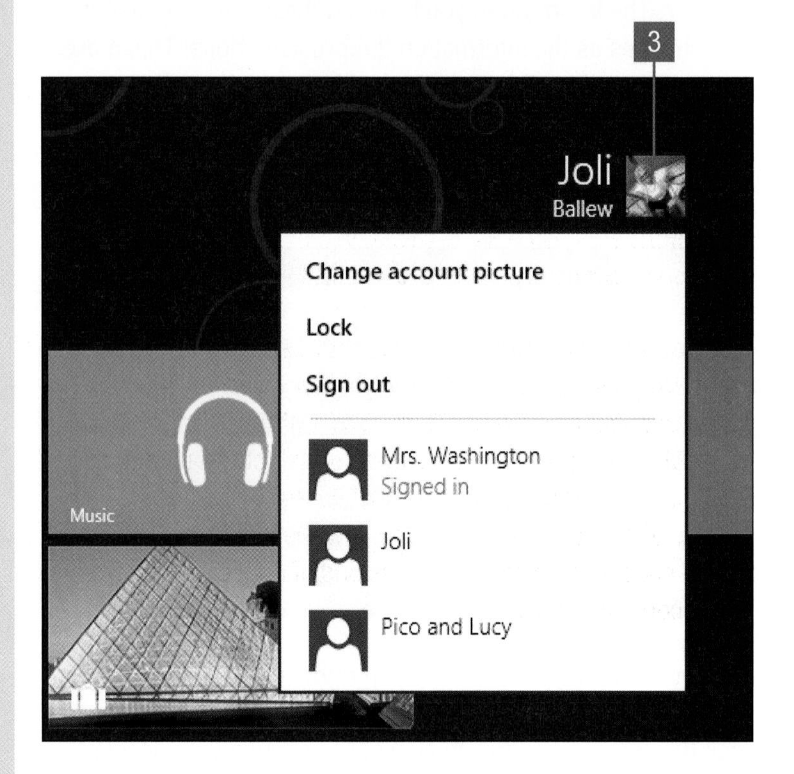

Once you're familiar with how the Start screen is configured and what it offers, you can start to concentrate on the tiles (and thus apps). When you're ready to explore, you simply click (or touch) a tile to open its related app. Because many apps get their information from the Internet, you'll also need to make sure you're connected to the Internet before you get started.

The first time you open an app you may be prompted to allow it to learn your current location, give your permission for the app to connect to a specific social account (such as Facebook), or enable the app to access other personal information already available on your computer. In most cases, if you want to use the app effectively, you'll have to allow these things. Once you've enabled the proper permissions, if applicable, the app will become functional.

## Explore the Start screen and its apps (cont.)



4 Click an empty area of the Start screen to hide the options under your user name.

5 If you have a touch screen, pinch in and out to zoom or flick your finger to scroll.

6 Position your mouse at the bottom of the screen and if you see a scroll bar, drag it from left to right to see additional apps.

7 Right-click an empty area of the Start screen. Click All apps.

8 Take a look at the list of apps available and then click the Windows key on the keyboard to return to the Start screen.

# Explore the Start screen and its apps (cont.)

## Use an app

1. From the Start screen, click Weather.
2. Click Allow to let the app discover your location.
3. Scroll right to see additional screens.
4. Right-click to view and hide options.
5. To return to the Start screen, press the Windows key on the keyboard.

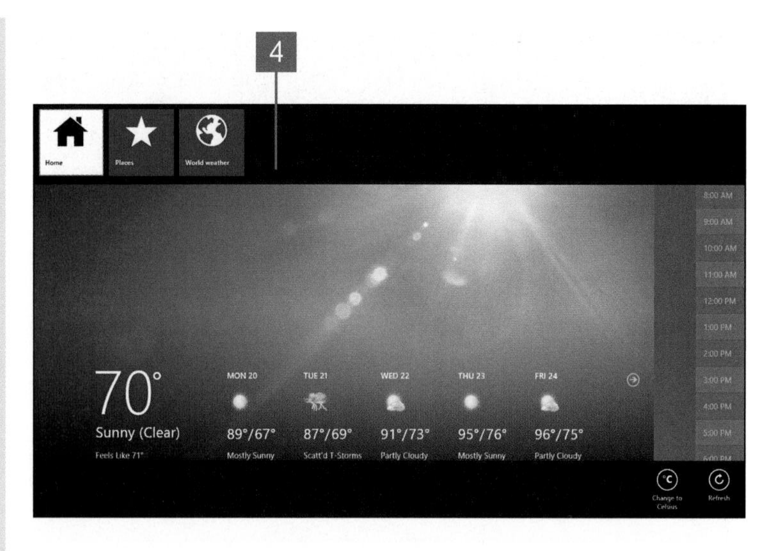


If you want to explore and use multiple apps, you'll have to know how to get back to the Start screen when you're in one. Yes, you can press the Windows key on the keyboard, but you can also:

- Move the cursor to the bottom left corner of the screen and click the Start screen thumbnail that appears.

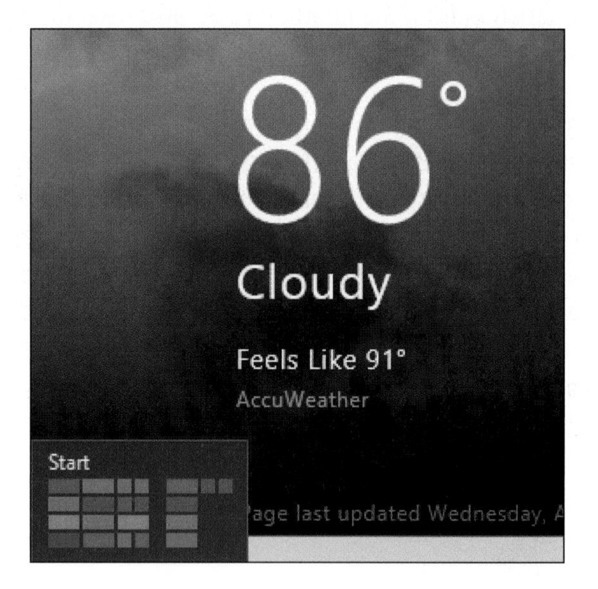


- Position your cursor in the top left corner of the screen and then slowly drag it downwards to access the Start screen thumbnail that appears (which also enables you to view and access other apps that are open).

## Explore the Start screen and its apps (cont.)

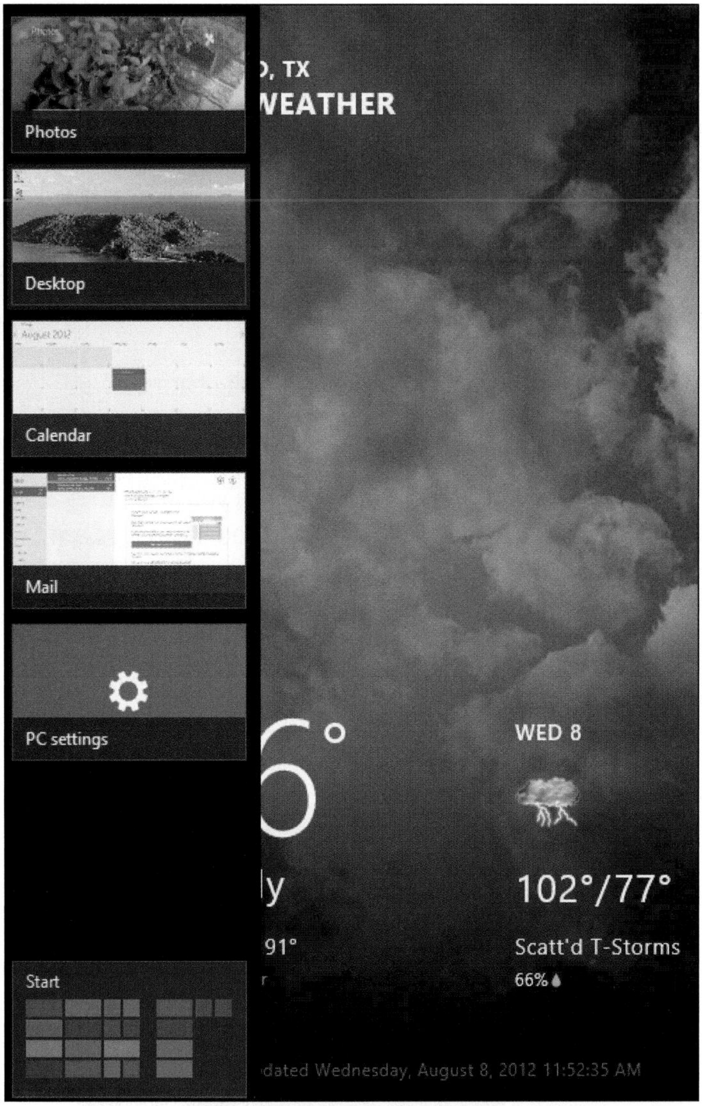

- On a tablet that offers touch only, press the Windows button on the device itself.
- Access the Start charm, detailed next.

Continue exploring apps now if you want to, otherwise move on to the next section.

## Access charms

### Access charms

- Using a keyboard, use the key combination Windows key + C.
- Using a mouse, move the cursor to the bottom right corner of the screen and when the transparent charms appear, move the cursor upwards. A corner that provides something when the cursor is positioned there is called a *hot corner.*
- Using touch, place your thumb in the middle of the right edge of the screen and flick left (inwards).

### Did you know?

The Shut Down command is available from the Settings charm, from the Power icon that appears there.

There are five default charms, and they enable you to configure settings, connect to networks and access the Start screen, among other things. You can access the charms in many ways, and charms are available from any screen and at any time. These default charms always open on the right side of the screen. Charms are not apps – they offer access to configuration options and settings related to your computer.

The following list describes the five default charms available in Windows 8, which can be accessed from the bottom right hot corner from any screen. What is available from these charms once you click them can differ depending on what app you have open when you access them. However, in general the charms offer what's listed here:

- **Settings** To personalise your computer, to get information about your computer or your network, to change the volume or brightness, to choose a power option, and more.

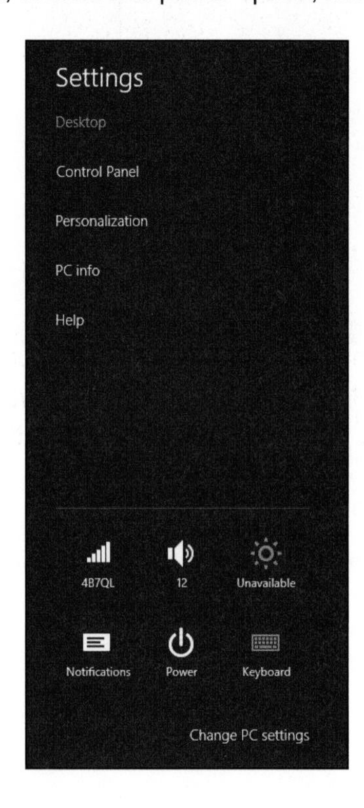

## Access charms (cont.)

- **Devices** To access and configure devices that are available for use with the current application. For instance, while in Mail, Devices offers access to available printers.
- **Start** To access the Start screen.
- **Share** To access share options applicable to the current activity or open application. While in Photos, you can opt to share a photo using Mail.
- **Search** To open the Search pane to search for anything on your computer.

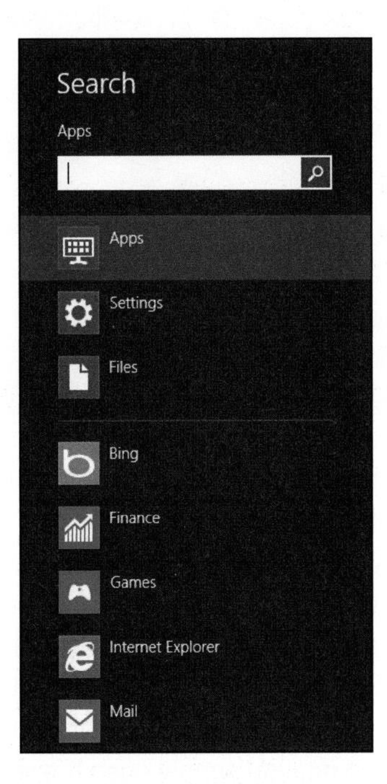


As you work through this book you'll learn more about these charms and what each one offers. Additionally, you'll learn that apps themselves offer their own options, and that you'll use those to work in the app when needed.

# Use the traditional Desktop and Explorer windows

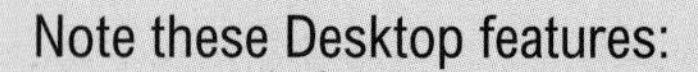

Note these Desktop features:

1. Recycle Bin – to hold items you delete.
2. Taskbar – to offer access to open windows and programs.
3. Internet Explorer – to surf the Internet using the traditional Desktop application.
4. File Explorer – to browse for files on your computer or network.
5. Action Center flag – to access the Action Center to resolve problems.
6. Network icon – to view the status of your network connection or connect to a network.
7. Volume icon – to change or mute the volume.
8. Time and date – to access time and date settings.

If you have a desktop computer, laptop, netbook or tablet, you'll have a tile on the Start screen named Desktop. This is the tile you'll use to access the familiar, traditional computing environment you're used to (if you've used a computer before, that is). The Desktop is what holds the Recycle Bin, the Taskbar, the notification area and the familiar background(s). This is where you've always accessed your personal folders and done all of your computing.

While at the Desktop you may notice that there is one major element missing. It's the Start button. No, your eyes aren't playing tricks on you! That's okay though, because if you are comfortable with the Start screen, you won't really need a Start button. You see, in Windows 8, everything ought to begin at the Start screen. So if you want to open a Desktop application, perhaps Notepad, WordPad, Paint, Control Panel, Windows Media Player and so on, you simply open it from there. When you do, the Desktop appears first and the application opens on it.

**For your information**

While on the Start screen you can simply start to type the name of the program you'd like to open and choose it from the resulting list. You'll learn more about this later.

Desktop

1

**Important**

Tablet computers that run Windows 8 RT have limited Desktop functionality.

# Use the traditional Desktop and Explorer windows (cont.)



## Access the traditional Desktop and use File Explorer

1. From the Start screen, click or touch the Desktop tile. (You can also press the Windows key + D.)
2. On the Desktop, locate the Taskbar, Recycle Bin, volume icon and so on.
3. Click the File Explorer icon.

# Use the traditional Desktop and Explorer windows (cont.)

4 In File Explorer, locate the tabs and tab commands.

5 In File Explorer, click the Pictures library in the left pane.

6 Click the View tab.

7 Click Extra large icons.

8 Continue experimenting as you wish.

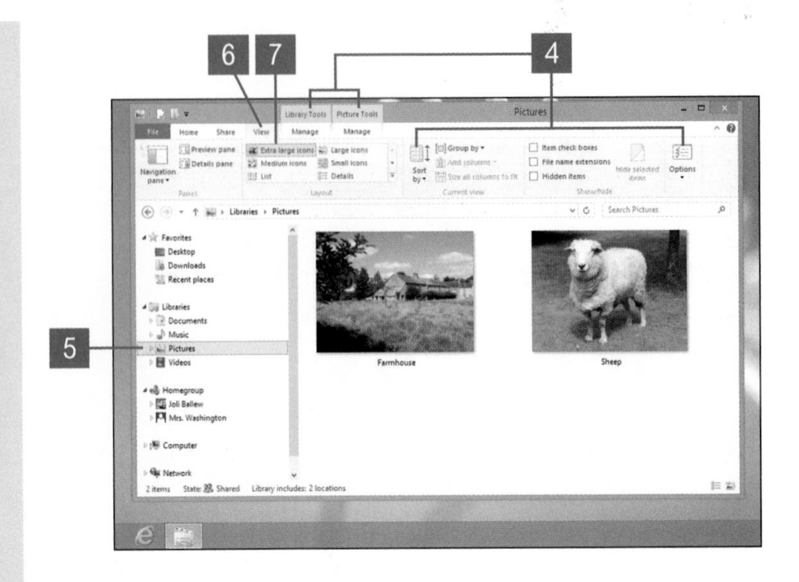


There is a shortcut to File Explorer on the Desktop's Taskbar. File Explorer (which used to be called Windows Explorer) helps you locate the data you've saved to your hard drive or any available networked computer(s). You can access your documents, music, pictures, videos and so on from one window. File Explorer also offers a 'ribbon' where you can perform tasks on data you select. You'll learn quite a bit about File Explorer as you work through this book. For now, it's important only that you understand these terms and features of File Explorer:

- **a** Tabs – tap or click to access options related to the tab's title. Common tabs include File, Home, Share and View.
- **b** Tab Commands – tap or click the commands as you wish. If a command is greyed out, it can't be used. Tab commands include options that enable you to work with selected files and folders.
- **c** Show/Hide the Ribbon – tap or click the small arrow located in the top right corner to always show the ribbon or to hide it.
- **d** Libraries – tap or click any library title to view the data you've stored there.
- **e** Favorites – tap or click any item under Favorites to access data in the folder.
- **f** Search – type keywords in the Search window to locate specific data in a folder.

## Use the traditional Desktop and Explorer windows (cont.)



?

**Did you know?**

A library is a virtual holding area that enables quick access to the related private and public folders. As an example, the Documents library offers access to My Documents and Public Documents. This makes access easy.

You'll use the Desktop and File Explorer when you want to organise the data on your hard drive. You can create folders, move and copy data, access data on networked computers and more. You'll also use the Desktop when you want to use *Desktop apps*. As you'll learn next, Desktop apps are those that require the Desktop to work and differ greatly from the apps you learned about at the beginning of this chapter.

## Know the differences between Start screen apps and Desktop apps

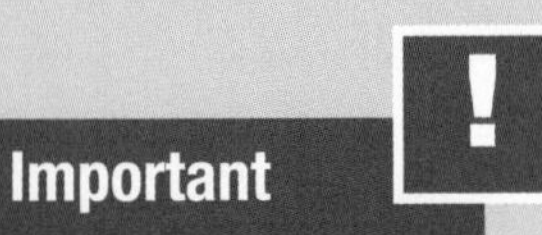

**Important**

Tablets running Windows RT are limited in desktop functionality. You can't install programs like Firefox or Photoshop, for instance. You can only install apps from the store.

The Desktop is where you'll do all of your traditional computing tasks, such as working in programs like Microsoft Word, Paint and WordPad. This is where you'll install and use third-party programs such as Adobe Photoshop Elements or Mozilla Firefox. It's also where you'll burn CDs and DVDs, configure power options, and so on. Thus, most of what you'll do while at the Desktop will be exactly what you've always done. In fact, some Desktop programs such as Internet Explorer and Windows Media Player haven't changed much at all. If you're looking for the traditional computing environment, you'll want to use the Desktop applications.

In contrast, the Start screen apps, including Weather introduced earlier, are just simple apps with minimal features. Those apps are more like what you'd see on a smartphone or an iPad. Start screen apps always have fewer features than Desktop apps, but because of this they are more streamlined and easier to use. Apps (Start screen apps) do not open on the Desktop. You won't see the Desktop background or Taskbar when you use them. You won't be bombarded with toolbars or menus; instead you'll have access to the app's specific charms. If you're trying to keep up with the latest technologies, and if you want to get a task done quickly and without all the fluff, you'll want to use the Start screen apps.

As you will learn throughout this book, some apps have both a Start screen app and a Desktop app counterpart. Internet Explorer is one of these. You'll learn about both versions in Chapter 9. For now though, so that you understand the

differences between streamlined apps and their fully fledged Desktop app counterparts, look at the interfaces of both. This is the Start screen's Internet Explorer app with its toolbar and available charms showing. You may be able to recognise the address bar (where you type the website name), and the backwards arrow which will refresh the page.

Next is the traditional Desktop app for Internet Explorer that you may already be used to. We've configured it so that all the toolbars and menus show, but they don't show by default. This is a full application and can do everything you want to do on the web. If you're looking for a traditional web browsing experience, this is the application you'll choose. Notice the Desktop shows behind it, and you have access to the settings available under Page, Safety and Tools, among other things.

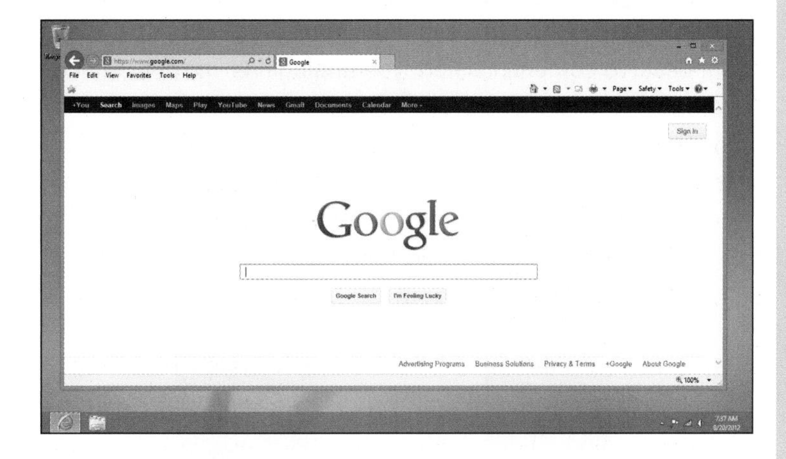


As you move forwards then, know that there are two kinds of applications. There are simple, easy-to-use apps, and there are much more feature-rich Desktop applications. As you work through this book, explore them all. If there is an application that has an app and a Desktop app version, make sure you give them both a try.

## Know the differences between Start screen apps and Desktop apps (cont.)

# Lock, sign out and shut down Windows 8

Your Windows 8 computer will go to sleep after a specific amount of idle time. You may be ready for it to go to sleep now! When this actually happens depends on several factors, including which power configuration you've selected and whether a tablet or laptop is plugged in or running on batteries. The sleep state is quite efficient and doesn't use much energy, so it's often okay to let the computer go to sleep instead of turning it off each time you've finished using it. Windows 8 also has a built-in security feature that requires you to input your password when you wake it up from sleep. You can access the sign-out and lock options from the Start screen – just click your user name.

There will be times when you want to turn off the computer or tablet completely. For instance, during aircraft takeoffs and landings, you'll be prompted to turn off all devices – you can't just let them go to sleep. Additionally, you'll want to turn off a desktop computer before you unplug it or move it. That command is a little harder to find, but is available from the Settings charms.

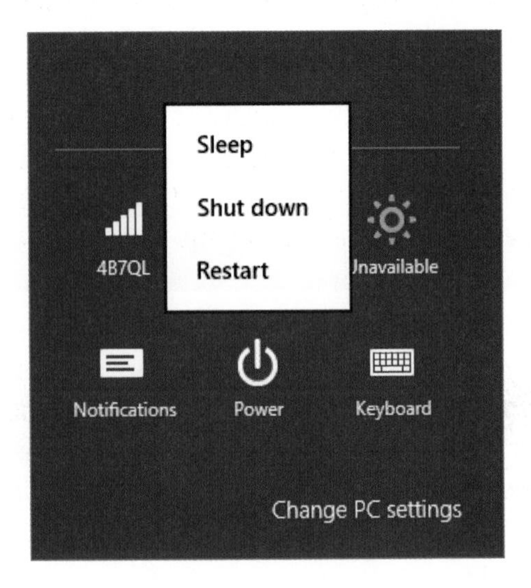


## Shut down Windows

1. Press the Windows key + I. (Alternatively, access the Settings charm using any other method.)
2. Click or tap Power.
3. Click or tap Shut down.

### Jargon buster

The Lock command locks the computer so that no one else can access it using your account. Your programs, windows and apps remain open and will be ready to use when you log back in. The sign-out command closes all your open apps and windows, and you are completely signed out of your account and your computer. When you log back in, you start a new session.

# Use apps

## Introduction

You learned a little about apps in Chapter 1; in fact, you opened and configured the Weather app there. You saw how easy it was to get information about the current weather quickly. There are more apps than Weather though. These other apps are all designed to be streamlined just like the Weather app, to enable you to do things and obtain information quickly and easily.

In this chapter you'll learn how to use and configure some of these additional apps. Specifically, you'll explore the most basic apps, such as Maps, Travel, Sports and Calendar, and two social apps, Messaging and People. (You'll learn about the Mail and various media apps later in this book.) Since most apps have common elements, such as the ability to right-click or flick up to access charms for configuring the app, and options to configure settings from the default charms, what you learn here will provide you with the framework you need to move forward successfully.

# 2

### What you'll do

**Get directions with Maps**

**Follow a team with Sports**

**Create an event in Calendar**

**Add contacts from social networks**

**Send and reply to an instant message**

**Read and reply to social networking posts**

**Create a tile for a contact on the Start screen**

**Upload a file to SkyDrive**

**Get a free app from the Store**

After you've used the apps for a while, you'll decide which app tiles you want to appear and where on your Start screen. You can reposition the tiles easily, add and remove tiles, and make rectangular tiles small and square. You can even change a tile so it does or does not show live information. In doing so, you make the computer easier to use and more personalised for you.

Finally, you'll use SkyDrive to store data online and the Store to obtain more apps. These are two additional apps you'll probably find you use often. By the time you've finished with this chapter, you'll be an app expert!

!

**Important**

Just about every app you'll use needs access to the Internet. We'll assume you're always online while reading this book.

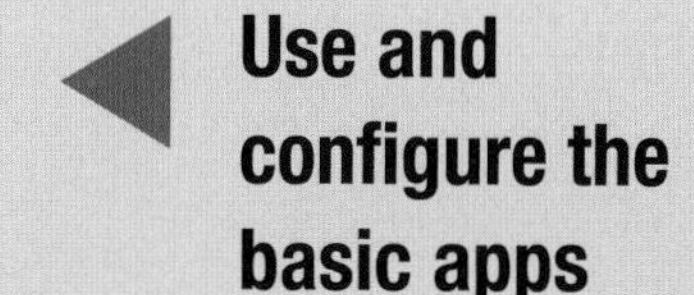


The best way to become comfortable with apps is to learn how to use the most basic ones. Maps is pretty simple and enables you to get directions to a location quickly. Apps like these are functional and provide a service. There are also Travel and Sports apps, among others. These types of apps let you browse articles, read the latest news, scores and stock quotes, configure personal preferences, and more. Another functional app that's pretty easy to use is Calendar. With it you can create events and appointments, invite others to join you there, create alerts, and even configure events (such as birthdays and anniversaries) to repeat every year.

Let's start with Maps.

## Use Maps

You can use the Maps app to locate a place or get directions from one place to another. By default, Maps will use your current location as the starting point, provided you allow it to access your position when prompted. If the information is available in your area, you'll also be able to view traffic conditions before you head out.

Go ahead and open Maps. If prompted, click Allow to let Maps learn your location. As with most other apps, you'll need to be online to use Maps effectively.

Every time you open Maps it will pinpoint your current location, which will be denoted on the map with a diamond. Click the diamond to learn more about where you are. Then you can right-click the screen to see the Maps toolbar and the available charms there. Here are the charms you'll find:

- Show traffic – click to view the current flow of traffic as green, yellow or red. Green means traffic is moving; red means it's extremely slow or stationary.

# Use and configure the basic apps (cont.)

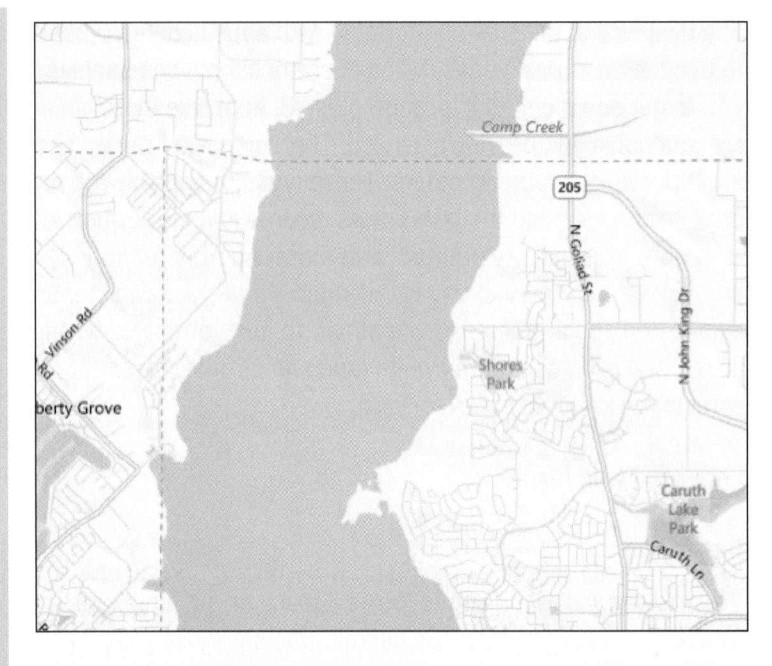

- Map style – to switch from the default Road view to Aerial view.
- My location – to place a diamond on the map to indicate where you are.
- Directions – to get directions from one place to another.

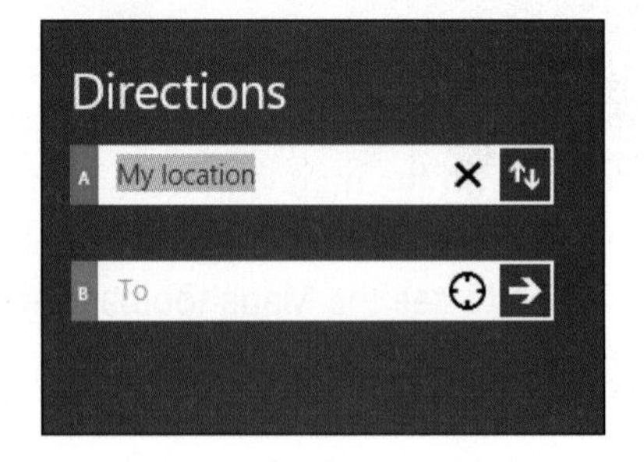

## Did you know?

You can click My location and then Map style to show an aerial view of your current location. Then use the scroll wheel on your mouse, double-click the mouse, or pinch with two fingers on the screen to zoom in. You may be able to view a picture of your home, business or current location as it appears from the sky!

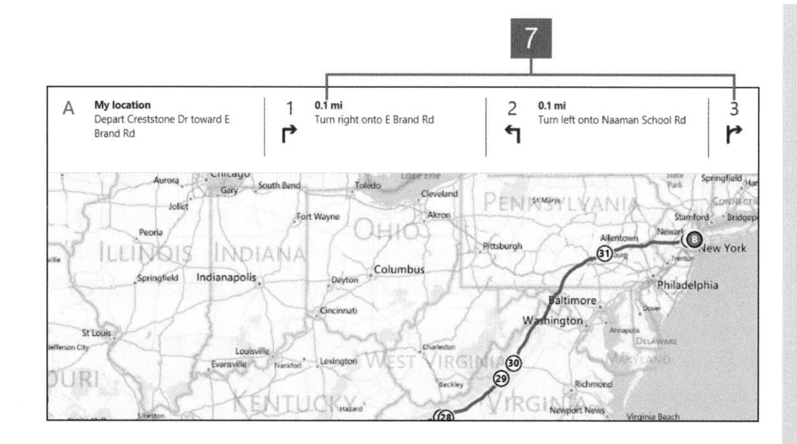


## Explore Travel

The Travel app is one of the easiest to use and is packed with information about places you might want to visit or read about. To browse the app's features, use the scroll wheel on your mouse, the scroll bar at the bottom of the app screen, or your finger to flick using a touch screen. You'll see various sections including Featured Destinations, Panoramas and Magazine Articles.

# Use and configure the basic apps (cont.)

## Get directions with Maps

1. Open the Maps app from the Start screen.
2. Right-click the map.
3. Click Directions.
4. Click ↓↑ to choose to start from your current location or end there.
5. Type a destination address.
6. Press Enter on the keyboard.
7. Note the directions.
8. To clear the directions from the map, right-click to access the Clear Map charm.

2

## Use and configure the basic apps (cont.)

While moving around in the app, try clicking city names, information icons, thumbnails and the back arrow that appears when you do (when you leave the main landing page). This will enable you to really get a feel for the app. Make sure you click one of the panoramas. Once there, you can click and drag your mouse to move around in the image, or flick with your finger. (Again, use the back arrow to return to the main Travel landing page.) Just look at this beautiful panorama of New York City.

Return to the Start screen when you've finished exploring the app. Notice that the Travel tile on the Start screen will now be 'live'. The tile will show various travel photos and city names as the information available in the app changes. (You may have noticed that the Maps tile is not a live tile and thus does not do this.)

### Use Sports

Like the Travel app, the Sports app also offers a host of information. There are articles, photos, sports schedules, plus the ability to add and then follow your favourite teams (which is explained in the panel here). It's a live tile too, so once you open the app and configure your favourite teams, the tile will show information about those teams as it becomes available, as well as information about sports in general.

Like the Travel app, you scroll through the features available with the wheel on your mouse, the scroll bar at the bottom of the screen, or by flicking with your finger on an available touch screen. As you do you'll see that there are sections named Top Story, News, Schedule, Favorite Teams and Magazine Articles.

You can also click the small dash that appears in the bottom right hot corner to access a different view (this works with other apps, too).

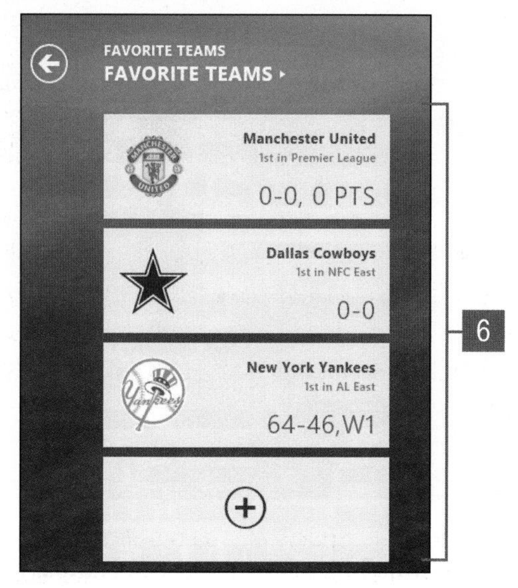


## Use Calendar

If you have a family calendar on your refrigerator, a personal calendar on your desk and a business calendar at work, you know how difficult it is to manage them all. You don't always have physical access, data is scattered across them and it's impossible to sync them in any real way. This is complicated even more when you also use a calendar on your smartphone or tablet.

# Use and configure the basic apps (cont.)

### Follow a team with Sports

1. From the Start screen, click the Sports tile.
2. Scroll through the available articles, schedules and so on.
3. On the far right, locate the Favorite Teams section. Click the + sign.
4. Type the team to follow and click Add.
5. Repeat as desired. Click Close.
6. Note the new entries – you can now click any of these to learn more.

**For your information**

Two more apps you should explore are News and Finance.

## Use and configure the basic apps (cont.)

Digital calendars store data on the Internet, thus solving these issues. You can access the calendar and the data you've saved to it from any device that offers Internet connectivity. In addition, changes you make to the calendar, say when you are at work, will be available when you access the same calendar at home. Windows 8 comes with an app that offers this kind of calendar. You input data, events and appointments to the calendar and then you can access that data from almost anywhere.

To get started, click the Calendar tile on the Start screen. If you've signed in to your Windows 8 computer with a local account, you'll be prompted to input a Microsoft account. This account will also be associated with the Mail, Calendar, People and Messaging apps. If you use a Microsoft account already, you won't be prompted.

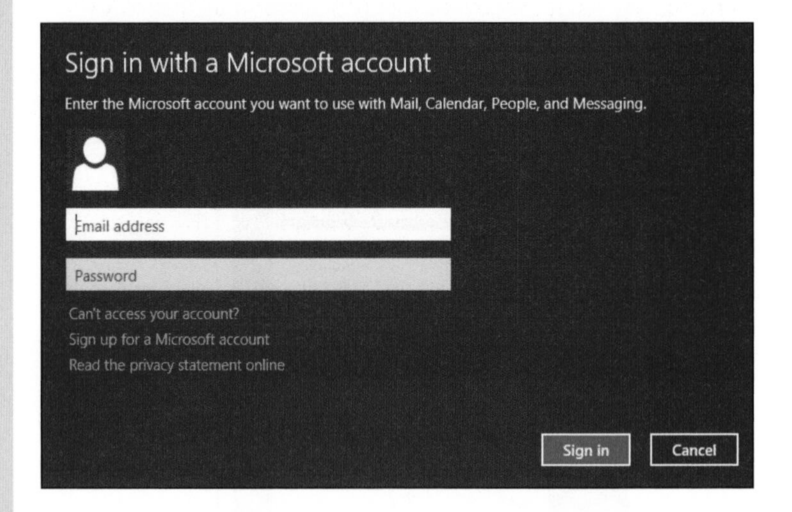


When the Calendar app opens you may see entries. What you see depends on whether or not you've previously input data to your account's associated calendar. Whether you see entries or not, you can input one to get started with the app.

## Use and configure the basic apps (cont.)

To change the view of the calendar, you must right-click inside it to show the toolbar and related charms. You can choose from Day, Week or Month, and you can click Today to immediately access today's date. You can also access the + sign to create a new entry.

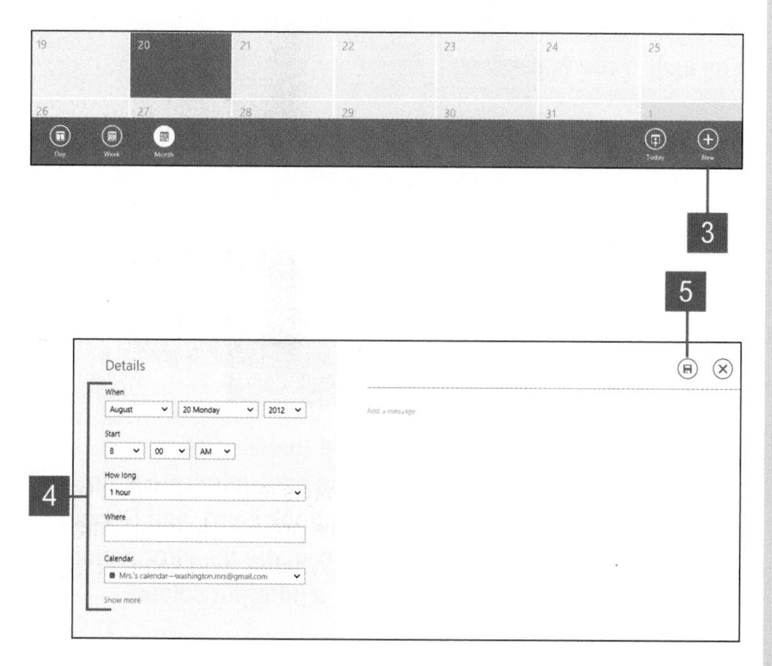


After you've input a few things, return to the Start screen. You'll notice that the Calendar tile is live. This means that as appointment and event dates approach, the tile will show the information on the Start screen.

### Create an event in Calendar

1. From the Start screen, click the Calendar tile.
2. Right-click with a mouse or flick upwards from the bottom of the screen with your finger to access the Calendar's charms.
3. Click New.
4. Input the required details. You can add information including but not limited to:
   - **a** Subject and notes.
   - **b** Where.
   - **c** When.
   - **d** Start time.
   - **e** Length.
   - **f** Show more – how often, reminder, status.
5. Click the Save icon located to the right of the subject.

### Did you know?

You can view your calendar from almost anywhere. It's on the web at https://calendar.live.com/.

# Use and configure the basic apps (cont.)

## Did you know?

You can subscribe to calendars other people have created, including those that mark national holidays, sports team schedules and even lunchroom menus. Do this from the web page associated with your calendar, not from inside the Calendar app.

Finally, the Calendar app offers various settings and configuration options (other apps do, too). You can access these settings from the Settings charm while the app is open. If you recall, Windows key + I can be used to open this charm. You can also position your mouse in the bottom right corner and click the Settings charm if you prefer. There are several entries under settings but only two you need to be concerned with right now:

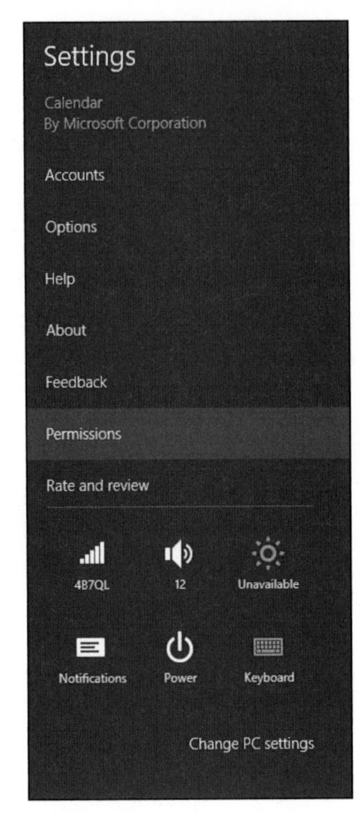


- Accounts – to add another account that also offers a calendar that you use. You can add accounts from Hotmail, Outlook (Exchange, Office 365, Outlook.com), and Google and Gmail. When you add these accounts the information in them appears on your calendar in a different colour.
- Options – to configure the colours for the multiple calendars you keep, if applicable.

Once you have input a few events, from any web browser visit https://calendar.live.com. You can do this from any computer – it does not have to be a Windows 8 computer. You can also use a tablet, such as an iPad. Once you've logged in to the website, you'll have access to your calendar.

## Use and configure the social apps

If you already use Facebook, Twitter, LinkedIn and the like, and if you already know how to send a text from your phone or an instant message from your computer, you'll be right at home with the social apps that are included with Windows 8. These apps let you access your social sites from a single app and enable you to send instant messages to others who use compatible message programs.

### The Messaging app

The first time you open the Messaging app, if you have logged in to your Windows 8 computer with a Microsoft account, you'll be greeted with a message from the Windows Messaging team. You can't reply to this message, but it does give you a sense of how you'll use the app in the future. To get started, click or tap the Messaging tile on the Start screen.

Read the messages and notice the reply area at the bottom of the screen. This is where you'd type a reply to a contact. You can also see which social networks you are currently connected to. At the very least, if you see the message from the Windows Messaging team, you'll see the Messenger icon. This is difficult to see here, but this icon is located in the top right corner of the screen beside Connected to.

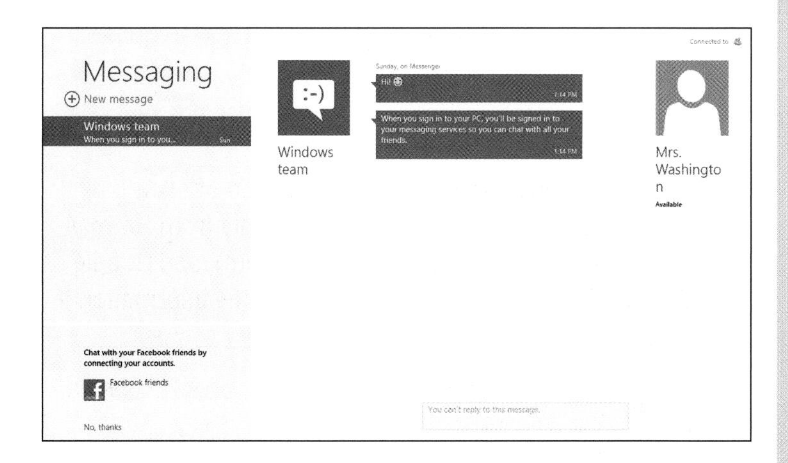


You'll need to have at least one contact to use the Messaging app. You can invite specific people by email or use the Messaging app to log in to whichever social networking service you use. When you do the latter, your contacts are

**Important**

You can't send text messages to mobile phones and smartphones from the Messaging app – you can only send instant messages, which is a different technology. If you want to send a text to a mobile phone, you'll have to use your phone to do so.

## Use and configure the social apps (cont.)

### Add contacts from social networks

1. While inside the Messaging app, access the default charms (Windows key + C or flick inwards from the right side of the screen).
2. Click the Settings charm and then click Accounts.
3. Click Add an account.
4. Choose the account from the resulting list.
5. Click Connect and input the required information.

automatically imported. This is a very easy way to populate your Windows 8 computer with people you know and have contact with. When you add contacts, they appear in a list in the People app, which you'll learn about shortly.

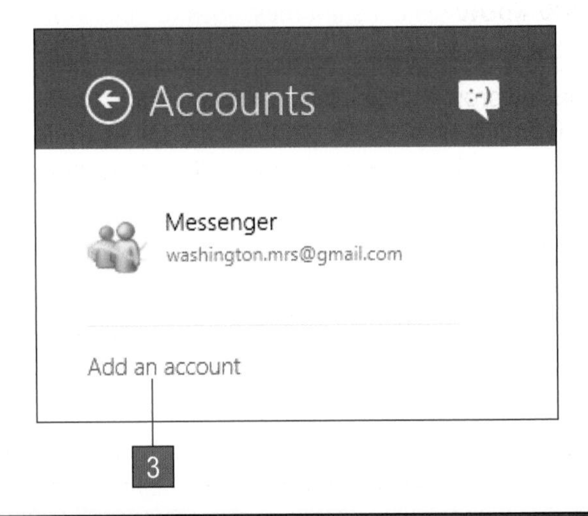


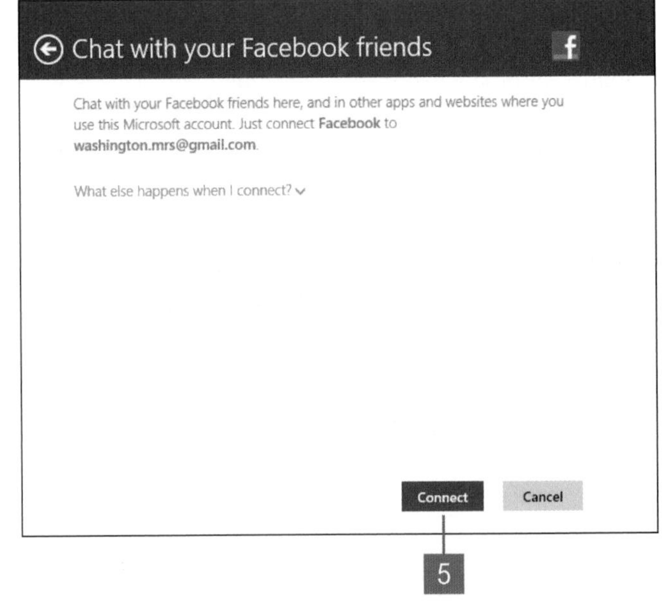


If you don't belong to any social networks, you'll have to add contacts manually. You do this from a different area of the Messaging app, from the Messaging toolbar. As with other apps, you access this toolbar with a right-click of the mouse or a flick up on a compatible touch screen. The toolbar offers options to change your status from online to offline, to delete a conversation, and to invite others to communicate with you using this method. When you click Invite, you'll see the option to Add a new friend.

?

**Did you know?**

If you click the option to invite people from the toolbar, you may be prompted to do a few things first, such as configuring Privacy settings, deciding which social network or service to choose from, adding passwords and giving permissions.

Once you've sent an invitation, the contact needs to accept it. If a contact does not respond and accept your invitation it means one of three things: they opted to reject your invitation, they do not have the proper communication option, or they never received it. In a similar manner, people can send you invitations. If you see invitations you will need to accept them to communicate using Messaging. When you accept an invitation to be friends in the Messaging app, the contact will also appear in the People app.

When you're sure you have some contacts, you are ready to send your first message. Any contact you communicate with will need to be online to receive it. Once that happens, they can reply to your message and then a conversation begins. A conversation is called a *thread*. After a while you may have multiple threads available.

## Use and configure the social apps (cont.)

**Important**

If you connect with lots of social networks, you'll probably end up with duplicate entries for the same contact in the People app. You may have to spend some time cleaning that up if so.

# Use and configure the social apps (cont.)

### Send and reply to an instant message

1. Click New message.
2. The People app will open. Choose the desired contact from the People tab and click Select.
3. Type your message in the text message window and press Enter.
4. Your message will appear at the top of the page.
5. When your contact types back, you can respond. Type your message and press Enter on the keyboard.

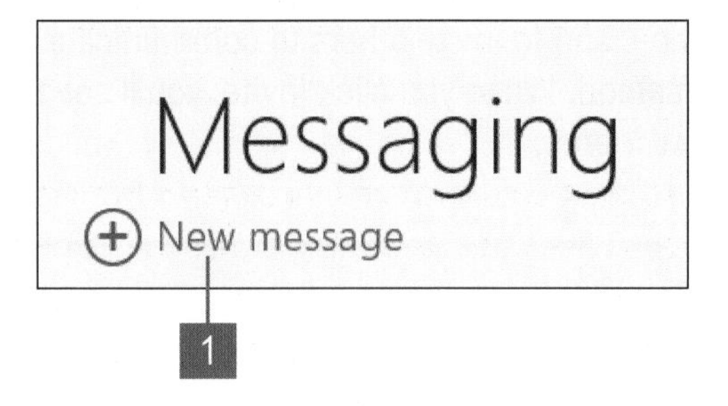


You can do a few more things with the Messaging app, but you can probably figure it out on your own. For instance, from the toolbar, you can delete a thread and change your status – there are charms for that. From the Settings charm (Windows key + I) you can add accounts and change configuration options.

### The People app

You use the People app to organise and make available information about your contacts. Contacts will automatically appear when you add social networking sites, connect with Messaging contacts, and log on with your own Microsoft account. What you see depends on how you've used your Windows 8 computer so far.

To see what's in the People app already, click People on the Start screen. Note the three areas:

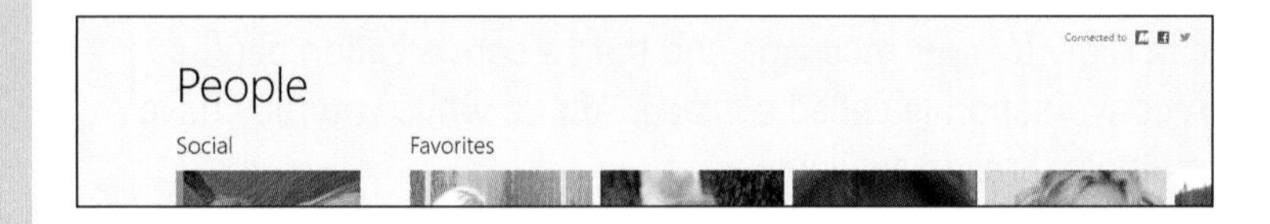


- Social – to access your social network information and to view new posts from those networks.
- Favorites – to view the list of people you communicate with often.
- All – to view all your contacts.

You can also see the social networks you're connected to. Although it's very small and in the top right corner, you can see icons for Messenger, Facebook and Twitter in the image here.

## Use and configure the social apps (cont.)

People What's new Me

Like the Messaging app, you can connect to networks using the options available from the Settings charm. The process is basically the same and if you signed in to those accounts from the Messaging app you're already signed in here. However, if you like, you can see what is available. Use the Windows key + I to get started.

You can also add a contact manually. Right-click an empty area of the screen or flick upwards and click New to get started. Type the desired information. Click any + sign to change the field name or the down arrow to select a different title option. When you've finished, click Save (not shown here).

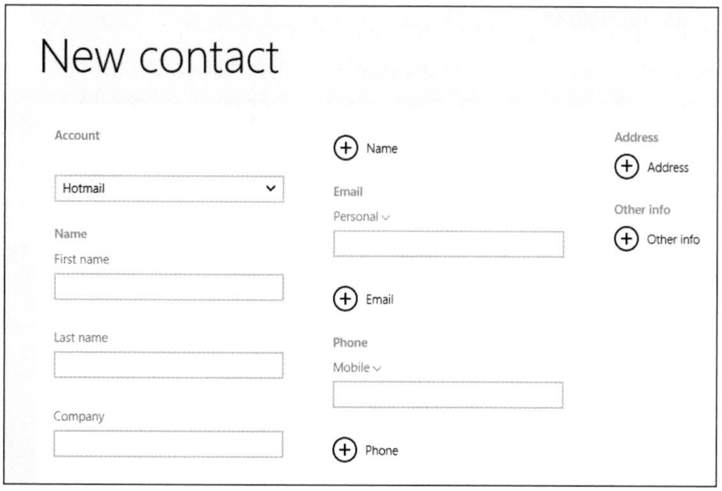

New contact

Account
Hotmail
Name
First name
Last name
Company
Name
Email
Personal
Email
Phone
Mobile
Phone
Address
Address
Other info
Other info

### Did you know?

To edit a contact after you've saved it, click the contact so that it is the only contact showing on the screen. Then right-click or flick upwards to access the Edit option (note the option to pin the contact to the Start screen, too) and input the information as desired.

# Use and configure the social apps (cont.)

## Read and reply to social networking posts

1. Open the People app.
2. Under Social, click What's new.
3. Locate an interesting post.
4. Click Retweet, Reply, Like or Comment, as applicable.

Once you have contacts and have connected to social accounts, here are a few things you can do in the People app:

- Position your mouse in the bottom right corner of the People app and click the – sign that appears. The screen will change from the large tiles you currently see for your contacts to small, alphabetic tiles you can use to go directly to that group of contacts. (Click any tile to change it back.)
- From the All area, if you see duplicate entries for a single contact, you can link the multiple contact cards. To get started, click the contact to edit so that it appears on a screen by itself, then right-click to access the Link charm.
- From the What's new area you can view other people's status updates, posts and tweets. You can click any option available under an entry to reply, like, retweet or respond, as applicable.

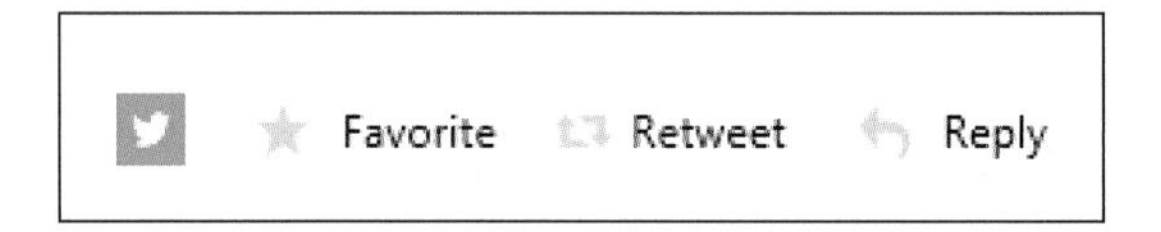


- From the What's new area, scroll right to continue to browse updates.
- From the What's new area, right-click to view the Filter option. You can then opt to show only data from a single network (such as only Facebook or only Twitter).

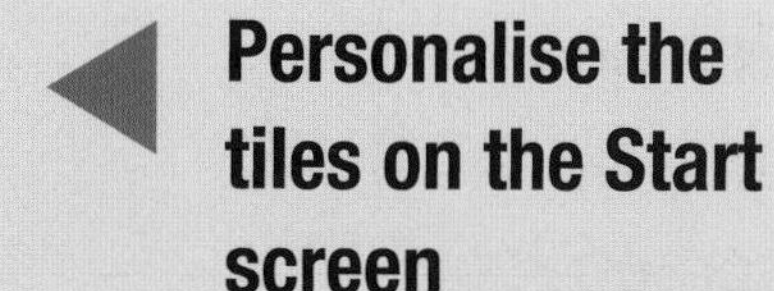

## Personalise the tiles on the Start screen

You've explored lots of apps. You may already know which apps you think you'll use most and which you'll probably never use. You may also be ready to turn off some of those live tiles, add tiles, remove tiles or even resize tiles. You'll learn how to do that and more, next.

### Reposition tiles

As you use your computer, over time you'll learn which apps you use most and which you use least. You may want to move the tiles for the apps you use regularly to the left side of the Start screen and the tiles for the apps you use less frequently to the right. There are many ways to move tiles:

- If you use a mouse:
  - **a** Left-click the tile to move and hold down the left mouse button.
  - **b** Drag the tile to its new location.
  - **c** Drop it there.
- If you use your finger on a touch screen:
  - **a** Tap and hold the app tile.
  - **b** Drag it to its new location.
  - **c** Drop it there.

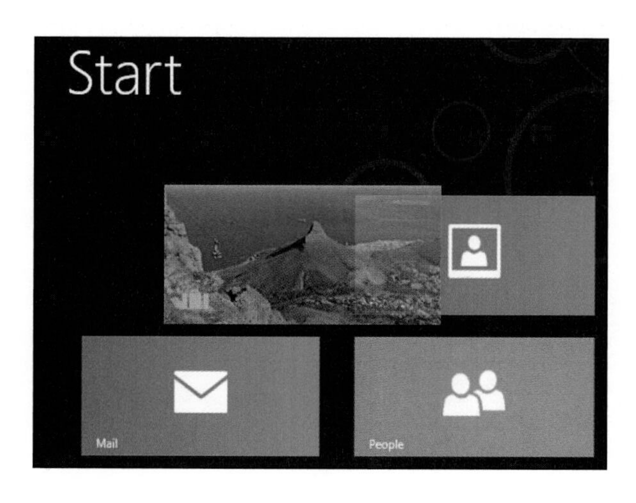

## Personalise the tiles on the Start screen (cont.)

It may take some practice to learn how to reposition an app's tile with your finger. Sometimes it helps to tap, hold and drag *downwards* first (all in one fluid motion) and then drag the tile to the desired location *after* it's been moved downwards from its current position.

### For your information

If a number appears on a tile on the Start screen, it means that there is new information or that the app needs your attention. For instance, a number on the Mail tile means you have unread mail.

### Remove or add tiles

You remove an unwanted tile from the Start screen by right-clicking it and then choosing Unpin from Start. If you like, you can select multiple tiles to remove at one time. If you use your finger to select a tile, you'll have to tap, hold and drag downwards. After you've removed unwanted tiles (and this is different from uninstalling an app), you'll probably want to reposition what's left by dragging the remaining tiles to the desired positions.

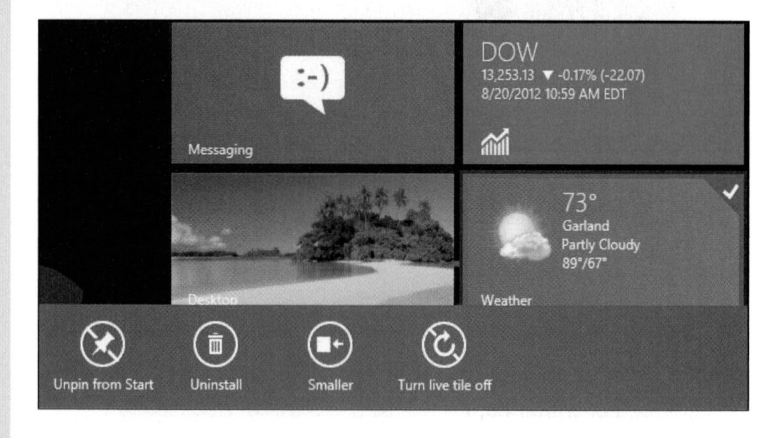

You can add more tiles to the Start screen, too. These tiles can be windows you open on the Desktop, tiles for third-party programs you've installed, tiles for websites you frequent, tiles for your favourite contacts, and more. Most of this, if you're reading this book from start to finish, may not be familiar to you yet. However, you do know about the People app and how to access contacts, so in this example you'll learn how to add a contact card for a contact on the Start screen. This enables you to contact this person with a single click instead of first having to open the People app and locate the contact.

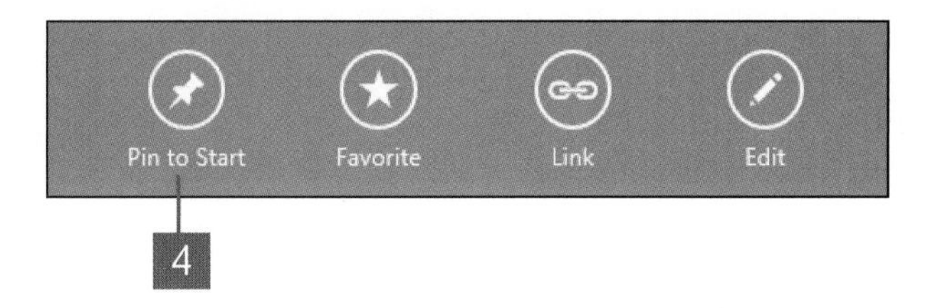


If you know a little about computers and you understand the differences between things such as apps, Desktop apps, Windows Accessories and Windows System tools, you can add tiles for your favourite items from the All apps screen. To do this, right-click an empty area of the Start screen and click All apps. From there, locate the item to add and right-click it. Then click Pin to Start. Here we're adding a tile Calculator.

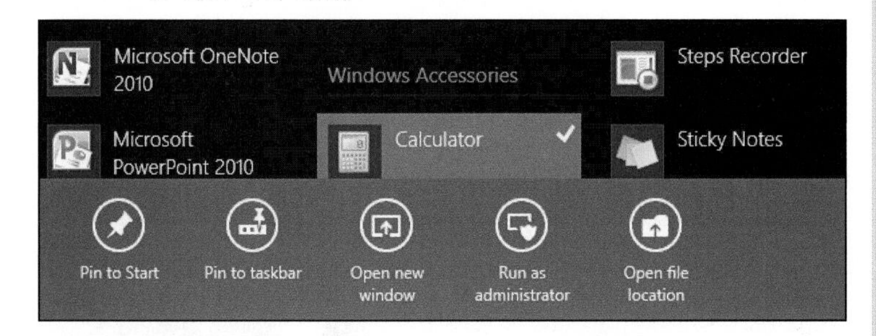


## Make additional changes

You can make additional changes to the tiles that appear on the Start screen. What is available for change depends on the tile you select. For instance, if you right-click the Messaging tile, you'll see options to unpin it from the Start screen, uninstall it, make it smaller or change the current live tile setting. As you might imagine, these options will change if you do make a larger tile smaller, or enable or disable a live tile.

# Personalise the tiles on the Start screen (cont.)

### Create a tile for a contact on the Start screen

1. Open the People app.
2. Click a contact.
3. From the screen that shows only that contact and nothing else, right-click.
4. Click Pin to Start, type the desired name and click Pin to Start once more.
5. Return to the Start screen and scroll right to locate the new tile.

# Personalise the tiles on the Start screen (cont.)

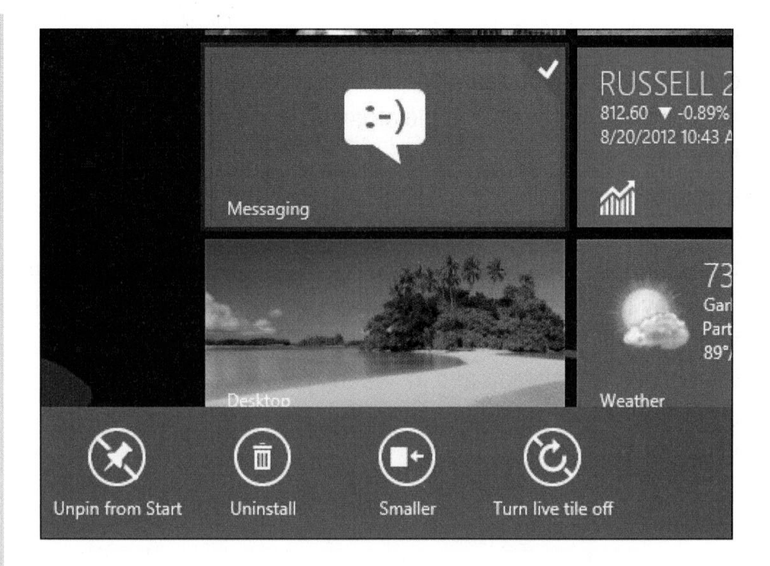


Some tiles can be made smaller, such as those that are rectangular by default. Some tiles (such as Maps) can't be enabled to show live information because there is nothing to show. You can experiment to see what's available. Finally, you can sometimes select multiple tiles and perform a single task with them. For instance, you can select multiple tiles and remove them all at once from the Start screen. You can't select multiple tiles to resize though, or to enable or disable live features.

**Important**

Do not uninstall any tiles just now!

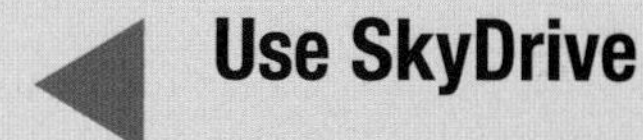

## Use SkyDrive

SkyDrive is an app that enables you to save data, including documents and pictures, to a place in 'the cloud'. When you save something to the cloud, you save it somewhere on the Internet. Where isn't important. If you created a Microsoft account and are logged in with it, you already own a piece of the cloud and it's accessible. Like data you keep in the Calendar app, you can access data you've saved to SkyDrive from any Internet-enabled computer – it does not have to be a Windows 8 computer. In contrast, you might save data to your computer's hard drive, to a backup drive, or even to a computer that is on your home network. But you can't access this data from just anywhere. That's why it is a good plan to save data you may need when you're away from home to your SkyDrive account.

### Jargon buster

The term SkyDrive means that you have access to a *drive* (like a hard drive) in the *sky* (which is actually the Internet). Because the Internet is often represented in technical documentation as a cloud, the word sky kind of fits here.

To get started, open SkyDrive from the Start screen. (If you've moved it, right-click the Start screen, click All Apps and locate SkyDrive there.) We have data stored in our SkyDrive account already, but you'll probably see only category titles.

If you want to save something to SkyDrive so that you can access it when you're away from your computer, you *upload* it to SkyDrive. As with other apps, there are charms to help you with this. You can right-click inside the SkyDrive app to access these charms or flick upwards with your finger. One of the options there is Upload. You use this command to add files to SkyDrive from your computer.

## Use SkyDrive (cont.)

### Upload a file to SkyDrive

1. Open SkyDrive.
2. Click Pictures. (You could also click Documents, Public or any folder you've created there.)
3. Right-click to access the charms, then click Upload.
4. Click a picture to add.
5. Click Add to SkyDrive.

In order to upload files, you must know where they are currently stored on your computer or network. Hopefully you've saved (or will save) your photos to the Pictures library, documents to the Documents library, and so on. If you do that, when you opt to upload a file to SkyDrive, it'll be readily available and you won't have to look for it. You may also be able to find what you're looking for by clicking Go up. If you don't see what you're looking for during the upload process and you don't know how to find it, refer to Chapter 11.

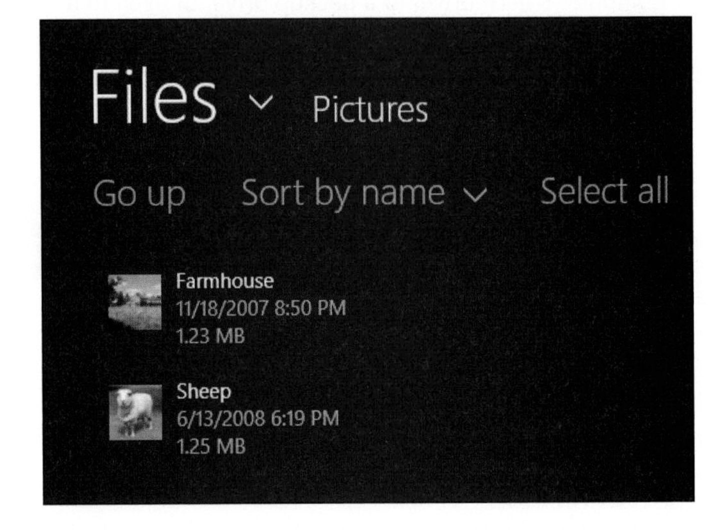


Once you've uploaded a few files, try accessing them from another Internet-enabled computer. Just use a web browser to navigate to https://skydrive.live.com/ and log in. You'll see your folders including Documents, Pictures and Public, you'll have access to their contents, and as a bonus you'll have the option to create new folders there and perform other tasks. (You can also create new folders from the SkyDrive app's charms.) New folders will be available from the SkyDrive app after you create them.

## Shop in the Store

So far you've been exploring apps that come with Windows 8. You can get additional apps from the Store, available from the Start screen. You'll need a Microsoft account to use the Store, even though many apps are free. Once you're logged in, you'll be able to browse many types of apps.

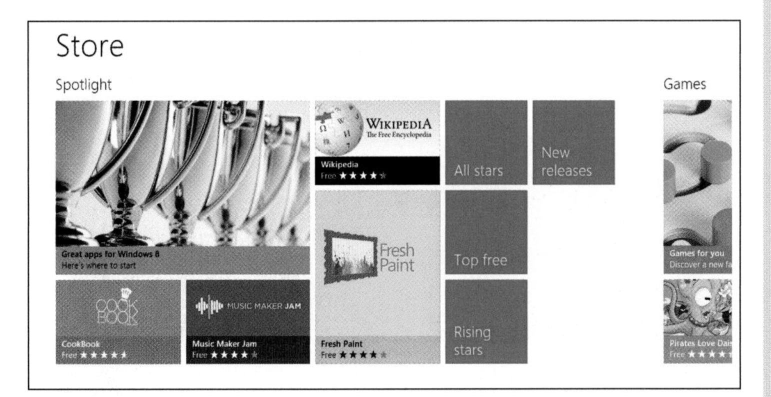


Here are a few of the categories you'll see:

- **Spotlight** – the Store team puts certain apps in the 'spotlight'. These are today's featured apps. You can sort what's here by All stars, Top free, New releases and Picks for you.
- **Games** – find games here, including Cut the Rope, Mahjong Deluxe! and others.
- **Social** – find social networking apps here.
- **Photo** – look for apps by photo sharing sites such as Photobucket and apps that let you fix your photos by removing red-eye, cropping, etc.
- **Music & video** – locate apps for Internet radio, learning song lyrics, and so on.
- **Sports** – keep up with your favourite sports teams with the apps you'll find here.
- **Books & reference** – locate third-party e-readers, as well as dictionaries, bibles and similar reference books.
- **News & weather** – look for apps from entities you recognise, such as msnbc.com, AccuWeather.com and more.

# Shop in the Store (cont.)

## Get a free app from the Store

1. From the Start screen, click Store.
2. Scroll, browse, navigate and explore the items in the Store using techniques you've already learned, such as scrolling and clicking.
3. Click Top free under any category.
4. Locate an app you'd like to own. Click it.
5. Read the information on the app's Details page, and if desired, click Install.

- **Travel** – find travel apps here that include maps, geographical information and popular tourist excursions.
- **Finance** – apps here can help you manage your finances, review stock prices and so on.
- **Government** – this category holds apps related to governing and government entities.

**Important**

Many apps are free, but many you'll have to pay for. If prompted to pay for an app, read the instructions for doing so and set up the required payment account.

After an app installs, it will appear as a tile on the Start screen, on the far right side. Like any other app, you click or tap to use it. Often, the app will offer setup information, help or instructions. Be careful though, some apps offer in-app purchases. This means you can pay for more 'bombs', 'lives' and various additional features. This can get expensive!

# Use Desktop applications

3

## Introduction

In the last chapter you learned about Start screen apps. These kinds of apps look, feel and act like apps you might use on any smartphone, iPad or Android tablet. They are somewhat like what you'd find at a kiosk at a photo store, bank or shopping centre. Start screen apps have charms that enable you to navigate and use them easily. Each of these apps has somewhat limited features, and they are not nearly as robust as the traditional applications and programs you may be used to. In this chapter you'll learn about these more robust apps, the Desktop apps.

Desktop apps always open on the Desktop, the traditional computing environment. These applications can be programs you install, such as Adobe Photoshop Elements, or programs that come with Windows 8, like Paint or WordPad. Applications can also be software you install with a new camera, printer or scanner. Additionally, they can be Windows Accessories, like the Calculator, Notepad, Snipping Tool and Sound Recorder. Windows Media Player is a Desktop application, and Control Panel opens on the Desktop, too, as does File Explorer. There are lots of programs and Windows features that need access to the Desktop to run.

In this chapter you'll learn how to locate the Desktop apps from the Start screen and how to use a few of them. From then on, whenever an application opens on the Desktop, you'll understand how to use it and why it's a Desktop app.

### What you'll do

# Find Desktop applications

The Start screen offers access to the applications, programs, accessories and features available on your computer. They don't all appear though. To see everything that's available, you have to right-click the Start screen and click All apps.

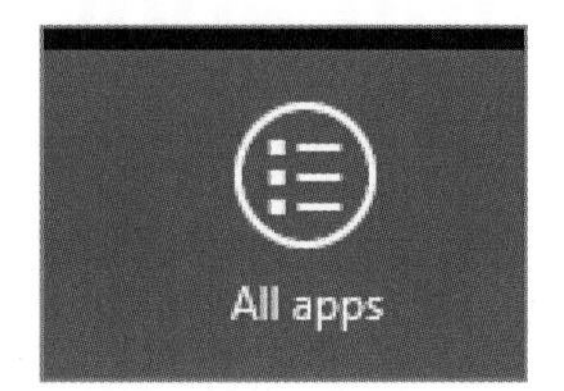


The first thing you'll notice about the resulting Apps screen is that it shows tiles for all the available apps and the utilities you've installed for printers, mice, scanners, etc. You'll also see tiles for your third-party software, Windows Accessories and various system tools. You can right-click any of these to pin them to the Start screen, and if it's a Desktop app, to pin it to the Desktop's Taskbar, as shown here. You click or tap any item to open it. Thus, you can find and open any Desktop app from the All apps screen.

You don't have to always access this screen though. You can open Desktop applications from the Start screen, even if they don't appear there. You only need to start typing while at the Start screen and a list appears that offers options. The more you type, the fewer the options. For instance, if you type 'Pai' at the Start screen, you can see Paint as an option. You click to open it.

**For your information**

To close any Desktop application, click the X in the top right corner.

## Find Desktop applications (cont.)

### Find Desktop applications

1. Press the Windows key on the keyboard to return to the Start screen.
2. Type Pai without quotes.
3. Verify that Apps is selected on the right side of the screen.
4. Click Paint to open it.
5. Note that Paint opens on the Desktop.

# Use WordPad

If your word-processing tasks involve simply creating a quick memo, note or letter and printing it out, or putting together a weekly newsletter that you send via email, there's no reason to purchase a large office suite like Microsoft Office (and learn how to use it) when WordPad will do just fine. You can't create and insert tables, endnotes, footnotes, WordArt, text boxes and the like as you can in Microsoft Word, but you may not need to. WordPad is quite functional and easy to use, and will suit the needs of many of you quite well.

## Write a letter with WordPad

1. Access the Start screen.
2. Type WordPad.
3. Select WordPad from the Program results. A new, blank document will open.
4. Type 'I am using WordPad'. (Alternatively, you could actually type a letter to a friend or family member.)
5. Select the text by holding down the left mouse key and dragging the cursor across the sentence.
6. Click the arrow next to the font size. Choose 72.
7. With the text still selected, click the slanted I located underneath the Font list. This will italicise the text.
8. Click the Bullets icon on the formatting toolbar. This will make the selected text a bullet.
9. Deselect the text by clicking at the end of the sentence. The cursor should be blinking after the word WordPad.
10. To close the program and save your work, click File, click Save As, click Rich Text Document.
11. Note that the file will be saved in your Documents folder in Rich Text Format. Type a name for the file and click Save.

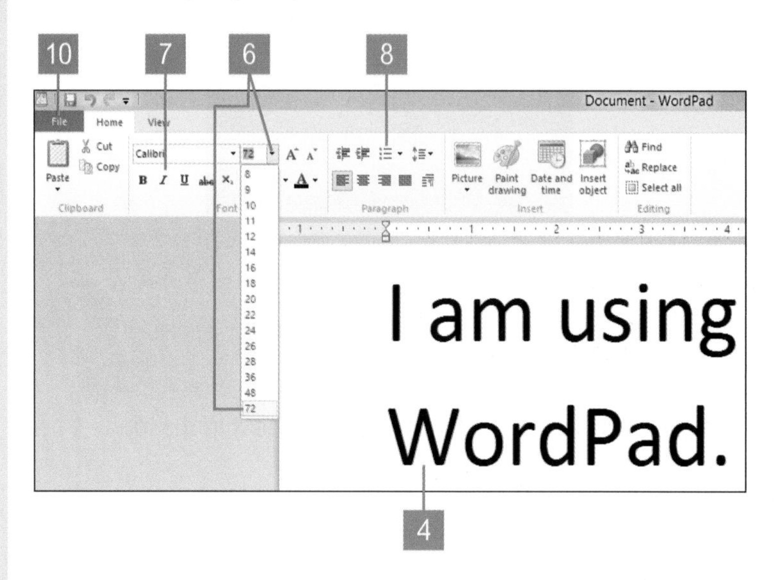

**Important**

You can open the file easily the next time you open WordPad by clicking the File tab. Recent documents are available there.

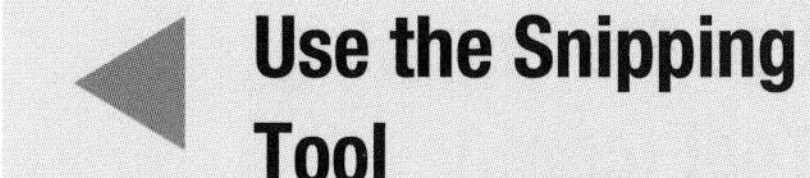

## Use the Snipping Tool

Sometimes you'll see something on your screen you want to capture to keep or share. It may be part of a web page (such as a great news story or a fabulous place to go on holiday), or an error message you want to share with your grandchild (who can probably resolve it). You can capture the screen using the Snipping Tool, another Desktop app.

The Snipping tool is easy to use – you really only need to click New and drag your mouse around the area to copy. Once you've captured the desired area you can perform edits on the snip. These include but are not limited to:

- Saving the capture to your computer.
- Sharing the capture via email.
- Copying the capture for pasting elsewhere.
- Writing on the capture using a pen or highlighter (in various colours) and erasing unwanted additions.
- Configuring options.
- Getting help and support.

You open the Snipping tool the same way you open any Desktop program – you either locate it from the All apps screen or type something like 'Snip' while at the Start screen. From the resulting screen, you can access the options to mark up, save or send the snip.

# Use the Snipping Tool (cont.)

## Capture the screen with the Snipping Tool

1. From the Start screen, type Snip.
2. In the results, click Snipping Tool.
3. Click New.
4. Drag your mouse across any part of the screen. When you let go of the mouse, the snip will appear in the Snipping Tool window.
5. Explore each menu: File, Edit, Tools and Help, and the options on the toolbar.
6. Click the arrow beside the pen, as shown here, and click Blue Pen. Repeat and select Customize.
7. Configure options as desired and click OK.
8. Use the pen to write on the snip. Use the Eraser to undo anything you've written.

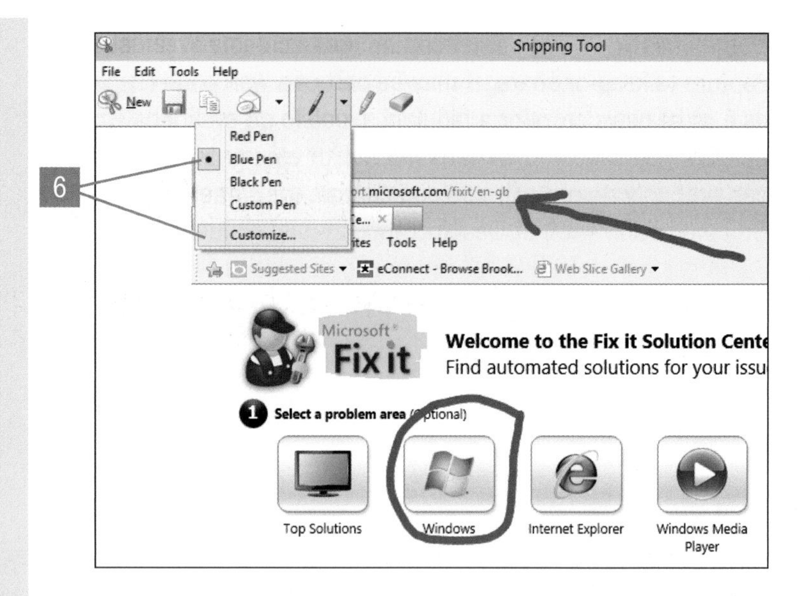


After you've acquired the snip and completed any other tasks, such as writing or highlighting on it, click the File menu to save or send it. To email the snip, choose Send to and then E-Mail recipient. When you do, the snip will be included inside the body of the email; if you opt to attach it, it will appear as an attachment when the recipient receives it.

### For your information

If you think you'll use the Snipping Tool often, pin it to the Start screen or the Taskbar on the Desktop.

As you can guess, there are many more Desktop apps to explore. Some you'll learn about in this book in other chapters, such as Internet Explorer in Chapter 8, Windows Media Player in Chapter 9, the Network and Sharing Center in Chapter 10, Windows Defender in Chapter 11, and so on. However, there are a few you can explore on your own. Open and explore these apps from the All apps screen (available by right-clicking the Start screen).

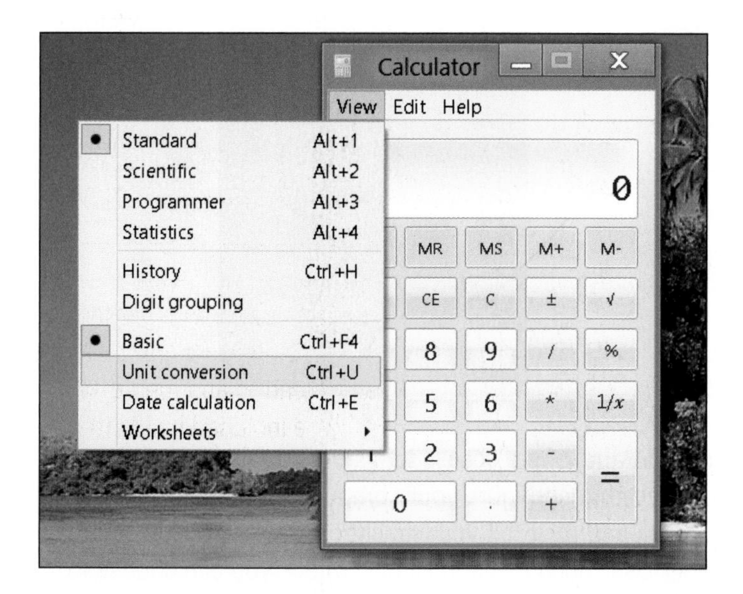


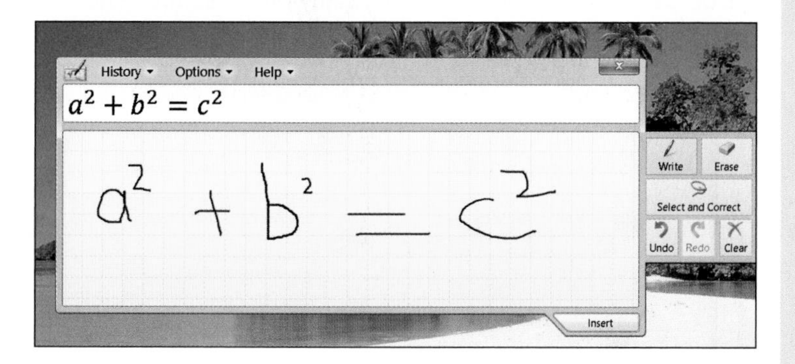

## More Desktop apps to explore

### Explore additional Desktop applications

- Calculator – perform simple and complex calculations. The View menu offers more options.
- Paint – create flyers, posters and similar media.
- Sticky Notes – create digital sticky notes to create reminders for yourself.
- Sound Recorder – record voice memos to save or share.
- Windows Journal – on touch screen computers and tablets only, write handwritten notes and transform them into text (among other things).
- Math Input Panel – write (with a mouse or a stylus) mathematical equations that can then be copied and pasted to a compatible program such as Microsoft Word.

3

# Use Control Panel

Throughout this book you'll use the features located in Control Panel to perform such tasks as configuring and checking for Windows updates, configuring security settings, optimising appearance and adding new users. You'll also use Control Panel to add printers, uninstall programs and perform routine maintenance on your PC, among other things. You can open Control Panel from the All apps screen and it opens on the Desktop.

Control Panel offers access to features, tools and windows you'll need to configure your computer. For instance, under Network and Internet, you can choose to set up file sharing. Under User Accounts and Family Safety, you can choose to set up parental controls. There are many other features and options to explore.

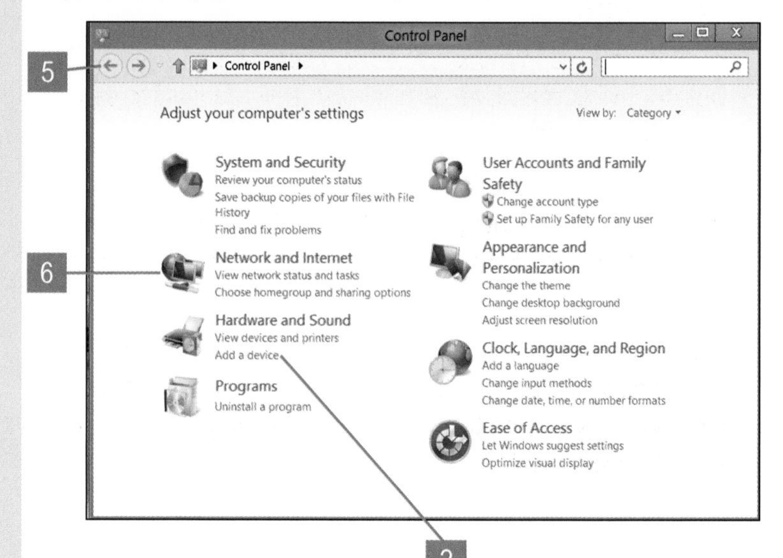


## Use Control Panel

1. Open Control Panel from the All apps screen.
2. Under Hardware and Sound, click View devices and printers.
3. Look at the listing of connected devices and right-click one of them.
4. Note the options, but do not click any.
5. Click the Back arrow.
6. Under Network and Internet, click View network status and tasks.
7. Review what's shown and click the Back arrow.
8. Continue to explore as desired, always clicking the Back arrow without making changes.

## Use Control Panel (cont.)

**Important**

If you open Control Panel and don't see what's shown here, specifically Category view, click the arrow by View By and select Category (as opposed to Large icons or Small icons).

The eight categories in Control Panel are used to group the various configuration, security and system options. Their features include but are not limited to:

- System and Security – to find and fix problems, secure your computer and create backups.
- Network and Internet – to view network status, fix problems, set up a homegroup and connect to networks.
- Hardware and Sound – to view and troubleshoot hardware and sound and to add devices.
- Programs – to view a list of and uninstall unwanted programs.
- User Accounts and Family Safety – to create user accounts, set up family safety settings, assign passwords and change account types.
- Appearance and Personalization – to set a theme, change the Desktop background, assign a screen saver, adjust screen resolution and so on.
- Clock, Language, and Region – to configure languages for Windows 8, to change how you input data with your keyboard, and to change the time zone, number format and so on.
- Ease of Access – to make the computer easier to use if you have a disability by optimising the display, changing how long pop-ups stay on the screen, and enabling and training speech recognition.

# Use Help and Support

Sometimes you need a little bit more than a book can give you. When that happens, you'll need to access Windows 8's Help and Support feature. You can access Help and Support from just about anywhere that supports a Desktop app or window. What the Help and Support feature offers when it starts depends on where you open it.

- Help and Support is available from the All apps screen. Help opens here with the Help home page that includes the category titles Get Started, Internet & networking, and Security, privacy, & accounts.

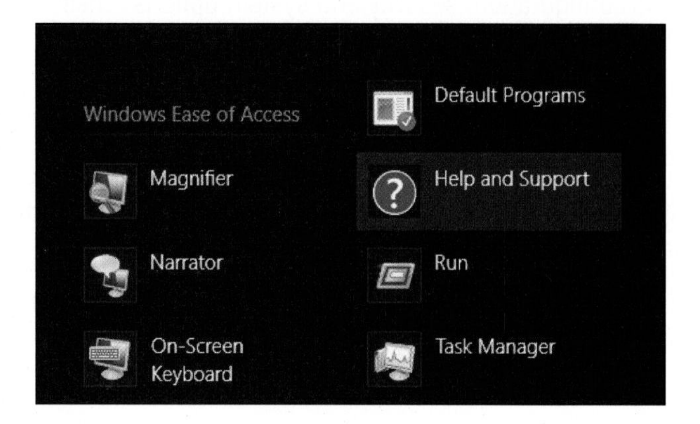


- The Help and Support icon is available from every Windows 8 Desktop application. Help opens in this instance with information about the open application.

- The Help and Support icon is available from every File Explorer window. Help may open here with information about libraries, how to work with files and folders, and so on.

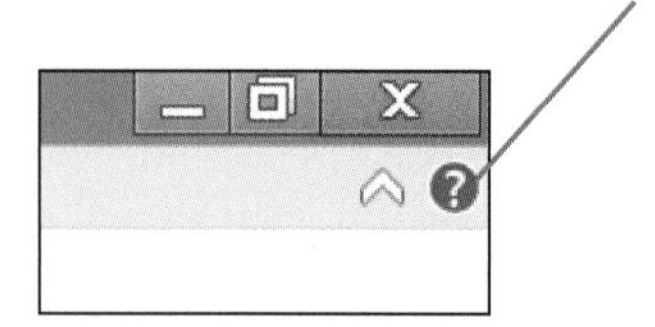

No matter how you open it, when you open the Help and Support Center you'll have several options for obtaining help and finding information. If you have time, click each option to see what it offers. You'll be surprised how much information is available. For instance, Get started offers articles on everything from using your mouse to fixing sound problems. If you want help on something in particular, such as Internet Explorer or Windows Media Player, type what you're looking for in the Search Help window and the articles that apply to that topic will appear.

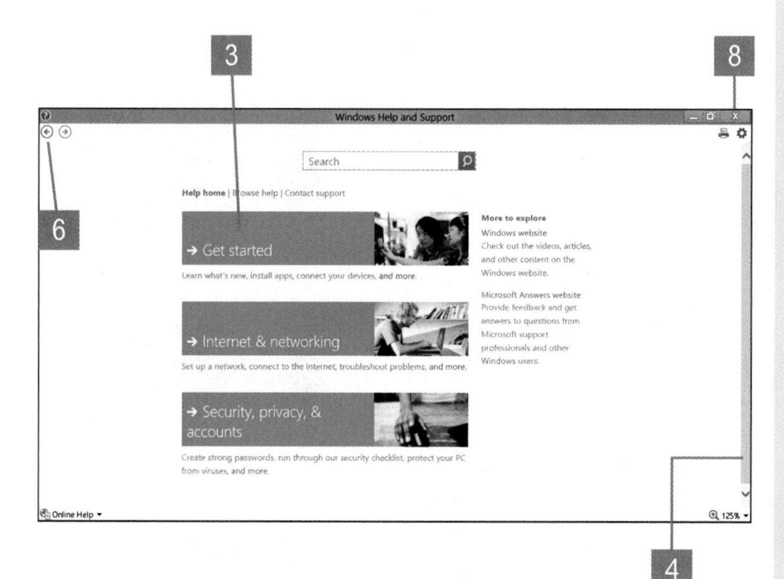


## Use Help and Support (cont.)

### Explore Help and Support

1. Open Help and Support using any method.
2. Review what's shown, then click Help home.
3. Click Get started.
4. Use the scroll bar to browse through the topics.
5. Select any topic to read more about it.
6. Click the Back button to return to the previous screen.
7. Repeat these steps as desired.
8. Click the X in the top right of the Help and Support Center to close it.

# Manage open apps, Desktop applications and windows

4

## Introduction

While using Windows 8, you will probably have multiple apps open at once. For instance, you may have the Mail, Weather, Calendar, Maps and SkyDrive apps open. This is perfectly fine because when an app isn't in use, it generally isn't using any system resources – it remains inactive in the background, waiting to be called on by you to perform a task or offer information.

Likewise, you may have multiple Desktop applications and windows open. For instance, you may have Control Panel, Windows Media Player, File Explorer and a third-party program from Adobe or something from Microsoft Office. Most Desktop applications use system resources behind the scenes, so it's best to close these when they aren't in use.

Even if you close unnecessary Desktop applications, you'll still probably have a lot of items open at any given time. You need to know how to move among these with ease. That's what you'll learn here. If you have a computer or tablet with a touch screen, there's a list of touch techniques you can use at the end of this chapter to help you learn how to navigate Windows 8 on a device without a mouse or keyboard (or one that offers a touch screen).

## What you'll do

**Move among open apps quickly**

**Use Snap to view two apps at once**

**Use Alt + Tab on the Desktop**

**Change the size of an open window**

**Shake windows to the Taskbar**

**Make Desktop icons easier to see**

**Use touch techniques**

# Work with multiple open apps

Apps are the items you open that appear in their own screen, offer toolbars and charms, and do not require the Desktop to run. You learned about apps in Chapter 2. When you have multiple apps open, there are many ways to move among them. You already know one way, which is to access the Start screen and select the desired app from it. There are many ways to access the Start screen. You can:

- Tap the Windows key on the keyboard.
- Move the mouse cursor to the bottom left corner of the screen and click once on the thumbnail that appears.

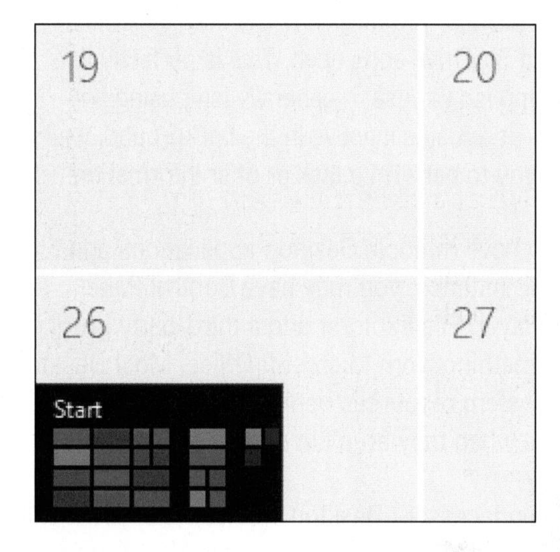


- Move the mouse cursor to the bottom right (or top right) corner of the screen to access the charms and click the Start charm.

## Move among open apps quickly

1. From the Start screen, open the Weather app, the Maps app, the Bing app and the Calendar app.
2. On the keyboard, press and hold the Windows key and the Tab key.
3. While still pressing the Windows key, press the Tab key four times.
4. Let go of both keys.
5. On the keyboard, press and hold the Alt key and the Tab key.

### Did you know?

You can access the five default charms by positioning the cursor in the bottom right corner or the top right corner. Both are hot corners.

## Work with multiple open apps (cont.)

As you probably know by now, always returning to the Start screen and clicking an app tile isn't an extremely efficient way to move among apps. You have to first *get* to the Start screen, then you have to locate the desired tile and click it. If that app is listed in the All apps screen, well, that's one more click of the mouse. There are better ways to move among apps that are already in use. Here are a few:

- Hold down the Windows key and press the Tab key to show thumbnails of each open app. Press Tab repeatedly until you get to the app you want to use, then let go of both.
- Hold down the Alt key and press the Tab key to show a row of open apps. Press Tab repeatedly until you get to the app you want to use, then let go.

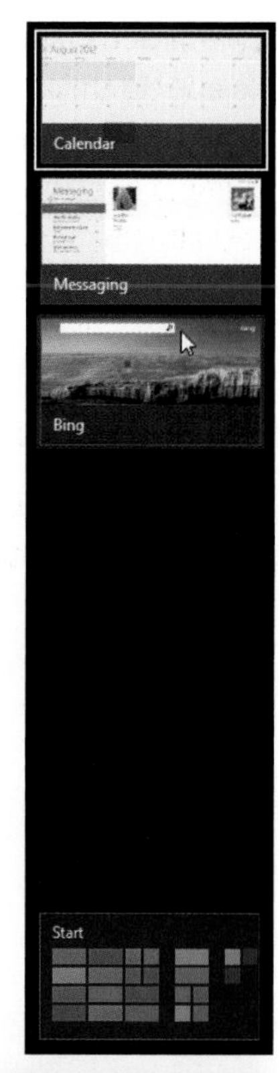


- Position your mouse in the top left corner of the screen to view and click the last used app. Don't click and then drag the mouse downwards slowly to view the other available apps.

Sometimes you'll need to work with two apps at once. As an example, you may need to hold a conversation in the Messaging app while you look up directions with the Maps app. It is possible to view two apps at once, using the Snap option.

To use this feature you must first open the two apps you want to use. Then, with one of the apps on the screen, you position your mouse in the top left corner, drag slowly downwards and

6. While still holding the Alt key, press the Tab key four times.
7. Let go.
8. Position your mouse in the top left corner of the screen.
9. Slowly drag your mouse downwards, keeping it as far to the left as possible.
10. Click any app to open it.

**Important**

The Alt + Tab and Windows + Tab key combinations work to move among Desktop applications too.



**Did you know?**

You can use a touch gesture to snap an app to one side of the screen. Position your finger in the middle of the left side, hold and drag from left to right. The new app will slide in. Remove your finger to snap the app to the screen.

# Work with multiple open apps (cont.)

## Use Snap to view two apps at once

1. From the Start screen, open the Messaging and Maps apps.
2. Make the Maps app the active app. View it on the screen.
3. Position your mouse in the top left corner of the screen and drag slowly downwards, keeping the cursor against the left edge.
4. Right-click the Messaging app.
5. Click Snap left.
6. Note that the two apps appear on the screen, with a divide bar you can use to reposition them.

right-click the app to snap. You can then choose where to snap the app, to the left or right. Here, the Maps app is open and we're going to snap the Messaging app to one side of the screen.

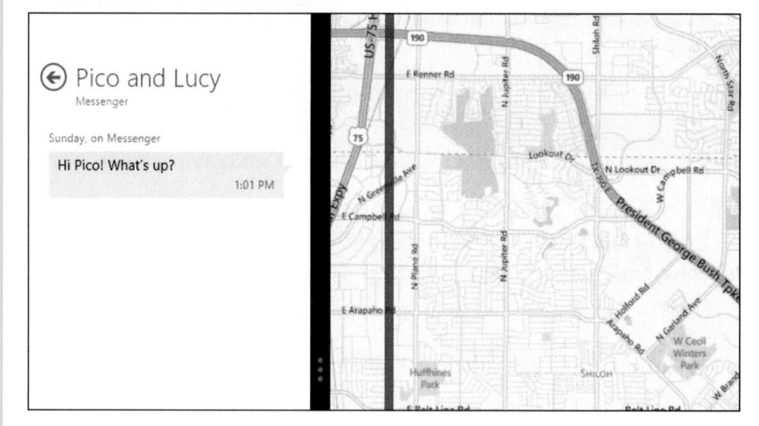

You can use the same techniques you learned in the previous section to move among multiple Desktop applications. You can use Alt + Tab and Windows + Tab to navigate to an open window or program, and you can use the top left hot corner to access thumbnails. When you're working only on the Desktop though, there are more options. You can change the size of the open windows, reposition them and minimise them to the Taskbar, among other things.

You can minimise and maximise windows on the Desktop, or click the Restore button so you can resize or move the window. A minimised window appears only on the Taskbar and is not on the Desktop. A maximised window is as large as it can be and takes up the entire screen. When the window is in *Restore mode*, it is neither maximised nor minimised, and you can resize the window by dragging from any corner or side, and even from the top.

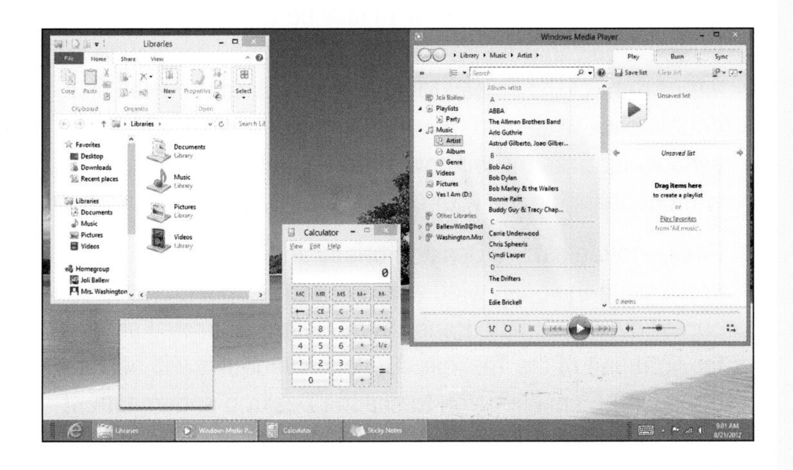


# Work with multiple open Desktop applications

## Use Alt + Tab on the Desktop

1. Open several Desktop windows. You might open File Explorer, Calculator, Windows Media Player and Sticky Notes, for instance.
2. With multiple windows open, on the keyboard hold down the Alt key with one finger (or thumb).
3. Press and hold the Tab key.
4. Press the Tab key again (making sure that the Alt key is still depressed).
5. When the item you want to bring to the front is selected, let go of the Tab key and then let go of the Alt key.

### Did you know?

An icon appears on the Taskbar for every open window or program.

# Work with multiple open Desktop applications (cont.)

## Change the size of an open window

- Maximise a window – click the square in the top right corner. If the icon shows two squares, it's already maximised. You can also drag from a window's title bar upwards.
- Restore a window – click the two rectangles in the top right corner of any maximised window. If you don't see two rectangles, it's not maximised. You can also drag from the title bar downwards.
- Resize a window – drag from any corner or edge of a window in Restore mode. A window is in Restore mode if there is a single square in the top right corner. You can also drag straight up from the top to cause the window to snap to the top of the screen.
- Minimise a window – click the dash in the top right corner of the window to minimise it to the Taskbar. Click it in the Taskbar to make it appear on the screen again.

You can move any window to a different area of the screen by dragging from its title bar. Just left-click with the mouse, hold and drag. Let go when it's in the proper location. You can also (in most cases):

- Drag upwards on any window's title bar while in Restore mode to maximise it.
- Drag downwards on any window's title bar when maximised to restore it.

### Did you know?

To bring any window to the front of the others while on the Desktop, click its title bar. This makes it the active window.

There are three additional options for working with multiple windows on the Desktop: Shake, Snap and Peek:

- **Shake –** to remove all but one window from the Desktop and minimise the others to the Taskbar. To use the feature, you click, hold, then shake the top of the window you'd like to keep. The other windows will fall to the Taskbar.
- **Snap –** to position a window to take up exactly half the screen. You can drag from the title bar of any window to the left or right of the screen to snap it into place. You can also double-click when you have the double arrow at the top of a window to make the window fill to the height of the screen without changing the width.
- **Peek –** to look at the Desktop briefly and see what's underneath the open windows. To use this, position your cursor over the small, transparent rectangle located at the far right end of the Taskbar. The open windows will become transparent, enabling you to see the Desktop underneath. If nothing happens, right-click and click Peek at Desktop.

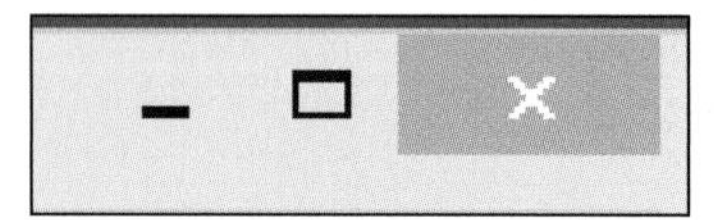

# Work with multiple open Desktop applications (cont.)

Here are a few more random tips for working on the Desktop:

- You can rearrange items on the Taskbar by dragging them to a different location. This may help you position the icons so they are easier to access.
- Using any open program's icon on the Taskbar, click and drag upwards to see a secondary menu. You can then opt to pin this program to the Taskbar to make it available from the Taskbar at all times. You can also choose to close the window.
- Hover your mouse over any icon on the Taskbar to see a small thumbnail of the window.

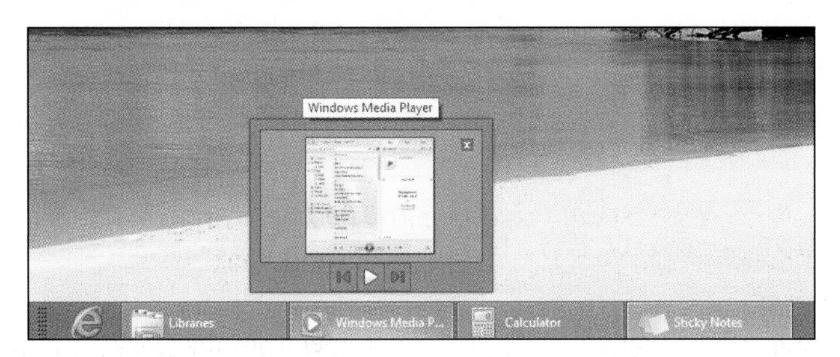


- Right-click an empty area of the Desktop, click Sort by and opt to sort the icons there by name, size, item type or date modified.
- Right-click an empty area of the Taskbar and click Properties to configure properties for the Taskbar, including using Peek to preview the desktop when you move your mouse to the Show desktop area at the end of the Taskbar.
- Drag the divider bars on the Taskbar to show or hide icons.
- Make Desktop icons easier to see by making them larger. This is explained in the panel.

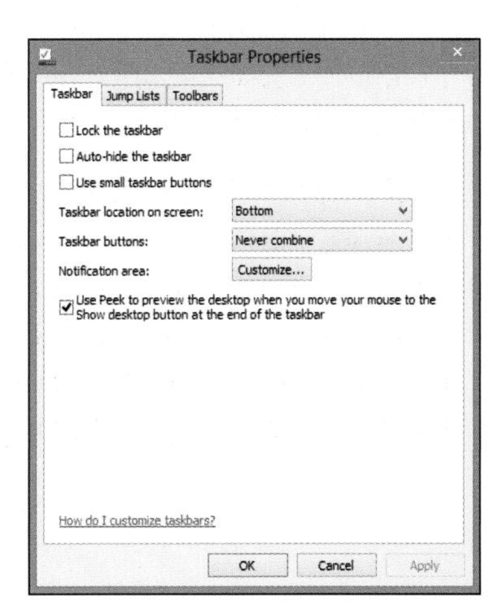


?

## Did you know?

If you have multiple monitors and opt to stretch the displays, you can drag windows from one monitor to another.

## Shake windows to the Taskbar

1. With multiple windows open on the Desktop, left-click the top of any open window.
2. While holding down the left mouse key, move the mouse quickly from left to right several times.
3. Watch while the windows are minimised to the Taskbar.
4. Repeat to maximise windows.

## Important

Close Desktop apps when you aren't using them. They will use resources in the background and could theoretically hamper performance.

# Work with multiple open Desktop applications (cont.)

## Make Desktop icons easier to see

1. Right-click an empty area of the Desktop.
2. Click View.
3. Click Large icons.

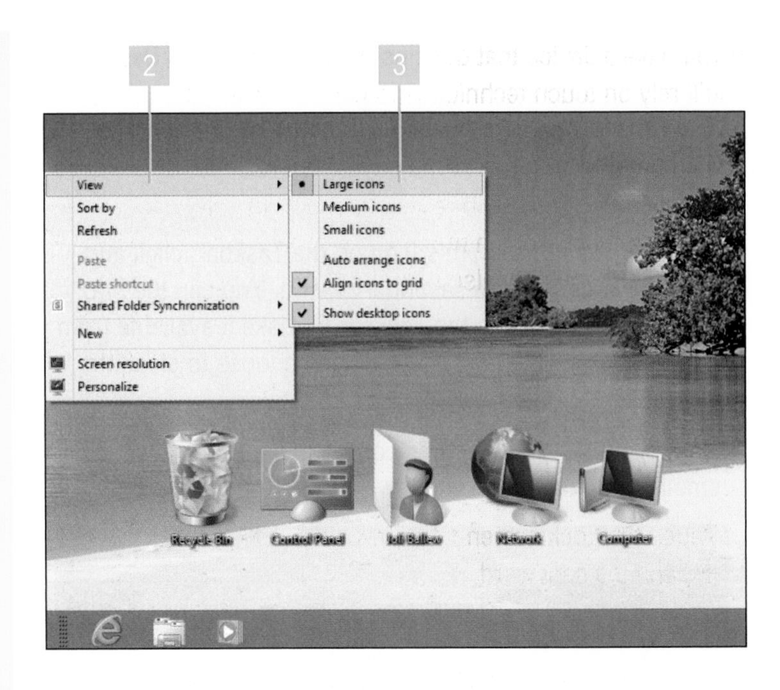


### Did you know?

If you have a tablet with a USB port, you may be able to connect a USB mouse or keyboard and use it instead of touching the screen. Likewise, if Bluetooth is an option, you may be able to connect Bluetooth input devices.

## Explore touch techniques

If you have a device that does not have a physical keyboard, you'll rely on touch techniques to perform tasks, access data, type text, select items, surf the web, move and resize windows and so on. If you have another device that supports touch along with a keyboard and mouse (perhaps a touch-screen monitor connected to a desktop PC), you may also want to learn and use these touch techniques.

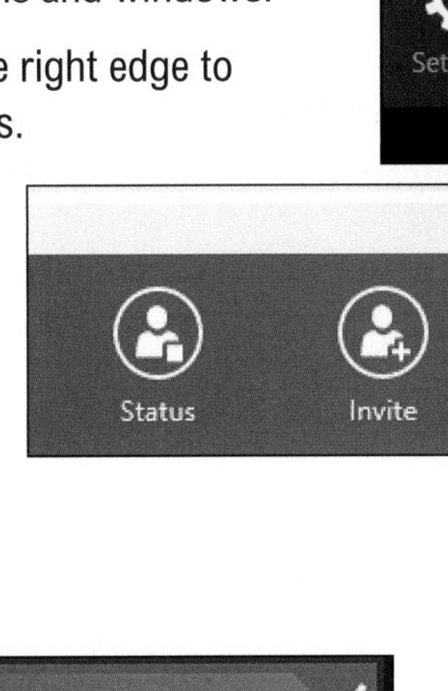

There are lots of ways to interact with touch screens. The touch techniques you'll use every time you use your touch screen-only device include:

- Touch the Lock screen to unlock your device and input a password.
- Touch a tile to open an app on the Start screen.
- Flick in from the middle of the left edge to move among open apps, applications and windows.
- Flick in from the middle of the right edge to access the five default charms.
- Flick up from the bottom of the screen while in an app to access additional charms unique to the app.
- Tap any item to open it.
- Tap and hold any item to select it.

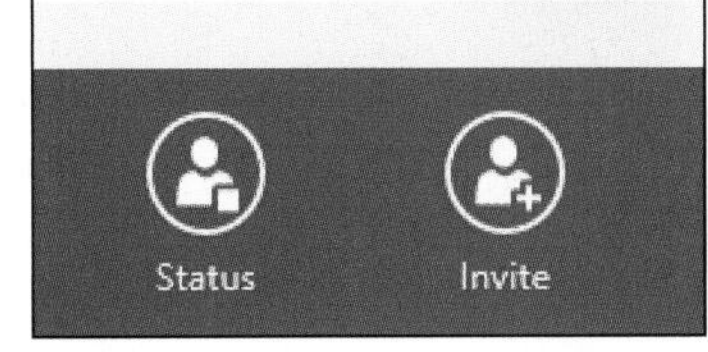

**Did you know?**

The tap-and-hold technique often produces what a traditional left-click does.

## Explore touch techniques (cont.)

### Use touch techniques

1. At the Start screen, tap the Weather app.
2. Flick up from the bottom to see the charms.
3. Flick again to hide them.
4. Flick inwards from the right edge, in the middle, and tap the Start charm.
5. Tap the Messaging app.
6. Flick inwards from the left edge, in the middle, to return to the Weather app.
7. Repeat.
8. If you have a Windows button, tap it; otherwise, use the charms to return to the Start screen.
9. Tap and hold the Weather tile, drag downwards, continue to drag and reposition the tile elsewhere.
10. Tap and hold the weather tile to select it. If this doesn't work, tap and hold again and drag it downwards slightly and quickly (and then let go) to select the tile and access the charms to manage it.

- Tap, hold and drag downwards a little to perform other tasks (such as to move an item).
- Double-tap an item on the Desktop to open it. This is equal to a double-click with a mouse.
- Tap and hold an icon on the Desktop to access the contextual menu.

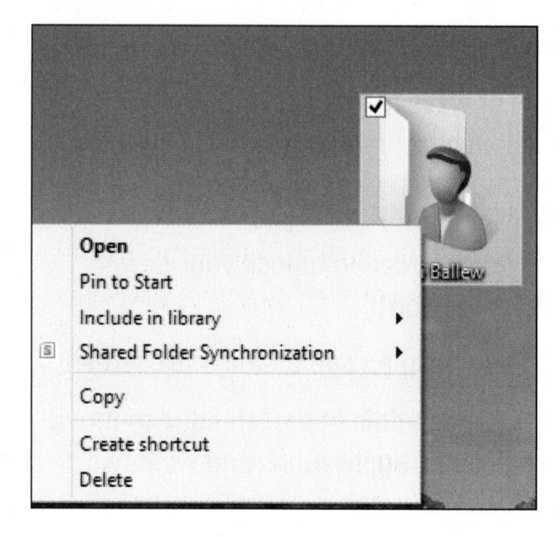


- Flick in and out quickly from the middle of the left edge to view all running apps.

# Personalising your computer

## 5

## Introduction

Now that you know a little about the Start screen, apps, Desktop applications and how to work among them, it's time to get personal! In this chapter, you'll learn how to personalise your computer to suit your needs and preferences.

The first thing you'll learn is how to personalise the Lock and Start screens. You don't actually have to do this – you don't have to change anything if you don't want to. Or you can make only a single change to get some experience, such as altering the colour of the Start screen or creating a four-digit PIN to unlock your computer. Of course, you can completely revamp the entire look and feel of Windows 8 by changing virtually everything, including colours, sounds, themes, fonts and so on.

Whatever you decide, there are three areas to make specific personalisation changes. You can make changes to the Lock screen and how you log in, to the Start screen and the designs and colours used there, and to the Desktop and Taskbar. There are basically two areas to perform these personalisation tasks: the PC Settings hub and Control Panel. The PC Settings hub is app-like; Control Panel is a Desktop application. If you've ever changed the background image or configured a screen saver on a Windows computer, you've used the latter. You may never have used the PC Settings hub.

Once you've finished these personalisation tasks you'll learn how to change the volume of your computer, improve the screen resolution, add hardware and install software, apply a power setting and perform a few other Desktop-related tasks.

### What you'll do

**Choose a new Lock screen picture**

**Log in with fewer keystrokes**

**Change the volume**

**Change the screen resolution**

**Change the size of the items on the Desktop**

**Add hardware**

**Install software**

**Apply a power setting**

**Improve performance with ReadyBoost**

**Personalise the Desktop with Control Panel**

**Create shortcuts**

**Configure the Taskbar**

Finally, you'll explore all the personalisation options in Control Panel and learn how you can personalise the Desktop with backgrounds and screen savers, configure the Taskbar to suit your needs, create shortcuts and more.

**Important**

You can't install familiar Desktop software on tablets running Windows RT.

## Personalise the Lock and Start screens

The Lock screen is the screen you must bypass to get to the log-on screen. There's a picture on the Lock screen that you can change, and icons for apps (called glyphs) that offer information about unread emails, the network, the time and so on. You can change almost all of this. Once you get past this screen you gain access to the screen where you choose your user name (if multiple users exist) and type your password.

Typing a long, complicated password might become tiring after a while, especially if you don't have a physical keyboard or if your password contains capital letters and small ones, numbers and special characters. It can be especially cumbersome if you use a tablet computer. You can change your log-in requirements so that you need only enter a numeric personal identification number (PIN) instead. You make changes to the Lock screen from the PC Settings hub. You can open this hub from the Settings charm – just click Change PC settings.

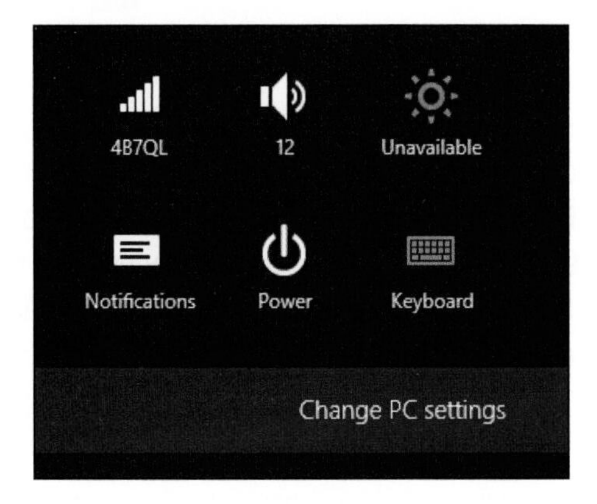


There are many other ways to access the PC Settings hub:

- From the Start screen, click your user name in the top right corner and click Change account picture.
- From the Start screen, type the name of any configuration option or something that can be configured, like *Lock screen*.
- Use the key combination Windows + I to access the Settings charm and click Change PC settings.

### Did you know?

The icons you see on the Lock screen run in the background and show quick status and notifications, even when the computer is locked.

# Personalise the Lock and Start screens (cont.)

## Choose a new Lock screen picture

1. Access the Settings charm. You can use Windows key + I.
2. Click Change PC settings.
3. On the left side, click Personalize; on the right side, click Lock screen (as applicable).
4. Click any picture shown there to use it. To use a picture of your own, click Browse, locate the picture and select it, and click Choose picture.

The PC Settings hub, once open, offers category titles on the left and options for those categories on the right. Here, Personalize is selected on the left side, and Lock screen is selected on the right. Often, as is the case here, category titles and options run off the bottom of the screen. There's a scroll bar available when you position your mouse appropriately.

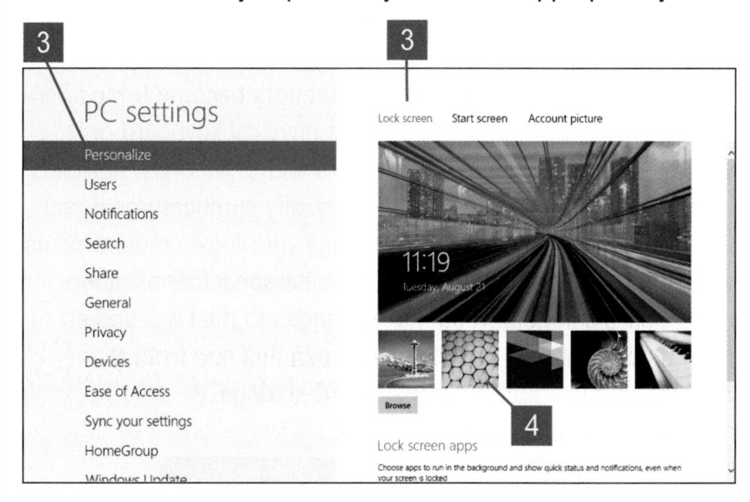


As you can see from the panel, it's pretty easy to choose a new, default Lock screen picture. Beyond that though, you can also choose the Lock screen apps that run in the background and whose icons appear on the Lock screen. By default, Messenger, Mail and Calendar information appear, but you can also add Weather or opt not to show detailed status at all.

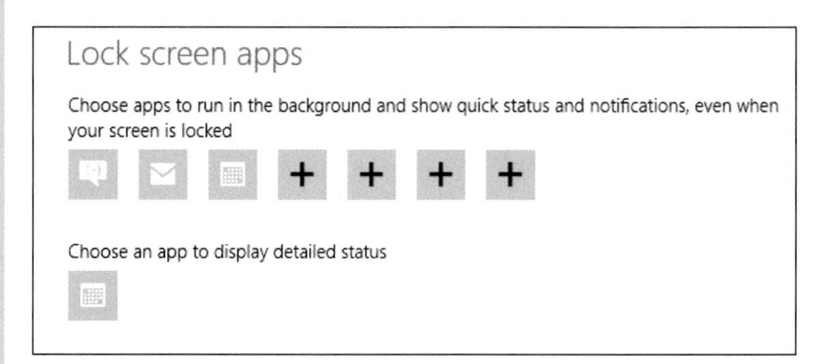


From the Personalize category you can change more than the Lock screen picture and the icons that appear there. If you click Start screen in the right pane instead, you'll notice you can choose a new background design and colour. Likewise, you click Account picture to choose a new account picture for your user account.

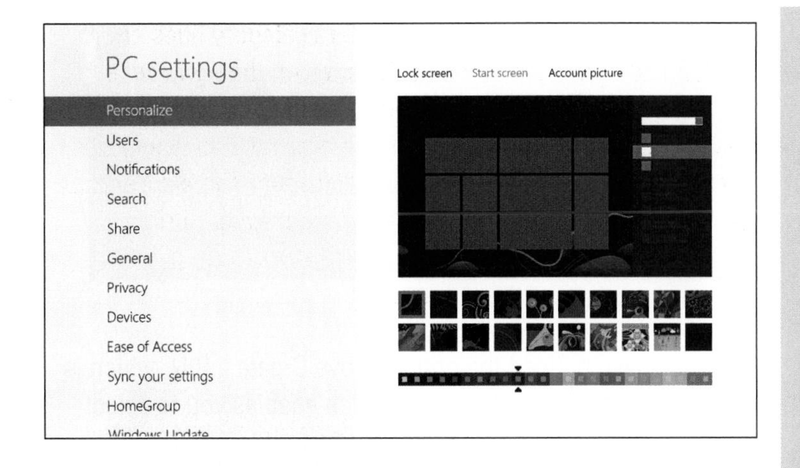


Although there aren't any more options available from the Personalize category in the PC Settings hub, there are other options under other categories. For instance, you can change how you log in from the Users category. One way is to switch from your complicated password to a PIN, such as one you may use at an ATM.

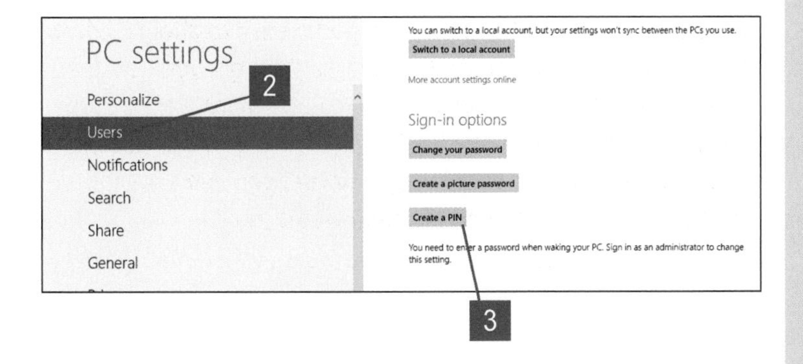


# Personalise the Lock and Start screens (cont.)

## Log in with fewer keystrokes

1. Open the PC Settings hub.
2. Click Users from the left pane.
3. Click Create a PIN from the right pane.
4. Type your current password, click OK, then enter the desired PIN twice.
5. Click Finish.

5

## Personalise the Lock and Start screens (cont.)

**Important**

When creating a PIN, try to avoid things like 1234 or 9876. Avoid using your birthday, too. (Make it at least a little difficult to guess!)

You may have noticed the option above Create a PIN, which is Create a picture password. This option enables you to select a picture and configure a touch pattern on it to unlock your computer. (You'll obviously need a touch screen to configure this.) A picture password is a unique way to unlock your computer. You choose the picture, you draw directly on the touch screen to create a combination of circles, lines and taps, and then you can use that pattern to bypass the Lock screen.

There are many ways to personalise how your computer looks and sounds. These options are numerous and you'll explore many of them later on in this chapter. There are some items you may want to explore right away though, especially if you have 'over-50 eyes' or if you have a hard time hearing system sounds and videos you play on the Internet. In this section you'll learn three things that relate to this: how to increase the volume, enhance the screen resolution and change the default sizes used by Windows 8.

## Personalise your computer

### Change the volume

If you have a laptop or tablet, there is probably a button on the outside for increasing or decreasing the volume. Likewise, if you have physical speakers connected to a desktop computer, they might have some sort of volume control. You may even have volume keys on your keyboard, probably engaged by holding down the Fn key while tapping them. However, if your speakers are built into your computer or tablet and you don't see any external controls, you'll have to change the volume using the Windows 8 interface.

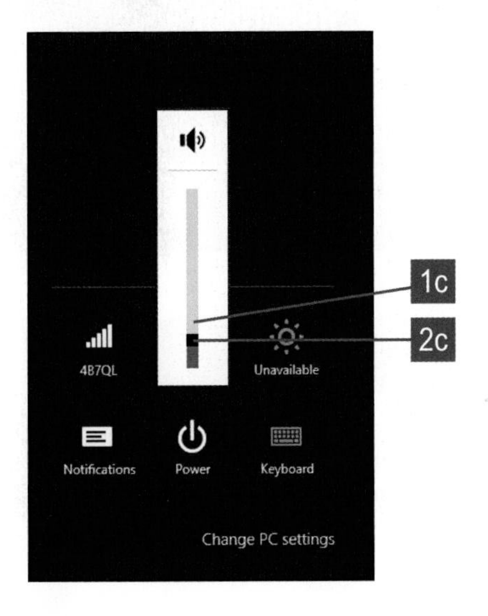


### Change the volume

1. Using a keyboard:
   - a Press the Windows key + I or otherwise access the Settings charm.
   - b Click the volume icon. This is just above the Power icon.
   - c Use the slider that appears to change the volume.
2. Using touch:
   - a Swipe in from the middle of the right side of the screen.
   - b Tap Settings and tap the volume icon.
   - c Use your finger to increase or decrease the volume.

?

**Did you know?**

Most all-in-one computers have speakers inside the unit itself, and often no external volume control.

### Change the screen resolution

Screen resolution defines how many pixels appear on the computer screen. Pixels are small units of colour information the computer uses to provide the image you see on the

# Personalise your computer (cont.)

### Change the screen resolution

1. Access the Desktop. You can use Windows + D.
2. Right-click an empty area of the screen and click Screen resolution.

screen. When more pixels are available, the quality of what's on the screen is increased; when fewer pixels are available, the quality of what's on the screen is decreased. (Think about the difference you see when you look at a picture taken with an inexpensive mobile phone vs one taken with an expensive digital camera. The mobile phone probably takes pictures at a lower resolution than the camera, thus explaining the quality difference.) There are a few common screen resolutions, so you can choose the one that is right for you. You may opt for a resolution that is low (800 × 600 or 1024 × 768) or high (1920 × 1080 or higher).

There is more to it than quality though, and while the science behind it is rather complex, suffice it to say that the lower the resolution, the larger your stuff appears on the monitor; the higher the resolution, the smaller your stuff appears on the monitor. So, if you have problems viewing what's on the screen, you should use a lower resolution.

**Important**

If you choose a resolution that is really low, you might see a message that states you may not be able to see everything on the screen. If this happens, choose a slightly higher resolution.

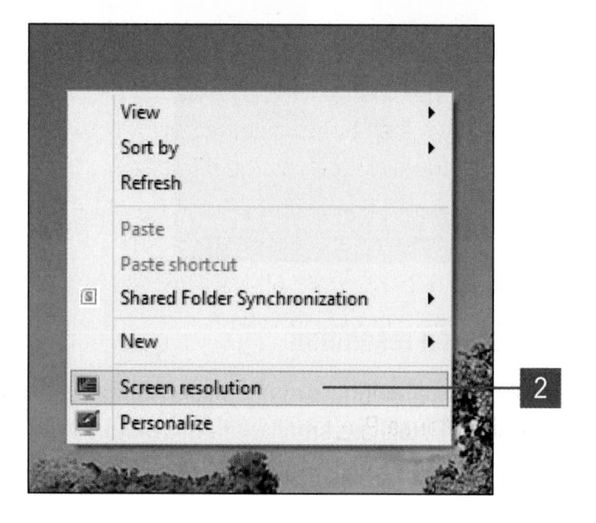

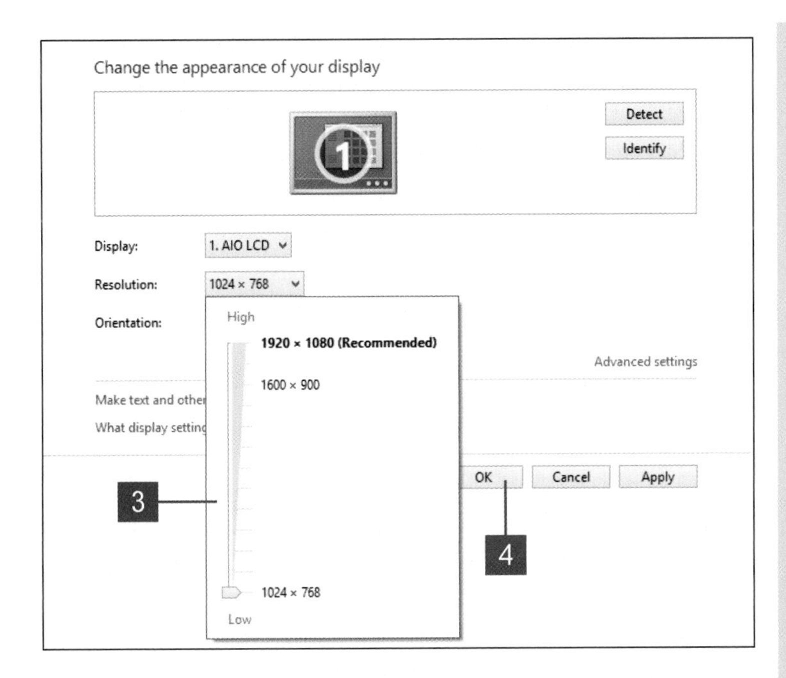


## Personalise your computer (cont.)

3 Click the arrow beside Resolution and select an option. For Snap to work, the resolution must be at least 1366 × 768.

4 Click OK.

5 When prompted, decide if you want to keep the selected resolution or choose a different one.

6 Click OK when you've finished.

**For your information**

From the Screen resolution settings window, click *What display settings should I choose?* if you are having a hard time deciding what's best for you.

### Make Desktop items easier to see

There are lots of ways to make what you see on the Desktop easier to make out beyond changing the screen resolution. You can change the size of all the items by magnifying everything to, say, 125%, or you can opt to change only the text size of specific parts of windows, such as the title bar or menus. As you have learned already, you can opt to show large icons on the Desktop vs medium or small (right-click the Desktop and click View). The best thing to try first is to change the size of everything, as outlined in the panel here.

You can also opt to change the size of the mouse pointer. You do this from the Mouse Properties dialogue box, which you can open by typing Mouse at the Start screen. (Just click the

# Personalise your computer (cont.)

applicable mouse options in the results that appear when you do.) If you have trouble seeing the cursor, consider choosing an 'extra large' scheme from the Pointers tab.

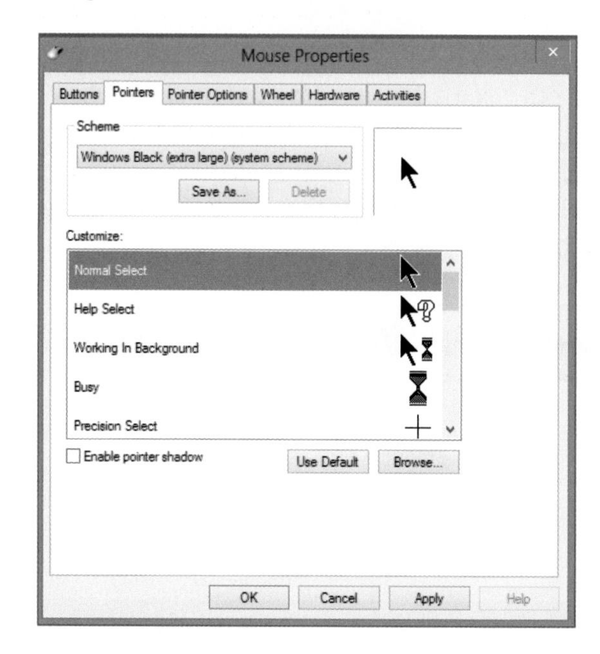


## Change the size of the items on the Desktop

1. Access the Desktop.
2. Right-click the Desktop and choose Personalize.
3. In the resulting window, on the left side near the bottom, click Display.
4. Select Medium – 125% or Larger – 150%. Note the warnings if they appear.
5. Click Apply.
6. If required, click Log off now to apply the settings. (You'll have to log back on afterwards.)

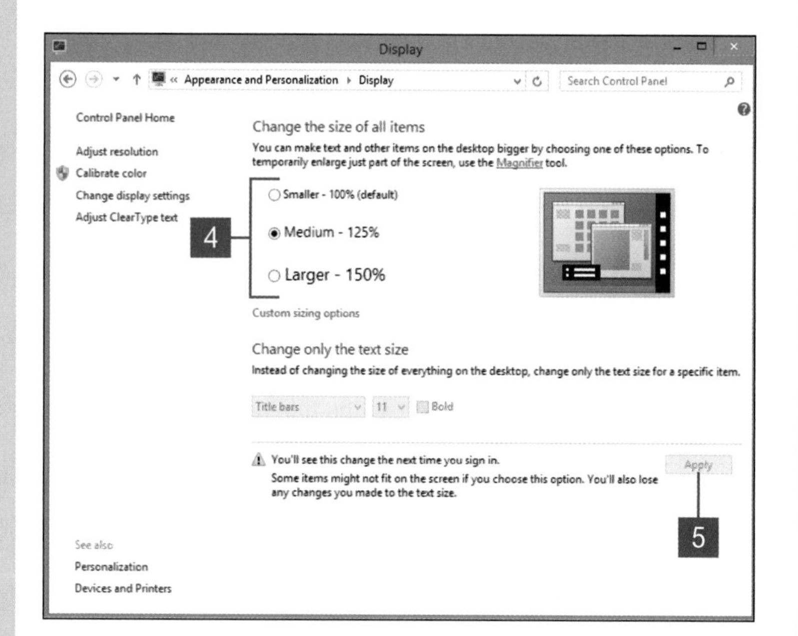

## Personalise your computer (cont.)

If you have tried to change the size of everything, as outlined in the panel, but didn't get the results you wanted, change the size back to Smaller, log off and log back on, and opt to change only the text size instead. You access these options from the same window you used to select 125% or 150% earlier. Note that you can change one or many things. Here, we've changed the text size for all title bars to 24 and made them bold. Notice the word Display at the very top of this screen. This is the title bar and it shows this change. Feel free to make changes as desired before moving on.

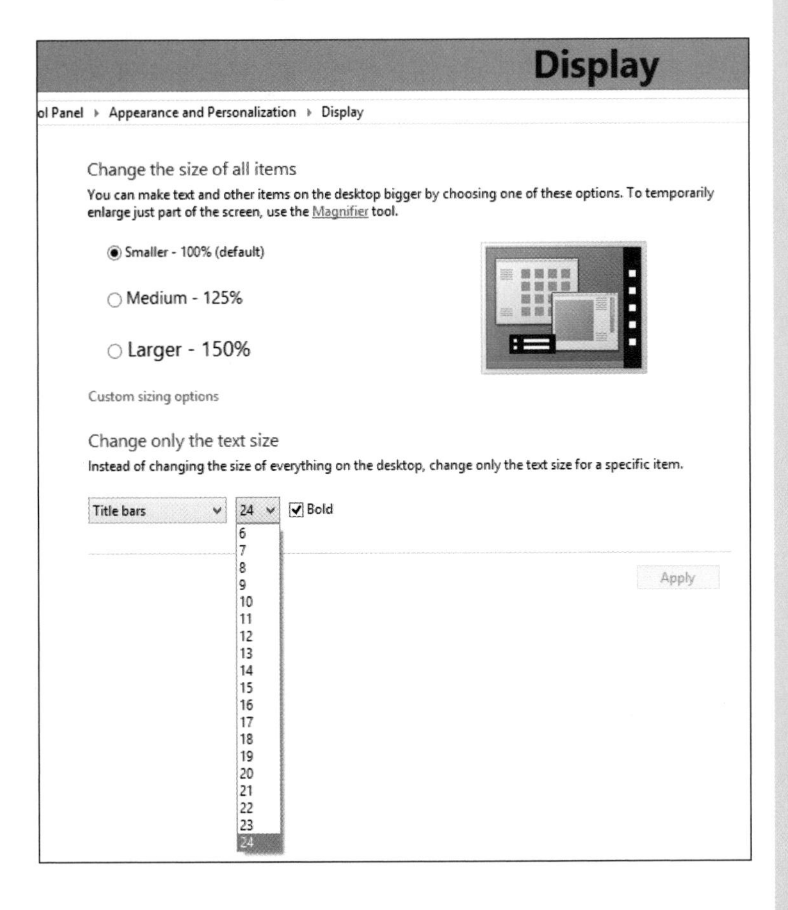

# Add and manage hardware and software

In this section you'll further personalise your computer by installing hardware and software, configuring a power plan and using ReadyBoost, an option to make your computer perform better. You'll also learn how to access your hardware so you can manage it.

## Install hardware

You probably have a printer, scanner, phone, music player or other gadget you want to connect to your Windows 8 computer (or already have). This hardware, as it's known, must be installed before it can be accessed and used from the computer. Most of the time, this is as easy as connecting the device and turning it on.

### Add hardware

1. Perform any setup tasks as applicable to your device:
   - **a** Insert batteries.
   - **b** Connect the device to a wall outlet and turn it on.
   - **c** Connect the device to the PC using the applicable cable.
   - **d** Insert the CD for the device if you have it.
2. If you see a prompt to run the installation file, click it and work through the setup process.
3. If you do not see any prompt and the device starts to install on its own, simply wait.
4. From the Start screen, type Devices, then Settings. Look for Devices in the results.
5. Click Devices and view the newly installed hardware.

?

**Did you know?**

Usually, installing hardware is easy. You simply plug in the device and wait for it to be automatically installed. Once it's installed, you can set what you'd like to happen by default. Before you start, make sure the device is charged, plugged into a wall outlet or has fresh batteries.

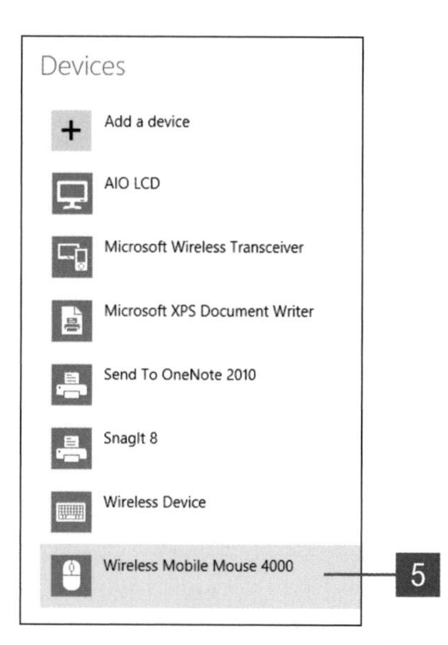

## Add and manage hardware and software (cont.)

### Important

Read the directions that come with each new device you acquire. If there are specific instructions for installation, follow those directions, not the generic directions offered here.

Once hardware is installed, you can view it from the PC Settings hub using the Devices category. All your devices will be listed on the right. If you want to manage that hardware though, you'll have to access Control Panel (which you can open from the All apps page and work with on the Desktop). From there you can see any non-functioning devices and troubleshoot them, share them with others, or remove them. Look at all the options for the wireless mouse we just installed. Also note the device called Gateway that has an exclamation mark beside it. This means there is something about the device that needs attention.

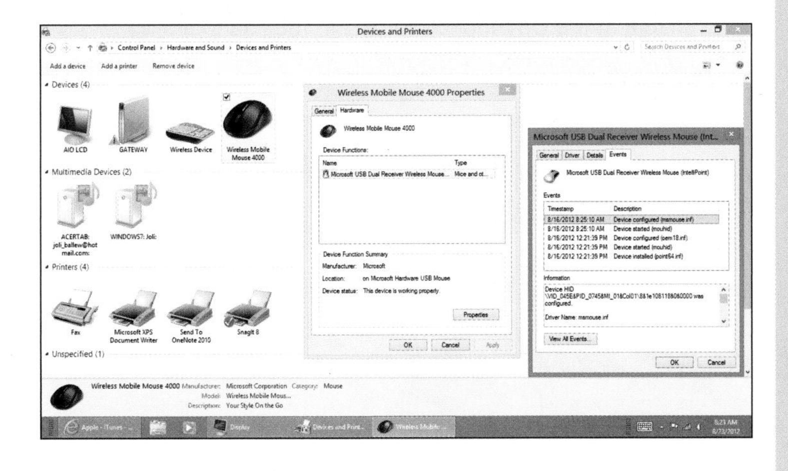


### Install software

You may have software applications you want to install, such as Microsoft Office or Photoshop Elements, or something you downloaded from the Internet, like iTunes. As with installing hardware, software installation goes smoothly almost every time. Just make sure you get your software from a reliable source, such as Amazon, Microsoft's website, Apple's website (think iTunes, not software for Macs only) or a retail store. Once you've obtained the software, on a CD, DVD or as a download, you must access the installation file.

Here are some tips for installing software:

- Insert the CD or DVD into the applicable drive bay and when prompted, opt to install the program.
- Be careful you know what you're installing. Some software asks to install things like toolbars, PDF readers and other add-ons you probably don't need (in addition to the software you do need).
- Always install the basic software that comes with printers, scanners, cameras and phones. You often need this software to use the device effectively.
- If a device won't work after you connect and try to install it, from the CD, install the driver.
- Files you download from the Internet and save will be available in the Downloads folder, in the File Explorer window. Double-click a file to run it.

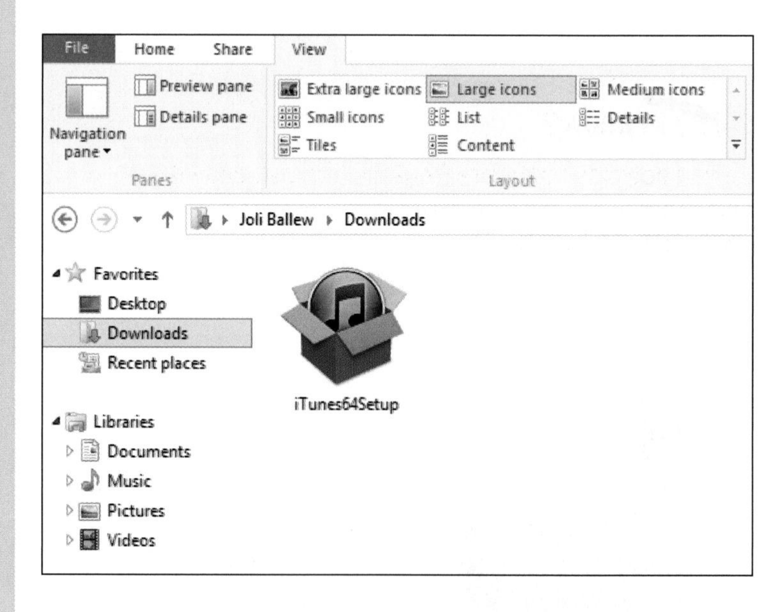

# Add and manage hardware and software (cont.)

## Install software

1. Download the installation file from the Internet and skip to step 4, or, insert the CD or DVD in the appropriate drive and proceed to step 2.
2. Click the prompt that appears in the top right corner to see your options. What you see may differ from what's shown here.
3. If you are not prompted or you miss the prompt, you can eject and reinsert the CD, or:
   - Open the Computer window. (You can type Computer at the Start screen.)
   - Double-click the CD or DVD drive in File Explorer.
4. Double-click the application file or do whatever else is necessary to start the installation.
5. Work through the installation wizard.

2

DVD RW Drive (D:) Oct 05 2011
Tap to choose what happens with removable drives.

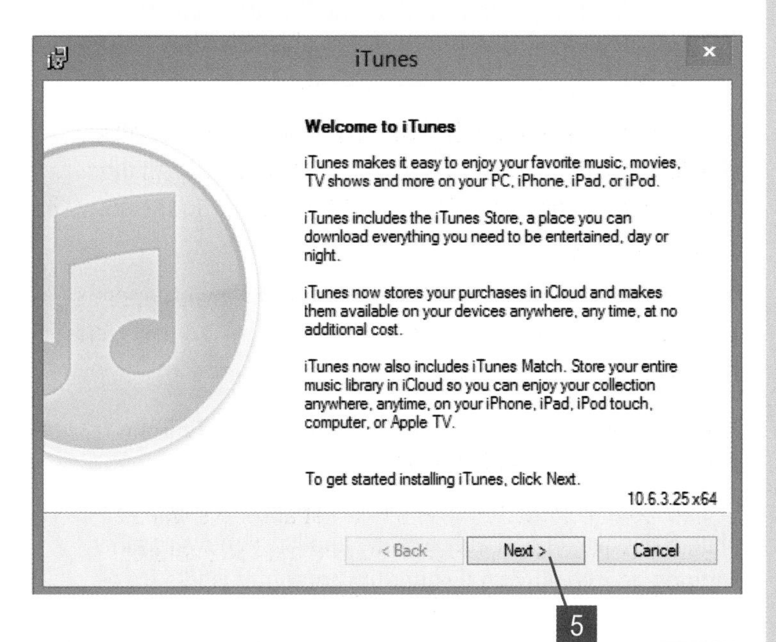


?

### Did you know?

If you download software from the Internet, copy the installation files to a CD or DVD for safe keeping and write the product ID or key on it.

!

### Important

To install software you must locate the application file or the executable file. Often this is named Setup, Install or something similar. If you receive a message that the file you are trying to access can't be opened, you've chosen the wrong file.

5

## Add and manage hardware and software (cont.)

> **Important**
>
> You can't install most common Desktop applications and software (and even some hardware) if you own a tablet that runs Windows RT.

If you install a software program but it doesn't work properly, you can run it in Program Compatibility Mode. This lets you run programs made for previous versions of Windows. Often this resolves software problems. To get started you must open the Program Compatibility application. You can do this by searching at the Start screen for *Program Compatibility*. With that done, work through the wizard to find the program and choose the default settings.

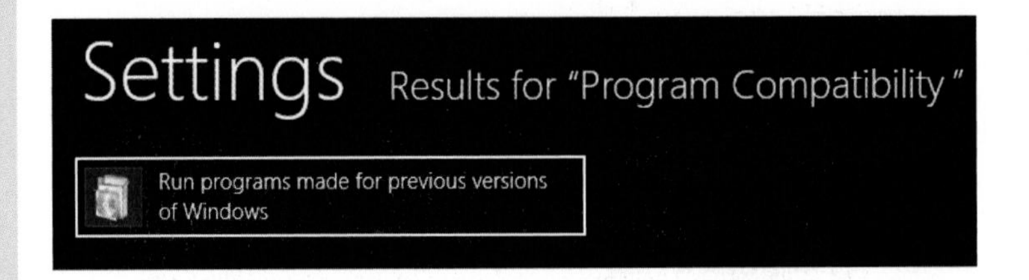


### Choose a power plan

A power plan contains settings that you can configure to tell Windows 8 when and if to turn off the computer monitor or display, and when or if to put the computer to sleep. The default plan, Balanced, is probably already applied. A power plan's settings go into effect only after the computer is idle for a specific amount of time. If you are happy with the current power plan, including when the computer monitor shuts down and the computer goes to sleep, you do not need to read this part of the chapter. If you'd like to tweak these settings, read on.

There are three power plans, but you can create your own if you prefer. The power plans offer options specific to your kind of computer, too. For instance, the power plans on a desktop PC let you configure when to turn off the display and put the computer to sleep. A desktop PC is assumed to always be plugged into a power outlet. However, on a laptop PC, you can configure when to turn off the display and/or put the computer to sleep when the computer is plugged in, or when it's using its battery.

The three plans included with Windows 8, regardless of whether the PC is a desktop or laptop, are Balanced, Power Saver and High Performance (you have to specifically opt to view additional options to see this one). When you select an option you're informed of the current default choices. You can make changes to the power plan or simply choose it. Likewise, you can create your own.

## Did you know?

It's actually better for a desktop computer if you leave it on and just let it go to sleep. Physically turning the PC on and off is hard on the internal parts.

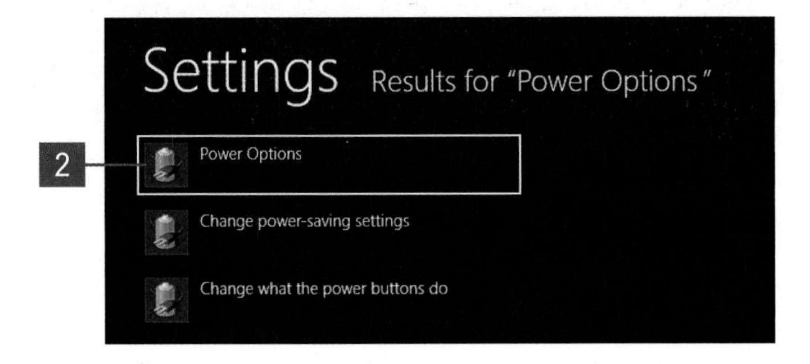


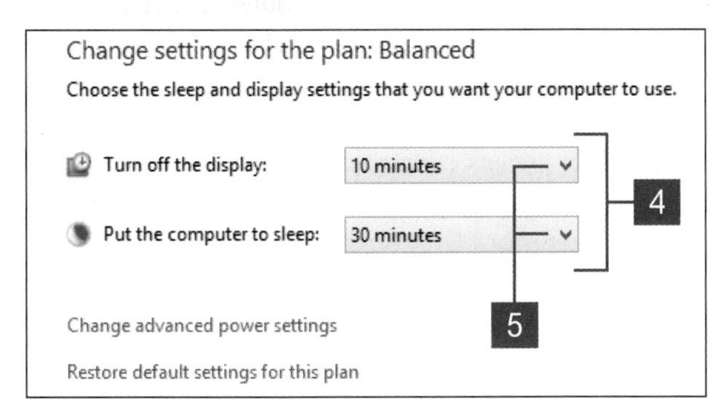


## Use ReadyBoost

RAM, or Random Access Memory, is installed inside your computer and holds data that is needed by the computer immediately, or is likely to be. The more RAM you have, the better the computer should perform. Adding RAM inside the case is difficult, a bit risky, and sometimes impossible. If you want to add more RAM but you can't (or don't want to), you can use ReadyBoost. ReadyBoost is a technology that enables you to use a USB flash drive or a secure digital memory card as

# Add and manage hardware and software (cont.)

## Apply a power setting

1. From the Start screen, type Power Options.
2. Click Settings and click Power Options.
3. In the Power Options window, next to Balanced, click Change settings for the plan: Balanced.
4. Note the settings for turning off the display and putting the computer to sleep.
5. Use the arrow keys to select the desired times for each entry.
6. Click Save changes.

# Add and manage hardware and software (cont.)

## Improve performance with ReadyBoost

1. Insert a USB flash drive, thumb drive or memory card into an available slot on the outside of your PC.
2. When prompted in the upper right corner, click to view your options.
3. Choose Speed up my system, Windows ReadyBoost.
4. Choose to dedicate the device to ReadyBoost and click OK.

cache (a place where data is stored temporarily and accessed when needed) to increase computer performance. (USB keys must be at least USB 2.0 and meet other requirements, but don't worry about that, you'll be told if the hardware isn't up to par.) ReadyBoost is kind of like RAM.

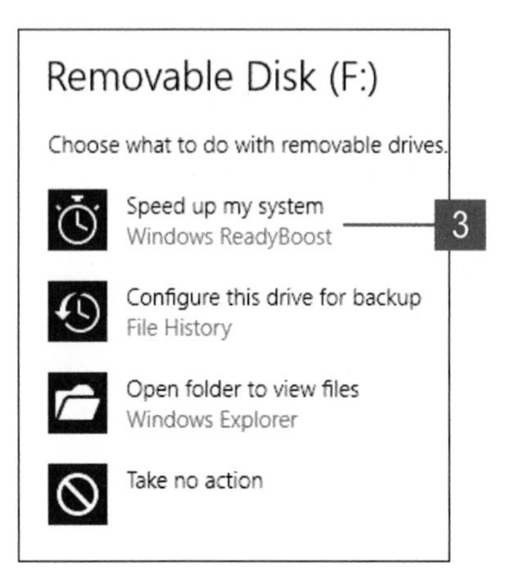

### Jargon buster

**Cache** – a temporary storage area like RAM.

**RAM** – random access memory is where information is stored temporarily so the operating system has quick access to it. The more RAM you have, the better your PC should perform.

## Personalise the Desktop

If you've ever used a computer, you probably have a little experience with the Personalization options available in Control Panel. This is where you select a new background picture, apply a screen saver, select a theme and more. There are hundreds of options here. It's fun to explore these and to apply different themes, mouse pointers, Desktop icons and so on.

### Apply a theme, new background or screen saver

You make changes to the Desktop background and so on from Control Panel. This is a Desktop application. You can make these kinds of changes using the PC Settings hub you learned about earlier as well.

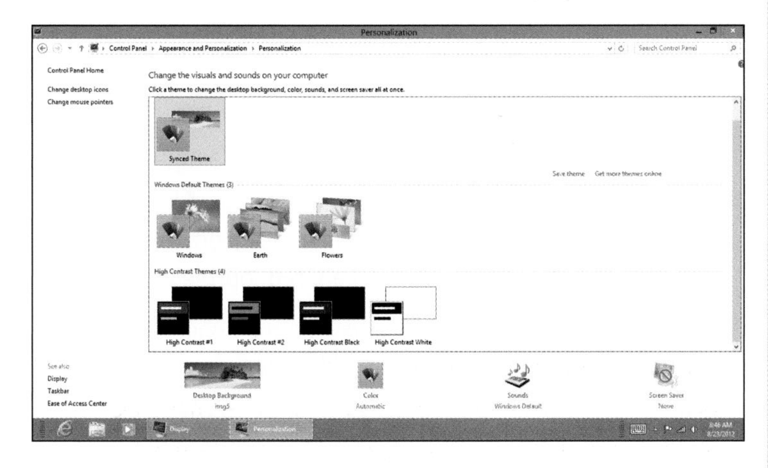


Here are a few things you can explore and change without worrying about causing any problems:

- Synced Theme – if you use a Microsoft account, you'll see a Synced Theme, which is the theme you'll see on every PC you log into with your Microsoft account. This enables you to configure your preferences just once and apply them easily to any other computer you use.
- Windows Default Themes – a theme is a group of settings that includes but is not limited to a background picture or multiple backgrounds that change often: screen savers, mouse pointers, windows colours, and sounds. When you apply a theme, just about everything changes.
- High Contrast Themes – if you have trouble viewing the default dark and coloured text on a mostly white

## Personalise the Desktop (cont.)

background, choose one of the first three high-contrast themes. This will apply a theme that uses white and other light colours for the text, and applies a black background. You can try High Contrast White for the opposite effect.

- Desktop Background – here you can choose what background(s) to use and how often to change them if you choose multiple backgrounds. You'll learn how to do this in the panel. There are many kinds of Desktop backgrounds, including:
  - Windows Desktop Backgrounds – the images are included with Windows 8.
  - Pictures Library – the images and pictures you've taken, acquired or otherwise saved to your computer.
  - Top Rated Photos – the images you've rated as your favourites.
  - Solid Colors – backgrounds that are all a single colour.
- Color – use this to change the default colour of the window borders and the Taskbar. You can choose from lots of colours, including pink, blue, green, red, purple and orange.
- Sounds – use this to choose a new sound scheme or change certain system sounds to something else.
- Screen Saver – apply a screen saver here. Read on for more information about screen savers.

### Personalise the Desktop with Control Panel

1. Right-click an empty area of the Desktop and choose Personalize.
2. Click Desktop Background.
3. Click the arrow beside Picture location and select Windows Desktop Backgrounds. (You could choose something else if you prefer.)
4. Deselect any pictures you do not like.
5. Choose how often to change the pictures.
6. Click Save changes.

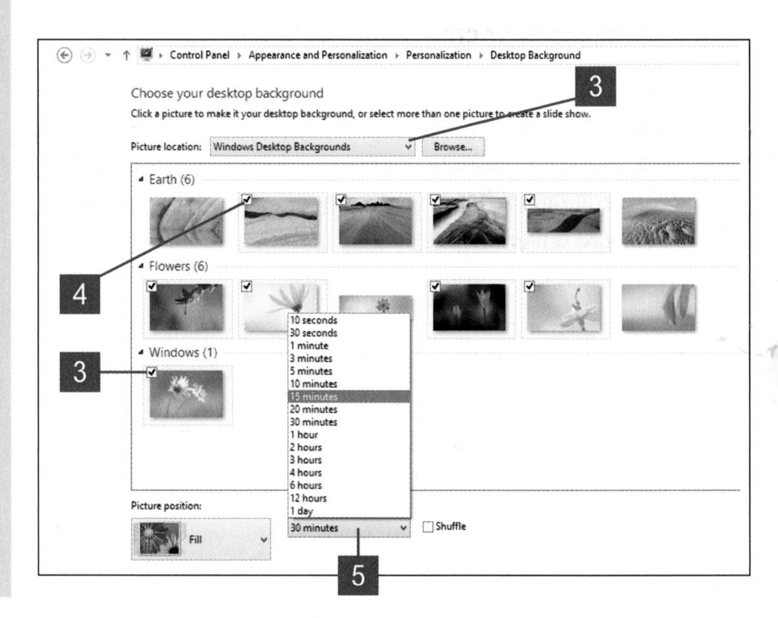

## Personalise the Desktop (cont.)

A screen saver is a picture or animation that covers your screen and appears after your computer has been idle for a specific amount of time that you set. It used to be that screen savers 'saved' your computer screen from image burn-in, but that is no longer the case. Now, screen savers are used either for visual enhancement or as a security feature. As an extra security measure, you can configure your screen saver to require a password on waking up, which happens when you move the mouse or hit a key on the keyboard. Requiring a password means that once the screen saver is running, no one but you can log on to your computer, by typing in your password when prompted.

Screen savers come in many flavours, and Windows 8 comes with several – the 3D Text screen saver is one of my favourites. As with other options, you access the settings by right-clicking an empty area of the Desktop and selecting Personalize.

You can also get screen savers online and from third-party retailers. However, screen savers from these places are notorious for containing, at the very least, annoying pop-ups or sales ads, and at worst malicious code and even viruses. Before you download and install a screen saver from a third party, make sure you've read the reviews and are positive it's from a worthy and reliable source.

### Add Desktop icons or create a shortcut

Beyond the Desktop backgrounds and screen savers, you can also choose which Desktop icons you want to appear. To get started, right-click an empty area of the Desktop, click Personalize and click Change desktop icons. From there you select what you'd like to see.

## Personalise the Desktop (cont.)

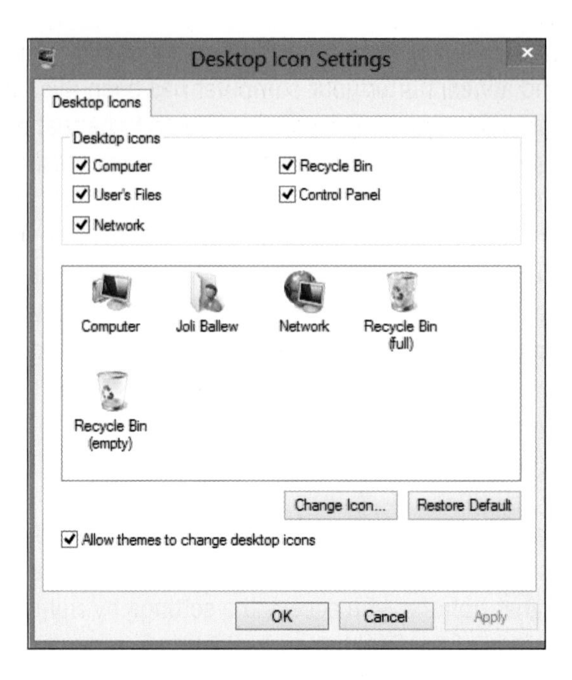


**Did you know?**

If you have more than one user account on your computer, each user can configure their Desktop as they wish.

Finally, you may want to create a shortcut to something that isn't available from any dialogue box. A shortcut always appears with an arrow beside it (or on it, actually). Shortcuts enable you to access folders, files, programs and other items stored on your PC without the hassle of drilling into various folders or libraries, accessing the folder on a network, or using the Start screen to search for it.

There are several ways to create a shortcut. One is to right-click an empty area of the Desktop, click New and then Shortcut. Performing these steps will result in the opening of a dialogue box where you can 'browse' to the location of the file, folder or program for which you want to create the shortcut. However, this method requires you to understand a bit more than you probably do about how files and folders are managed and stored in Windows 8, as well as where program files are located and which file actually starts the program. Although we cover this in depth in Chapter 6, this is really the long way round the issue anyway. There's a better way, and that involves finding the item to create a shortcut for in File Explorer and dragging it to the Desktop, or locating the item and right-clicking it.

When you right-click a shortcut on the Desktop, you'll see lots of choices. One is to create a shortcut, interestingly. When you click Delete, you are prompted to move the shortcut to the Recycle Bin. Since it's a shortcut, that's fine; you can delete any shortcut without worrying about deleting actual data.

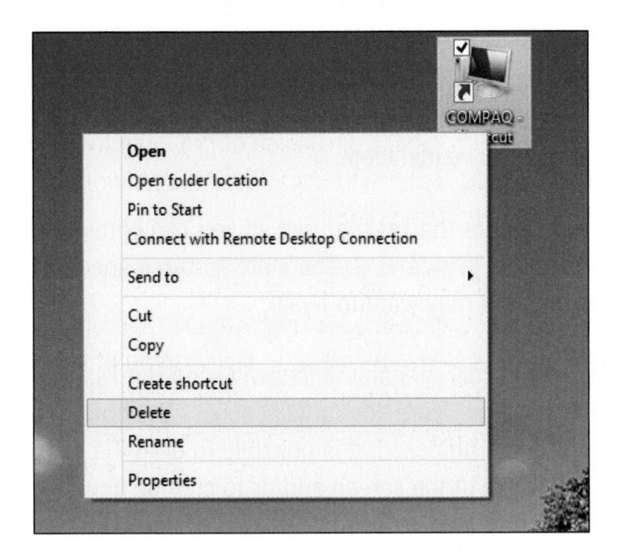


# Personalise the Desktop (cont.)

## Create shortcuts

1. Access the Desktop.
2. Use File Explorer to locate the item for which you want to create a shortcut.
3. Right-click it and drag it to the Desktop. Note that as you drag a shortcut arrow appears.
4. Let go of the mouse and click Create shortcuts here.

# Personalise the Desktop (cont.)

**Important**

If the icon you want to delete does not have an arrow by it, and it's data you created such as a picture or a file, deleting it from the Desktop will delete the actual data. You should delete only items that have the shortcut icon on them, just to be safe.

## Explore the Taskbar

The Taskbar is the transparent bar that runs horizontally across the bottom of your screen. It can contain the following items:

- Icons for programs you use often – by default, icons for Internet Explorer and File Explorer appear on the Taskbar. You can add icons for programs you use often. These icons always appear on the Taskbar, whether they are open and in use or not.
- Icons for open documents, pictures, spreadsheets or other data – by default, when you open a program to view, edit, listen to or manage any kind of data, an icon for that open program appears on the Taskbar. When you hover the mouse over the icon, a thumbnail will appear.
- Icons for system notifications – by default, the Taskbar offers 'system icons' for the date and time, the network icon and the system volume. These appear on the right side of the Taskbar. Notification icons can also appear including but not limited to the Action Center, Media Center Network and programs you've installed.

You can configure the Taskbar just as you can configure the other aspects of Windows 8. There are features specific to the Taskbar that you may want to tweak:

- Lock the Taskbar – enabling this will keep the Taskbar in its default position, lying horizontally across the bottom of the screen. When unlocked, it is possible to drag the Taskbar to other areas of the screen and/or to change how thick the

## Personalise the Desktop (cont.)

Taskbar is, as shown here. (To move or resize the Taskbar, just click an empty area of the Taskbar and drag it to another area of the Desktop.)

- Auto-hide the Taskbar – enabling this will cause the Taskbar to disappear when not in use. It will reappear when you move your mouse over the area of the screen where the Taskbar lies.
- Taskbar Buttons – configuring this will allow Taskbar icons to be combined when the Taskbar is full and allow you to hide labels. Combining Taskbar icons will offer a less crowded Taskbar when multiple programs are open.
- Use Peek – enable this to preview the Desktop when you move your mouse to the Show desktop button at the end of the Taskbar.

### Did you know?

You don't have to configure the Taskbar. If you're happy with it the way it is, just skip this section.

# Personalise the Desktop (cont.)

## Configure the Taskbar

1. Right-click an empty area of the Taskbar, towards the middle of it.
2. Click Properties.
3. In the Taskbar Properties dialogue box, select or deselect any feature by clicking in its tickbox.
4. Explore the other tabs: Jump Lists and Toolbars.
5. Click OK when you've finished.

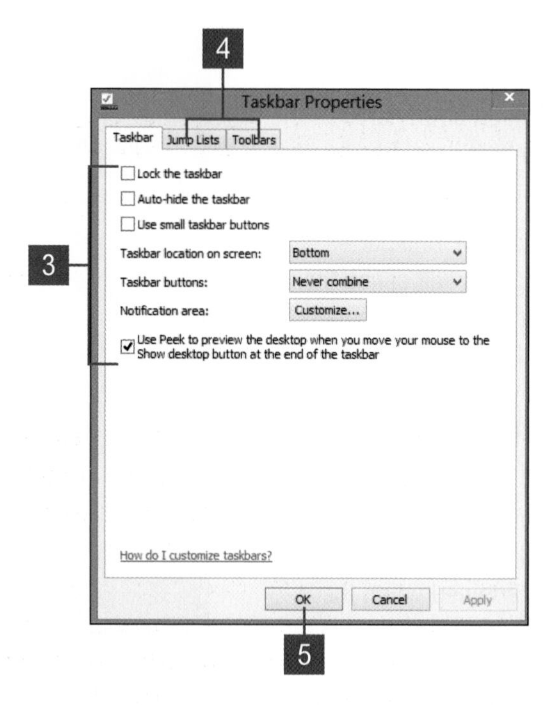

# Manage files, folders and libraries

6

## Introduction

You're going to have data to save. That data may come in the form of letters you type on the computer, pictures you take using your digital camera, music you copy from your own CD collection, music and media you purchase online, address books, videos from a DV camera, holiday card and gift lists, and more. Phew! Each time you click the Save or Save As button or option under a File menu, on a tab or on a menu bar (which is what you do to save data to your PC most of the time), you'll be prompted to tell Windows 8 where you want to save that data.

To be able to save data effectively and appropriately, you need to understand where files are saved by default. For the most part, documents go in the Documents folder, Music in the Music folder, Pictures in the Pictures folder, and so on. Once you understand the system already in place, you can then grasp the importance of personalising that system with your own folders and subfolders. You'll learn how to create those folders here. With that system expanded, you'll learn how to copy, move and delete files and folders, how to use the File Explorer ribbon, and how to view data in different ways. All of this happens on the Desktop, using File Explorer.

## What you'll do

**Save data to a library from WordPad**

**Locate a file from a Start screen app**

**Create subfolders**

**Create your own libraries**

**Copy or move a file**

**Restore data from the Recycle Bin**

# Explore your libraries

There are four libraries already available to you for saving and storing data: Documents, Music, Pictures and Videos. You'll find them in File Explorer, a window that opens only on the Desktop. The first step in understanding how Windows 8 organises the data you keep and where to save data you create or acquire in the future is to understand these libraries.

Briefly, a library is a virtual storage area that makes it possible for you to access data that is stored in a personal folder (such as My Documents) and the related public folder (like Public Documents), and any other folders or libraries you've created and/or specifically made available there. When you save a file to one of these libraries, by default it's saved to the related personal folder (My Documents, My Pictures and so on.) If you want to save it to the related public folder or some other folder you've included, you have to specifically choose it during the save process. You can view these libraries and their related folders from File Explorer. To get started, access the Desktop (Ctrl + D will work) and click the folder icon at the bottom of the screen on the Taskbar.

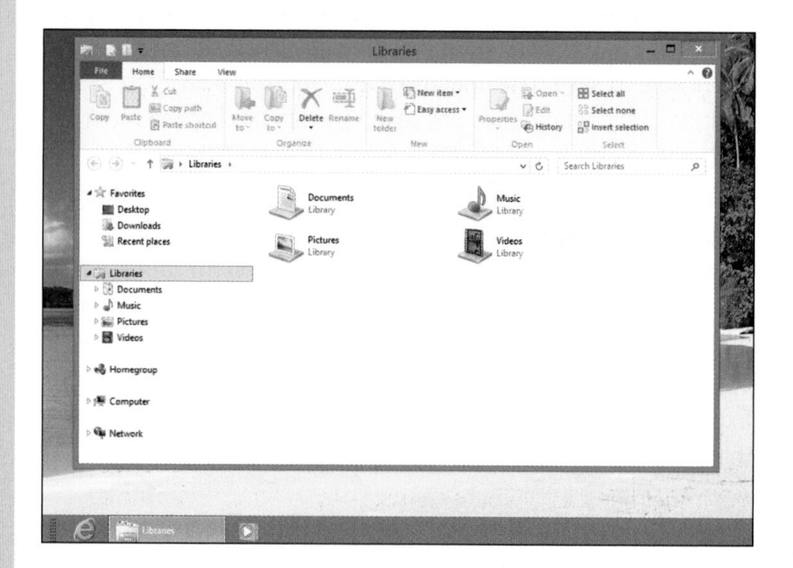


Now try the following:

- Position the cursor over Libraries and if you do not see a down-facing arrow as shown next, click Libraries to show it (and the libraries underneath).

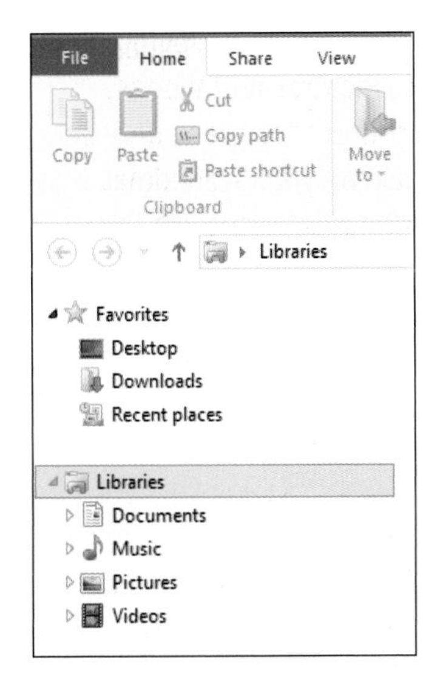


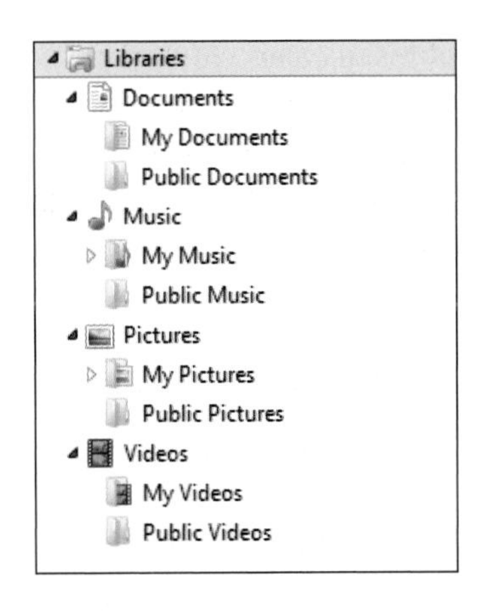


- Click the right-facing arrow by each library entry so that it becomes a down-facing arrow. Note the folders that appear underneath. You store data here.

Depending on how you've used your computer up to now, you may see more folders than the personal and public folders you see here. These additional folders will be available if you have purposely created or included them in a particular library.

?

## Did you know?

If you click a library in the Navigation pane, you'll see what's in both the personal and public folders; if you click only one related Library folder, the data will be separated appropriately.

You must become adept at saving data to the proper library or folder to keep your computer organised. Sometimes you will save data using a Desktop app's File menu. Other times you will use a download dialogue box. And in other cases, you may use a graphic like the one you see when uploading data with an app such as SkyDrive. You may even use something completely proprietary, such as a menu or option in a software program you use with a digital camera or scanner. In all

## Explore your libraries (cont.)

of these cases, you must know how to navigate the folder hierarchy already provided for you.

- In a Start screen app such as SkyDrive, you locate data you've saved or want using a graphical interface like the one shown here. You can opt to 'go up' to move up the file structure hierarchy, or if you see what you want, you can simply click it. You can also click the arrow beside Files to select any other folder.

- In any Save or Save as dialogue box in a Desktop application, locate the desired library in the Navigation pane. You may need to expand a library to locate your required location.

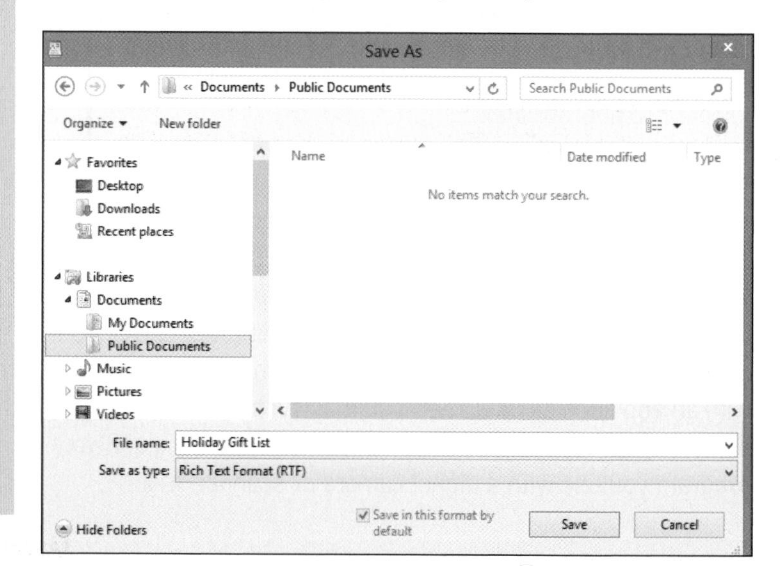

- In the Desktop app Internet Explorer, when prompted to save a file, click the arrow beside Save and click Save as. You may opt for the Downloads folder.

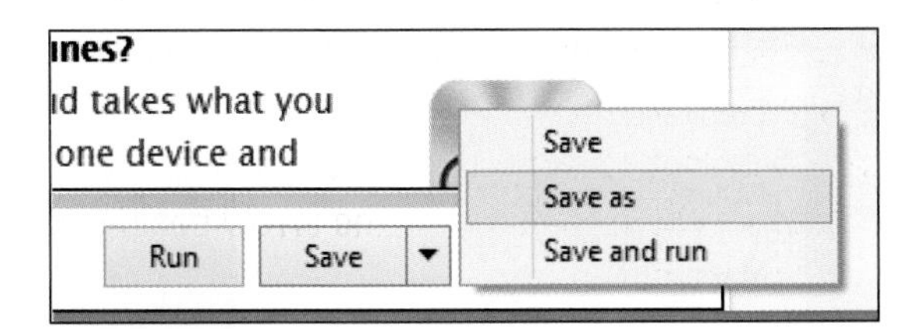


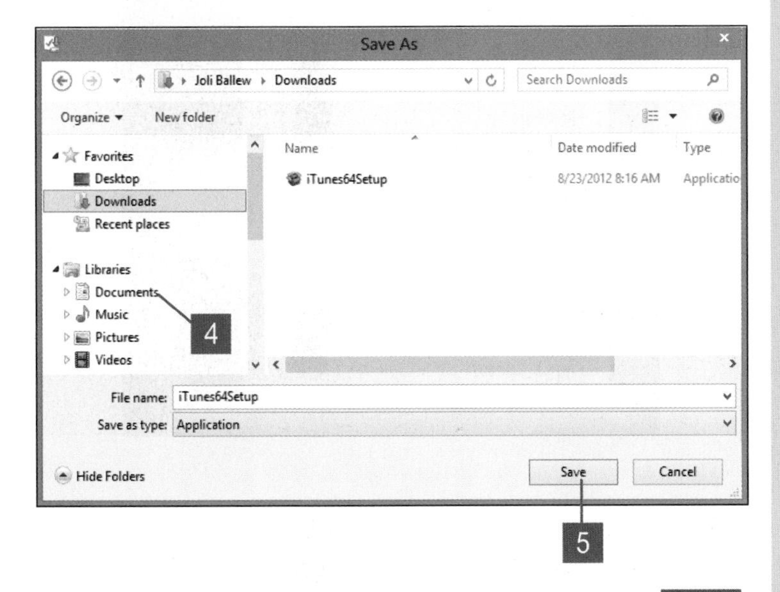


## Did you know?

You can save the file to a different computer on your network or a different drive on your computer from the Network and Computer options, respectively.

# Explore your libraries (cont.)



### Save data to a library from WordPad

1. From the Start screen, type Word and select WordPad in the results.
2. Type a few words and click the File tab.
3. Click Save as.
4. In the Navigation pane, under Libraries, click Documents.
5. Type a name for the file and click Save.

# Explore your libraries (cont.)

## Locate a file from a Start screen app

1. From the Start screen, open the SkyDrive app.
2. Right-click and then click Upload.
3. You may see the data you expect. If so, you can select it and add it to SkyDrive. To experiment though:
   a. Click Go up. Note the options to select a different library.
   b. Click the arrow beside Files. Note the option to select any library or folder, your Homegroup, or even Computer or Network.

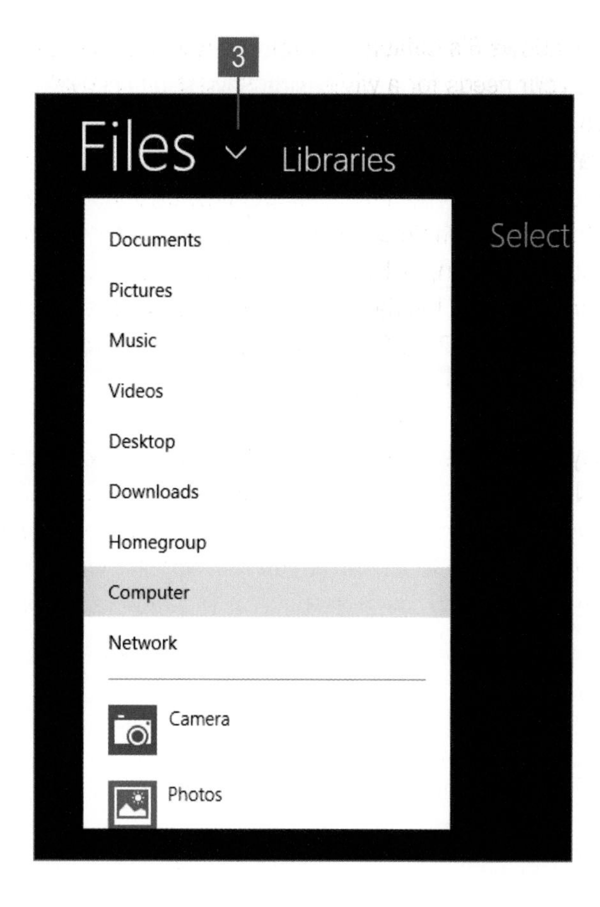

While Windows 8's default libraries and the folders in them will suit your needs for a while, it won't last. Soon you'll need to create subfolders inside those folders to manage your data and keep it organised. For instance, inside the My Documents folder, you may need to create a subfolder called Tax Information to hold scanned receipts, tax records and account information, or Health Records to hold sensitive health information. Inside the Pictures folder you might create folders named 2012, 2013, 2014, and then populate those with subfolders named Weddings, Holidays, Grandkids and so on.

It's easy to create a folder or a subfolder. Using File Explorer, in the Navigation pane, select the folder inside which you'd like to create a subfolder. Then, from the Home tab, select New folder. All you have to do after that is name the folder. (You can rename a folder by right-clicking it and selecting Rename.)

## Enhance the library structure

6

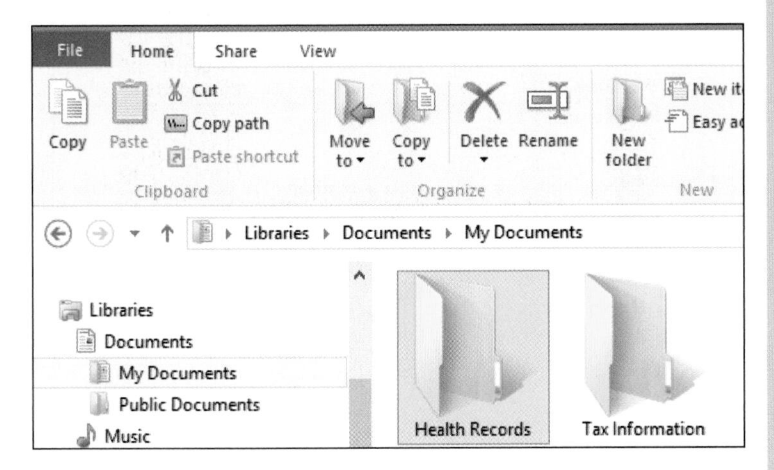


### For your information

The tabs in File Explorer, when clicked, provide a ribbon that contains the commands and tools you need to perform tasks. For instance, the Home tab offers options to create a new folder, rename a file or folder, or even move or copy a file or folder.

# Enhance the library structure (cont.)

### Create subfolders

1. In the Navigation pane of File Explorer, under Libraries, click Documents.
2. Click the Home tab and then click New folder.
3. Type a name for the folder and press Enter or Return on the keyboard.
4. Repeat as desired, and make sure to create subfolders inside the Pictures library (perhaps Children, Pets, House, etc.).

Creating subfolders in the existing folders often works just fine. Sometimes, though, you may have specific hobbies or interests that require you to create your own library structure. In this case, you'd extend what's in the left pane of your library by adding your own link under Libraries to the mix. Here, I've created a new library called Grandchildren, and its associated icon appears in the main window of my Libraries folder. I've also 'included' three folders, one for each grandchild, named Abigail, Nathan and Allison.

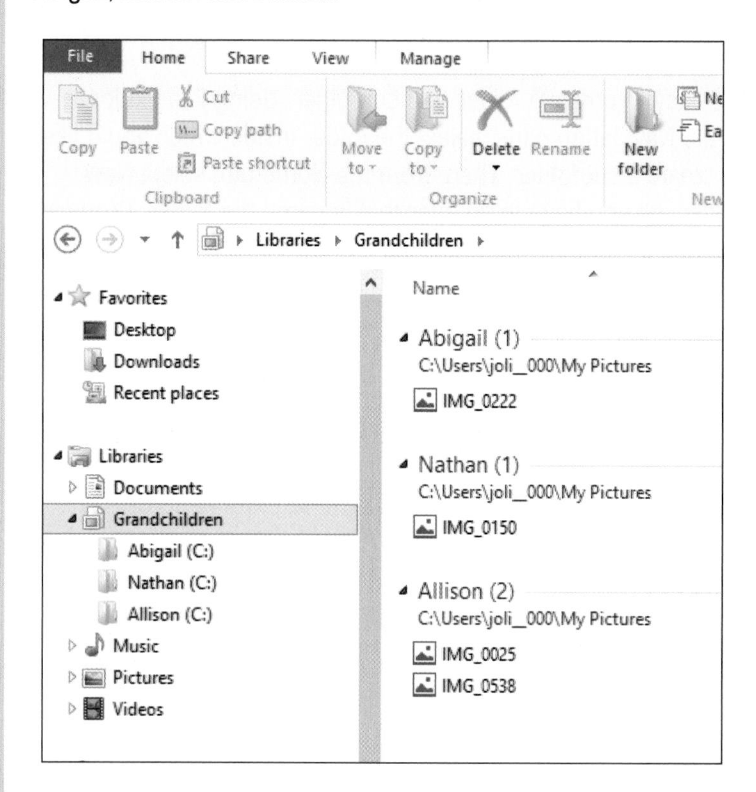

### Jargon buster

Library – a top-level organisational folder.

Folder – a second-level organisational folder.

Subfolder – a third-level organisational folder you create.

## Enhance the library structure (cont.)



The idea behind extending Windows 8's library and/or folder structure is to personalise it to meet your needs. If you travel a lot, you might want to create an entirely new library called Travel and make folders and subfolders available there that are named appropriately and hold similar data. (You'll need to first create these folders.) You could keep everything related to travel there, including maps, documents, pictures and videos, and ignore Windows 8's existing folders altogether.

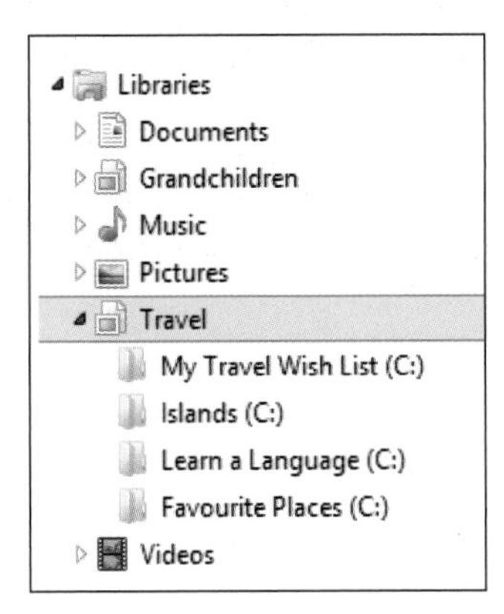


Other libraries or folders you might consider creating include:

- Graduations
- Genealogy
- Places to Visit
- Quilting Patterns
- Bike Trails
- Lakes and Campgrounds
- Letters to Family
- Pets
- Doctor and Hospital Information
- Recipes
- Home Improvements
- Scanned Receipts

Make sure to consider this. Don't stray very far from the default file structure. Create any new libraries, folders and subfolders inside the existing structure. This will make your data easy

### Did you know?

You can create a new folder just about anywhere: on the Desktop, in an existing folder or in a folder you create yourself. If you have an external hard drive or networked computer, you can create a folder called Backup in any of the public folders and store backup data there.

# Enhance the library structure (cont.)

to find and will also make it easy to back up. Just about any backup program will automatically back up everything there. If you have folders scattered about the hard drive, you'll have to manually tell the program where they are and that you want to back them up – that is difficult.

## Create your own libraries

1. Open File Explorer.
2. In the Navigation pane, click Libraries.
3. From the Home tab, on the ribbon, click New item and then Library. If you're more comfortable with the old way of doing things:
   a. Right-click an empty area of the Content pane.
   b. Click New and click Library.
4. Type a name for the library. To rename it, right-click the new library and click Rename.
5. Click Enter (or Return) on the keyboard.
6. Click the library in the Navigation pane to open it. Click Include a folder.
7. Locate the folder to include. Click Include folder.
8. To add more folders:
   a. Click the Manage tab.
   b. Click Manage library.
   c. Click Add.
   d. Locate the folder to add.
   e. Click Include folder.
   f. Repeat as desired.
   g. Click OK.

**Important**

If you don't see a ribbon but instead see only menu titles, click the down arrow located to the left of the Help button and below the red X in the top right corner of the window.

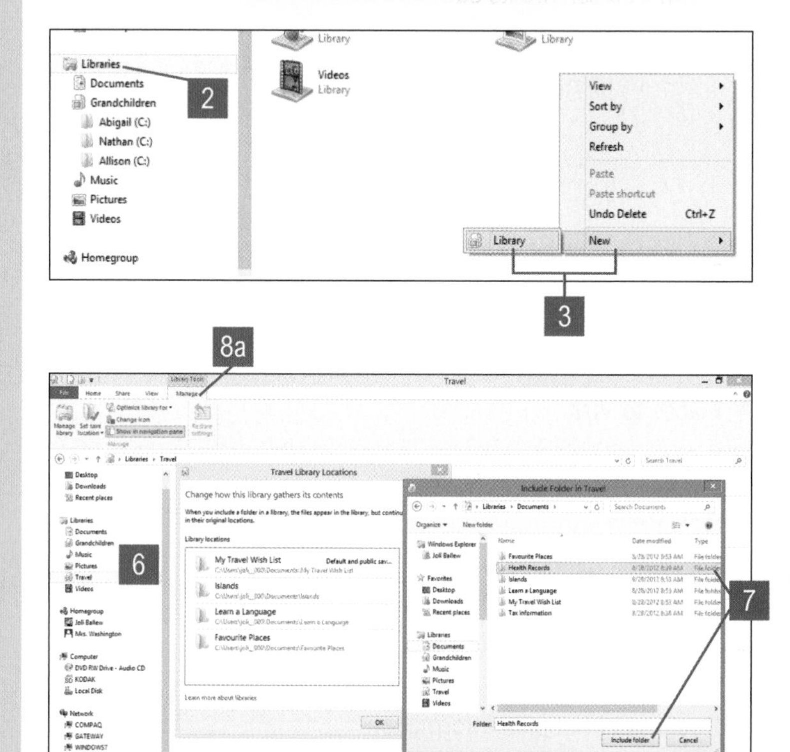


The libraries and the subfolders you create are not the only places you can save data; you have a personal user folder with additional folders, although you probably won't access them nearly as often as you do libraries. To access these folders, you must know how to navigate there.

## For your information

Locate the View tab at the top of the File Explorer window. Change the view to Medium icons or Large icons if you have trouble viewing what's on the screen.

To access your personal user folder, from File Explorer in the Navigation pane, click Computer. Then, in the Content pane, double-click Local Disk, then double-click Users and double-click your user name. The 'path' appears in the File Explorer window. You can create subfolders here, too.

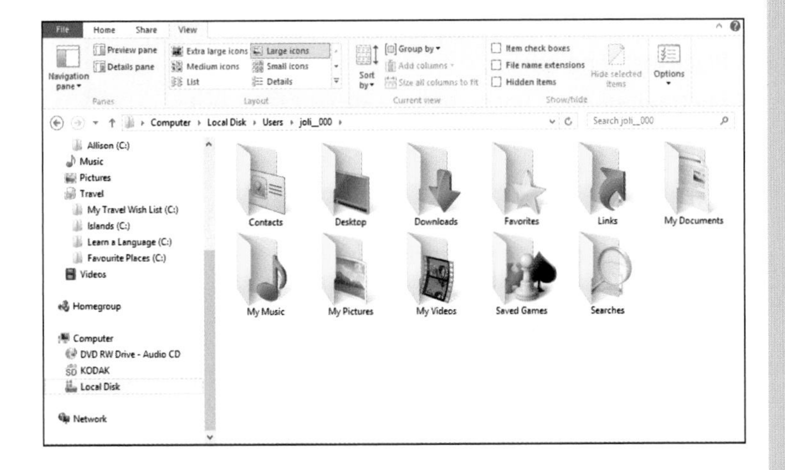

# Enhance the library structure (cont.)

## For your information

Your personal folder contains the following folders, which in turn contain data you've saved:

**Contacts** – might contain information about the contacts you keep, such as email addresses, phone numbers, home and business addresses and more.

**Desktop** – contains links to items on your Desktop.

**Downloads** – does not contain anything by default. It does offer a place to save items you download from the Internet, such as drivers and third-party programs.

**Favorites** – contains the items in Internet Explorer's Favorites list.

**Links** – contains shortcuts to the Desktop and Recent Places, among others.

**My Documents** – holds documents you save and subfolders you create. This is the same data you see in the Documents library.

**My Music** – contains music you save. This is the same music you see in the Music library.

**My Pictures** – holds pictures you save. This is the same data you see in the Pictures library.

**My Videos** – contains videos you save. This is the same data you see in the Videos library.

**Saved Games** – contains information about the games you play.

**Searches** – contains information about searches you've performed.

It might be helpful to think of libraries and folders in a more physical way, letting libraries represent the drawers of a filing cabinet, and folders as their, well, folders. For instance, you could allot an entire physical file cabinet drawer to documents, name the drawer Documents and then create subfolders to organise, sort and manage the printed documents you have. You can do the same thing on your computer, except on a computer the data is all digital, not physical. Thus, the next logical step after creating libraries, folders and subfolders is to put data into those folders. This will help you keep the data organised and easily available, just as you would in a filing cabinet.

You may want to start with your pictures. Often, the Windows 8 My Pictures folder becomes filled with unorganised pictures from your digital camera, the web, emails, or other sources. (In my case it becomes chaotic with screen shots for books!) To organise the data inside that folder, you create subfolders inside the Pictures folder and then move pictures into them to arrange and manage them.

Before we start moving data around though, it's important to understand the difference between copying and moving. When you copy something, an exact duplicate is made. The original copy of the data remains where it is and a copy of it is placed somewhere else. For the most part, this is not what you want to do when organising data – you want to move the data. If a picture of a graduation needs to be put in the Graduation Pictures folder, you need to move it, not copy it.

When you back up data, you want to copy it. This is about the only time you will want to copy data. And you'll want to copy the data to a source you'll keep away from your PC. You can copy data to a CD or DVD drive, to an external hard drive, or to a network drive. Copying allows you to create a backup of the data in one place, like your kids' houses or a safe deposit box, while keeping a local copy available for immediate use.

To move and copy data, you have quite a few choices. The first is to drag and drop with the mouse. You can left-click and drag and drop the data using a mouse, or you can right-click and drag and drop the data with the mouse. Left-clicking is easier,

## Manage files (cont.)

but there are rules to remember; when you right-click, there are no rules to remember. If you are used to dragging and dropping, always use a right-click to do so. When you let go, you get to choose whether you want to move or copy.

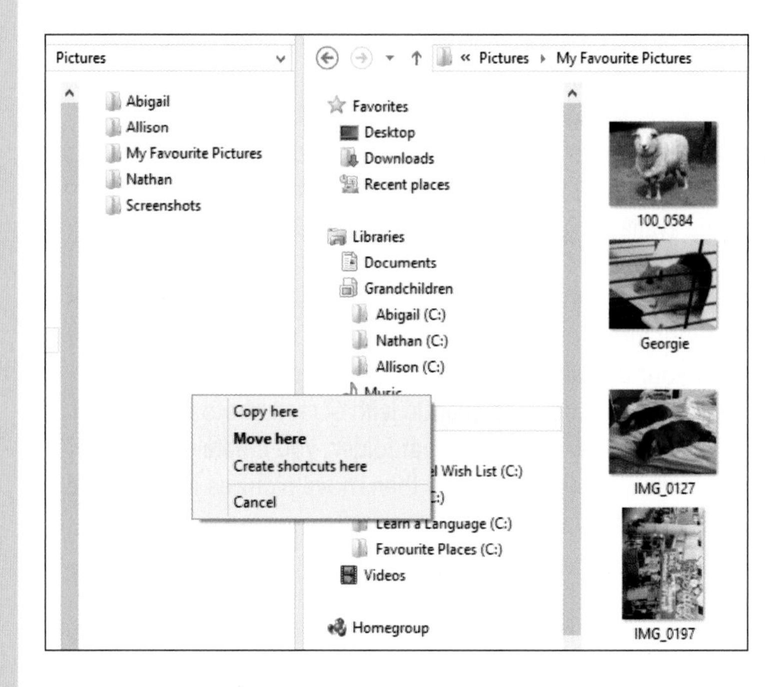


### Did you know?

You can also right-click a file, multiple selected files or folders and choose to Cut or Copy. You can then choose to Paste elsewhere. Choose Cut when you want to move the data, choose Copy when you want to copy it.

Right- and left-clicking, whether to drag and drop or to choose Cut or Copy, is old school. That means it's out of date and out of favour! Now you do your moving, copying and even deleting from the File Explorer ribbon.

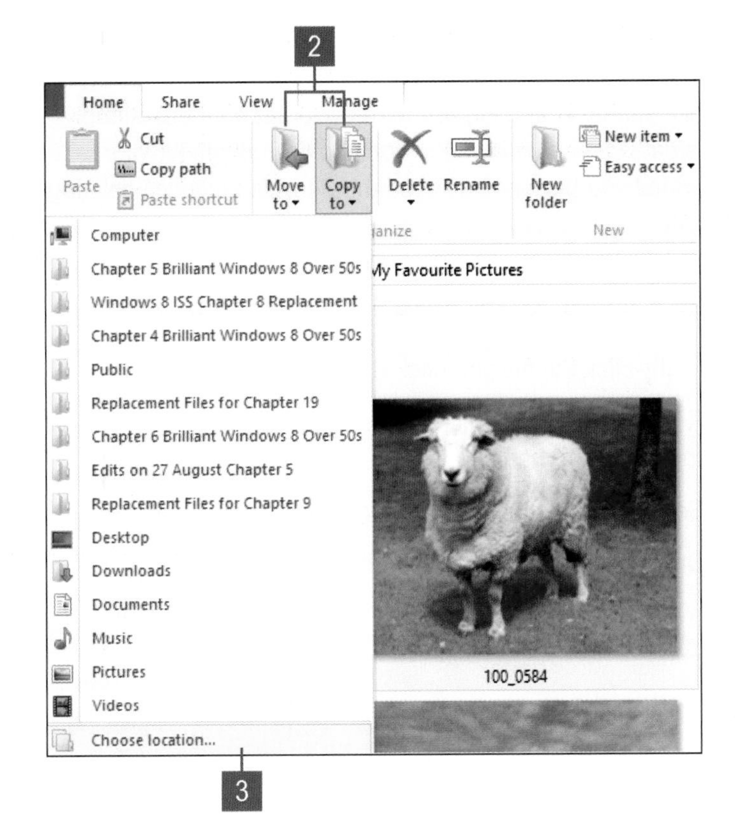


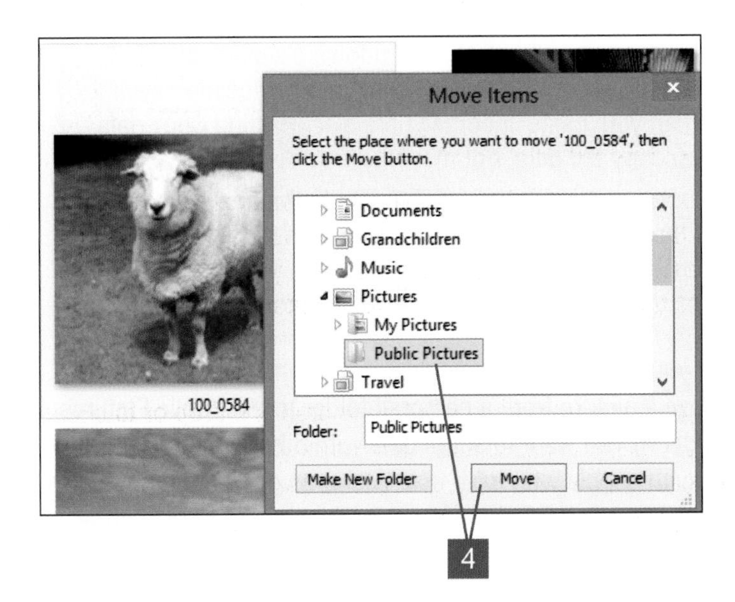


# Manage files (cont.)

6

## Copy or move a file

1. In File Explorer, locate a file to copy or move. Click it once to select it.
2. From the Home tab, click either Move to or Copy to.
3. Choose the desired location from the list. If you don't see it:
   - **a** Click Choose location.
   - **b** In the Move Items or Copy Items dialogue that appears, locate the desired folder.
4. Click the folder and then click Move or Copy.

?

### Did you know?

You can hold down the Ctrl key to select non-contiguous files or the Shift key to select contiguous ones. Then you can perform tasks on multiple files at once.

## Manage files (cont.)

When you are sure you no longer need a particular file or folder, you can delete it. Deleting it sends the file or the entire folder (contents and all) to the Recycle Bin on the Desktop. This data can be 'restored' if you decide you need it later, provided you have not emptied the Recycle Bin since deleting the file.

There are many ways to delete a file:

- Right-click the file and click Delete.
- Right-click the file, click Cut and then repeat and opt to Paste the data elsewhere.
- Select the file, and from the Home tab, click Delete.
- Drag the file to the Recycle Bin.

### Jargon buster

Cut – copies the data to Windows 8's clipboard (a virtual, temporary holding area). The data will be deleted from its original location as soon as you 'paste' it somewhere else. Pasting Cut data moves the data.

Copy – copies the data to Windows 8's clipboard. The data will be not deleted from its original location even when you 'paste' it somewhere else. Pasting Copy data will copy the data, not move it.

Paste – copies or moves the data to the new location. If the data was cut, it will be moved; if the data was copied, it will be copied.

As you can see in the image and the panel, we've opted to move a picture from a personal folder to the Public Pictures folder. If you want to share data with others on your network or with people who have user accounts on your computer, this is the best option. Using the public folders to hold pictures you want to share is only the beginning, though. It's often best, for instance, to put all the music you own in the Public Music folder – you can then access that music from anywhere on your network. The same is true of videos. Read on to learn more.

You can share your personal data with Windows 8's built-in public folders. There are other ways to share, but public folders are extremely easy to use and require no knowledge of permissions, user accounts or network sharing rules. With public folders, you simply move, copy or save the data you want to share in the appropriate public folder and anyone with an account on the computer can access it. You can also configure the Public folder to share files with people using other computers on your local network. The nice part is, there's very little configuration involved.

Public folders are a great way to keep multiple-user PCs organised and to avoid multiple copies of data. Instead of having two copies of your last holiday, one copy under your account and the other under your husband's account, you can have one copy and store it in the Public Pictures folder. There, you can both access the pictures and don't need two copies of it. The same is true of videos. You can even create your own public subfolder for email attachments. Save funny attachments there instead of emailing them to your partner (who uses the same PC) and you'll reduce the clutter created by having two copies of the email and attachment on the PC.

If you don't want everyone who has access to the computer to be able to view shared data, you'll have to choose another option for sharing data. There are several, including manually sharing personal folders and setting the required permissions, sharing on CDs and DVDs, sharing via email, and even sharing using instant messaging programs. However, public folders are the easiest to use and manage, and the easiest to keep organised.

These are the existing public folder options:

- Public Documents
- Public Downloads
- Public Music
- Public Pictures
- Public Videos.

## Learn more about public folders

### Important

When you copy something, an exact duplicate is made. The original copy of the data remains where it is and a copy of it is placed somewhere else. For the most part, this is not what you want to do when organising data – you generally want to move the data.

## Learn more about public folders (cont.)

You can save any file to any public folder by browsing to it using the application's Save As dialogue box. Here is WordPad's Save As dialogue box. Notice we've browsed to the Public Documents folder. Because virtually all Desktop programs offer a Save As dialogue box, it's possible to save all your data in public folders if you wish. To do so, when saving, simply choose to save to one of the public folders instead of your personal folders.

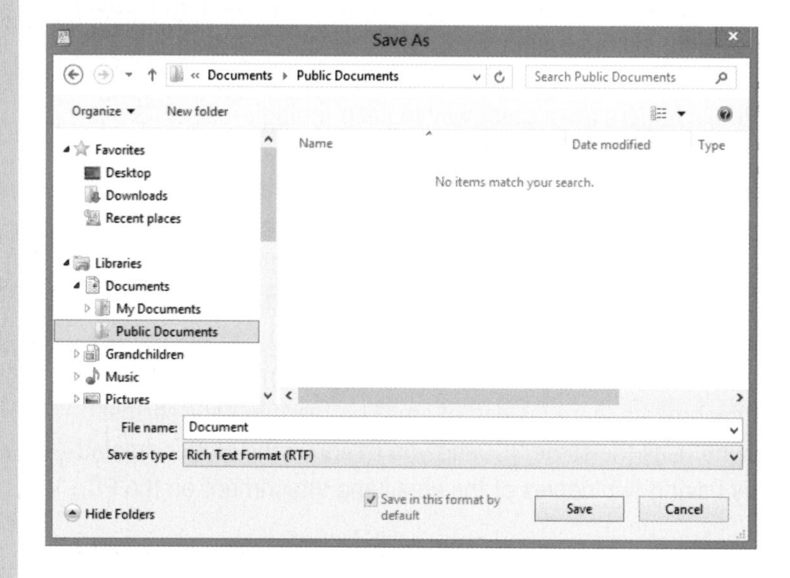

Since you've learned to delete files and folders in this chapter it's only fair to tell you how to recover them if you delete them accidentally. Every file or folder you delete is sent to the Recycle Bin. Until the Recycle Bin is emptied, which you must do manually or using Disk Cleanup, you can 'restore' the file, which means you will put it back where it was before you deleted it. The Recycle Bin sits on the Desktop. Double-click it to open it. Notice that the Recycle Bin opens using File Explorer, and the familiar Navigation pane, Content pane and ribbon are available.

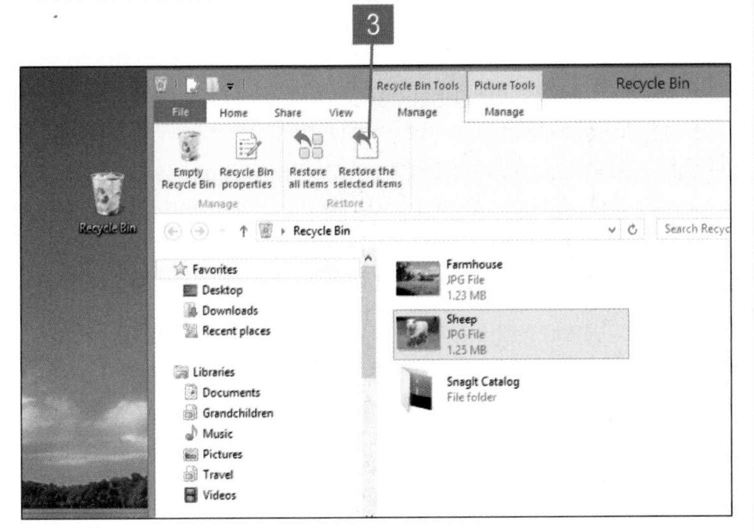


If you find a file you want to restore (recover), click it and click Restore the selected items. The file will reappear in the same location it was in prior to deleting. You can also restore all items, although you probably won't want to.

## Restore folders (and files) from the Recycle Bin



### Restore data from the Recycle Bin

1. Double-click the Recycle Bin (it's on the Desktop).
2. Click anything you did not mean to delete. (Hold down the Ctrl key to select additional files.)
3. From the Manage tab, click the applicable restore option.

## Explore more features of the File Explorer ribbon

**Important**

If you can't see all the tabs, or if the items on the tabs seem condensed, maximise the Windows Explorer window.

Before we end this chapter and move on, let's take one last look at the ribbon in File Explorer. The ribbon runs across the top of the File Explorer window and offers tabs. This is true even when Recycle Bin is the focus. You click these tabs to access the groups, options and tools available for the particular task you are performing. Each time you click a new tab, what's shown on the ribbon changes.

To understand how to use the ribbon in the long term, you must know which tabs will appear the most and what is available under these tabs. Then, when working with libraries and folders, you'll click the tab that most likely offers the tools you need. Here are the most common tabs you'll encounter:

- File – use this tab to open a new window, access folders you visit often, clear your history with this item, and more. Most of the time what you see under the File menu is the same no matter what you have selected in the Navigation pane.
- Home – when a compatible item is selected in the Content pane, you can cut, copy and paste the selected data. You can also move data, delete data, rename data, create a new folder and select data, among other things. What you see here depends on what is selected.
- Share – when a compatible item is selected, you can send files in an email, compress (zip) files, burn selected files to a CD or DVD disk, print, and more, as applicable. (You can't print a video you've selected, for instance, so Print will be greyed out in that case.)
- View – choose how files appear in the window (Extra Large Icons, Large Icons, Medium Icons and so on). You may also be able to hide or show the various panes, choose how to sort the data in the window, and show or hide file name extensions.
- Additional tabs, such as Manage – use these tabs to perform tasks specific to the selected data. You can play a slide show of pictures in a Pictures folder, for instance.

# Configure and use Mail

7

## Introduction

Mail is an app available from the Start screen. Because it's not a fully fledged Desktop application, Mail will look and feel more like something you'd experience on a smartphone than what you may be used to on a computer. That's OK, and it's exactly what Microsoft wanted to provide, something really easy to use. Even though it is streamlined, it does enable you to view, send and receive email, open and send attachments, and access your contacts, among other things.

If you sign in to your Windows 8 computer or tablet with a compatible Microsoft account such as one from Hotmail.com or Live.com, Mail is already set up and ready to use. You can skip the bit that deals with the setup process. If you have another email account, you'll have to add that account manually, though. Once your email accounts are ready, accessing new mail and composing your own is a simple process.

?

**Did you know?**

If you have been using a web-based email account from Hotmail or Google and you've created folders to store your mail there, you'll see them in Mail when you open it.

### What you'll do

**Set up an email address**

**View an email**

**Open and view an attachment**

**Print an email**

**Send an email**

**Reply to and forward email**

**Attach a picture**

**Check junk email folders for legitimate mail**

# Configure an email address

As noted above, you might open Mail and notice that your email account has already been configured. If that is the case and if you do not have another email account to add (perhaps one from Gmail or a second Hotmail or Live account), you can skip this section.

**Important**

If you need an email account and you don't know where to start, get a free one from Microsoft at **https://signup.live.com**. You can be sure it'll be compatible with Mail if you do.

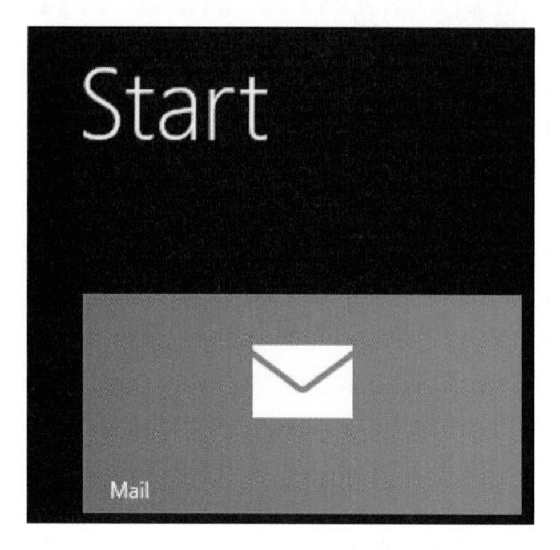


Depending on the email address you want to add, you may need to type some or all of the following information, which you can get from your Internet service provider (ISP) or email provider:

- Email address – this is the address you chose when you signed up for your email address. It often takes this form: yourname@something.com. Email addresses are not case sensitive.
- Password – the password you chose when setting up your email address. Passwords are case sensitive and should contain letters and numbers.
- Username – this is often your email address, but occasionally it can be something else.
- Mail Servers – these are the servers that receive and deliver your email. There are two: an incoming mail server and an outgoing mail server. Often the server names look something like *pop.yourispnamehere.com* and *smtp.yourispnamehere.com*.

- Ports – these have numbers that are used by your email provider to deliver and obtain mail. Ask your ISP what the port numbers are if you are prompted to enter them.

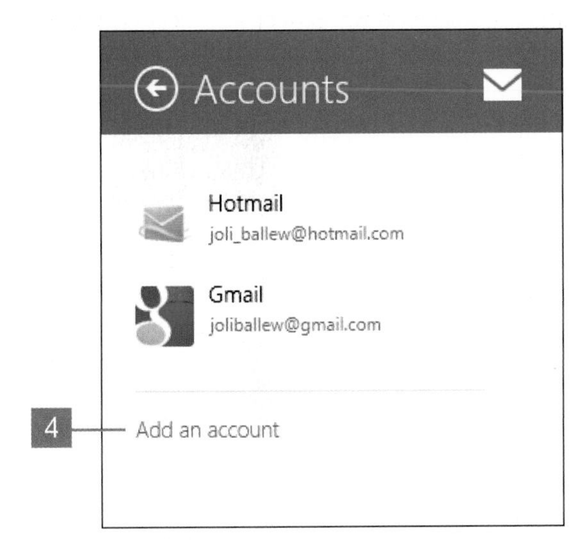


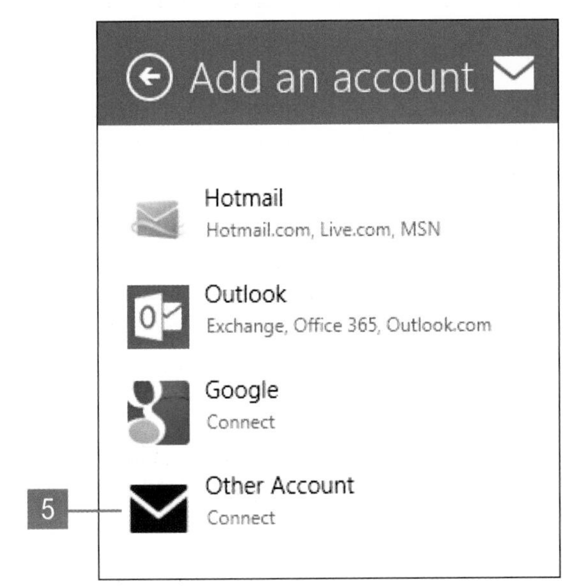


?

**Did you know?**

If you configure more than one email account in Mail, you must click the account name in the left pane to access that account's email. Email from multiple accounts is not combined into a single repository in Mail.

# Configure an email address (cont.)

7

## Set up an email address

1. Click the Mail icon on the Start screen.
2. Use Windows + C to access the charms. Click Settings.
3. From the Settings options, click Accounts.
4. You may see existing accounts. Click Add an account.
5. Click the type of account to add. If it is not listed, click Other Account.
6. Fill out the information when prompted, which will include at least your email account and password.
7. If applicable, choose to include or not include the account's related contacts and calendar information.
8. Click Connect.

# Get to know the Mail interface

Now that you have your email address(es) set up, you can explore how Mail is configured. There are three sections to the Mail interface:

- Accounts are shown on the far left. This is where you select the account and the desired folder available from that account. The folder you'll spend most of your time in is the Inbox, but you may also see Sent, Trash, Junk and others. If you've created your own folders, you'll see them here, too.
- Emails in whatever folder you've selected are shown in the middle. When in an Inbox for an account, this is where you select the new email to read.
- Email content is on the right. This is where you read the content of emails you've received, sent, kept or deleted, and then selected in the middle pane.

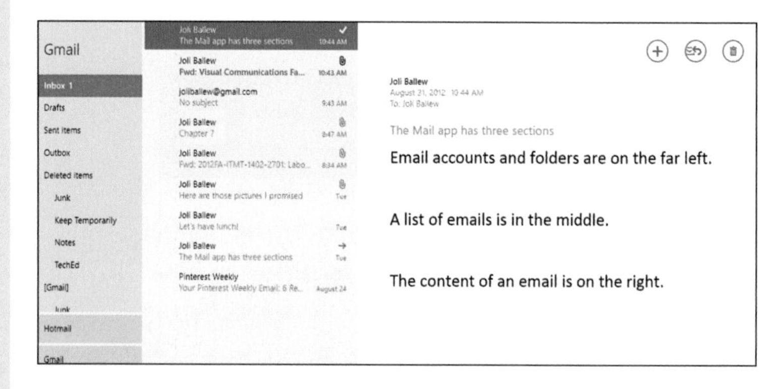


If you right-click an empty area inside Mail (or flick upwards from the bottom), there are some options:

- Sync – to check for new mail. By default, Mail will offer email as it arrives.
- Pin to Start – to pin the selected account to the Start menu.
- Move – to move selected email to a different folder.
- Mark unread – to mark selected email as unread.

And finally, from the Settings charm (Win + C) there are various options including Accounts, Help, Rate and Review, and others. When you click Accounts from here you can reconfigure existing accounts and add new ones as well.

Mail displays new email about the same time it arrives in your Inbox on web mail servers from entities such as Gmail, Outlook and Hotmail. You may experience a delay with ISPs, though, depending on how they are configured. You'll know you have new email when a number appears either on the Mail tile on the Start screen or next to the name of the account in Mail's left section. Here is an example of both.

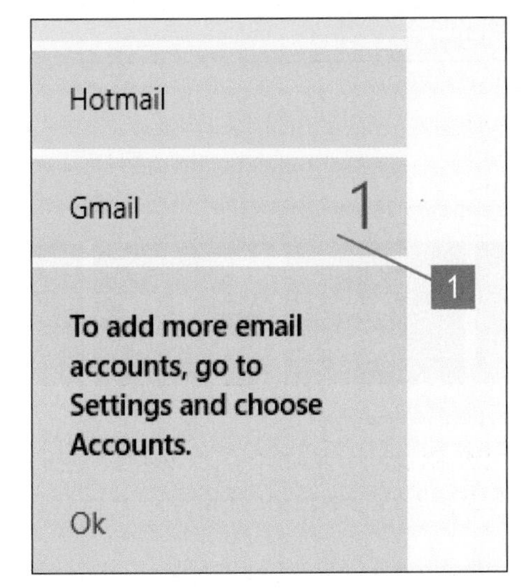


To read the new email you must select the proper account if multiple accounts are configured and access the Inbox of that account. As soon as you click the email in the middle section of Mail, the number associated with it disappears.

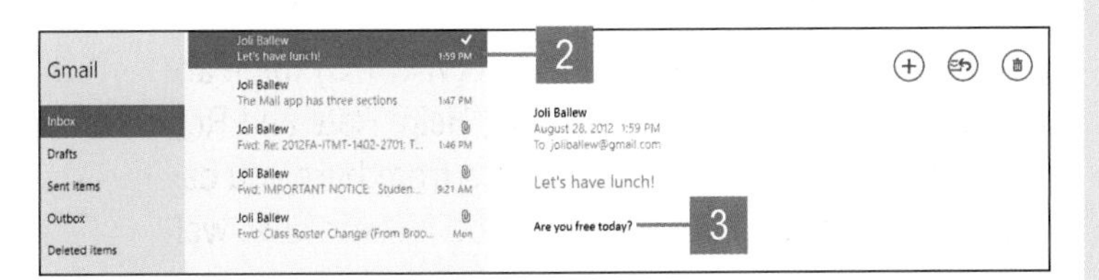


## Receive and view an email

### View an email

1. If you have more than one email account configured, select the account to use.
2. Click the email to read.
3. In the right section of Mail, read the content.

# Receive and view an email (cont.)

Some email arrives with an attachment (or multiple attachments). These attachments are denoted by a paperclip on the email in the middle section of Mail. In the content area, you'll see the actual attachment(s).

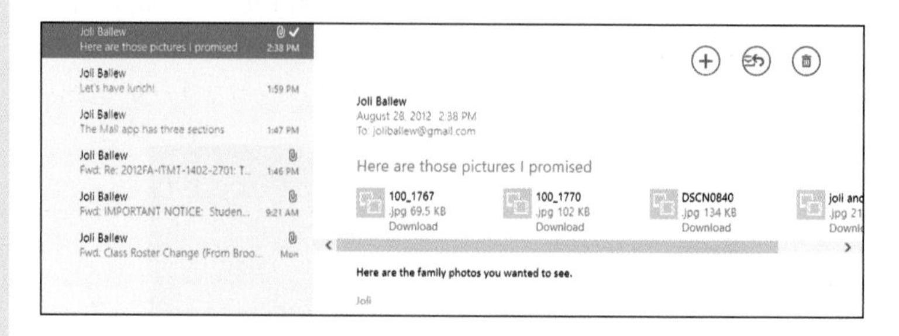


You must click the attachment in this pane to download or open it, as applicable. You only need to click the attachment once. Here's what the same email looks like after downloading the attached pictures.

Sometimes attachments can't be downloaded or opened because they are not compatible with Windows 8 and Mail. If this happens you'll have to reply to the sender and ask them to send you the attachment using another method. Perhaps they can copy and paste the information, embed the images or text, or save the file as a different file type before resending it.

Finally, you must be very careful that you only open attachments from people you know, and only open the attachments that you expect. Attachments can contain viruses, so it is perfectly fine to email the sender and ask what is in the attachment prior to opening it. It's also important to note that your bank, credit card company, Gmail, Hotmail, Outlook and so on will never send attachments. If you get an email like this, it's probably fraudulent.

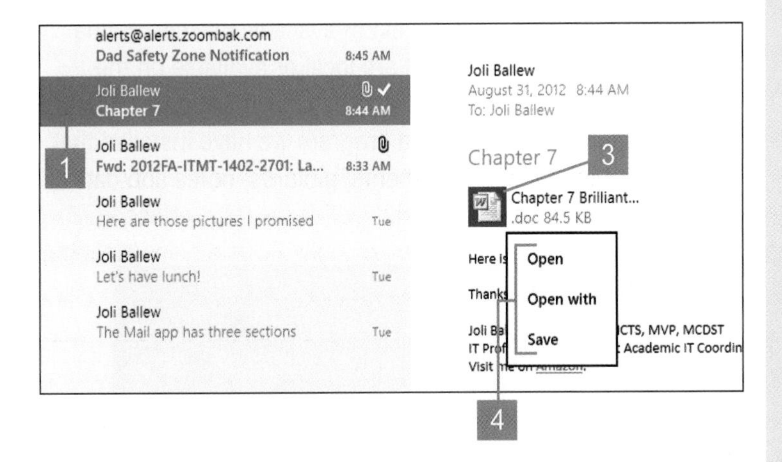


## Important

Hackers, scammers, thieves and con artists send attachments that look like they are from legitimate companies, banks and online services. Do not open these. Companies rarely send email attachments.

# Receive and view an email (cont.)

### Open and view an attachment

1. Click the email that contains the attachment.
2. If you see a message that says 'Get the rest of this message', click it.
3. Locate the attachment. Here it's Chapter 7 Brilliant. Click it.
4. Click the appropriate option: Open, Open with or Save.
5. The attachment opens.

# Print an email or an attachment

Sometimes you'll need to print an email or its attachment. The email could contain a receipt, a great joke you want to share with your friends who don't have or use email, or test results from a doctor. It may be an email with pictures embedded in the email itself. Whatever the case, Mail makes it easy to print – provided you have a printer connected and turned on!

To print an email, you'll need to access the Devices charm. You may never have used this charm before. When you click the Devices charm, you will see a list of available devices. Some might be physical devices that are local or available on the network, like an actual printer, and others may appear in the list that are virtual, like OneNote, a program we have installed that can be used to manage documents, pictures, notes and data from various sources.

## Print an email

1. Select the email to print.
2. Bring up the default charms (Windows key + C will show these) and click Devices.
3. Select the printer to use.

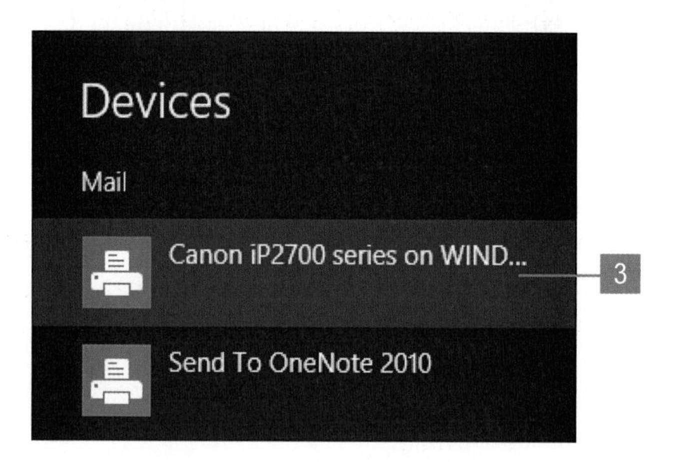


After you choose a device, the preview pane will appear where you can set the number of copies, orientation, colour mode and more. If an email contains attachments that are embedded, such as pictures, those attachments will print with the email content. If the attachment is actually attached, such as a Word document, presentation or spreadsheet, you'll have to open the attachment before you can print it.

### Did you know?

To bring up the Devices charm, use the Windows key + K shortcut.

### Did you know?

If you'd rather use a keyboard, the shortcut Ctrl + P will open the Print window. From there, select the printer and configure printer options, then print.

# Print an email or an attachment (cont.)

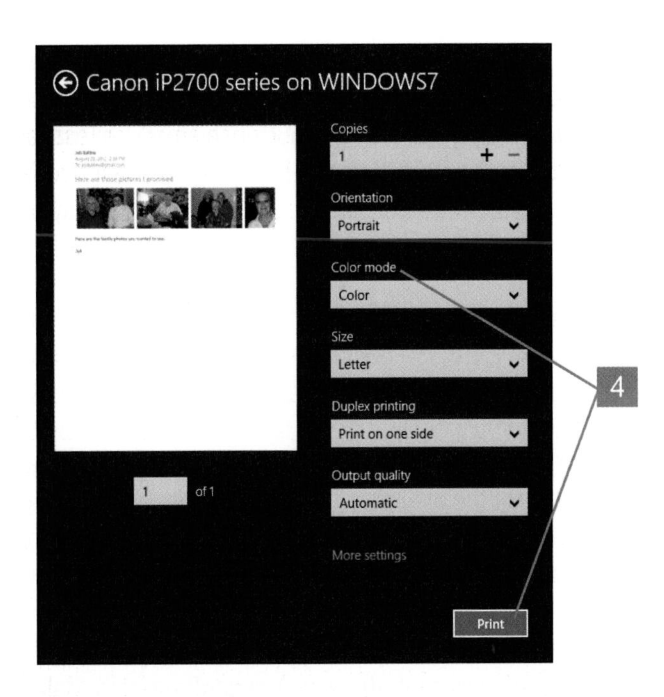


4 Configure the print options and click Print.

It's important to note that printing an attachment is a little bit different than printing an email. If you want to print an attached document, you'll have to open the document first. Then you'll need to access the Print command from the program it opens in.

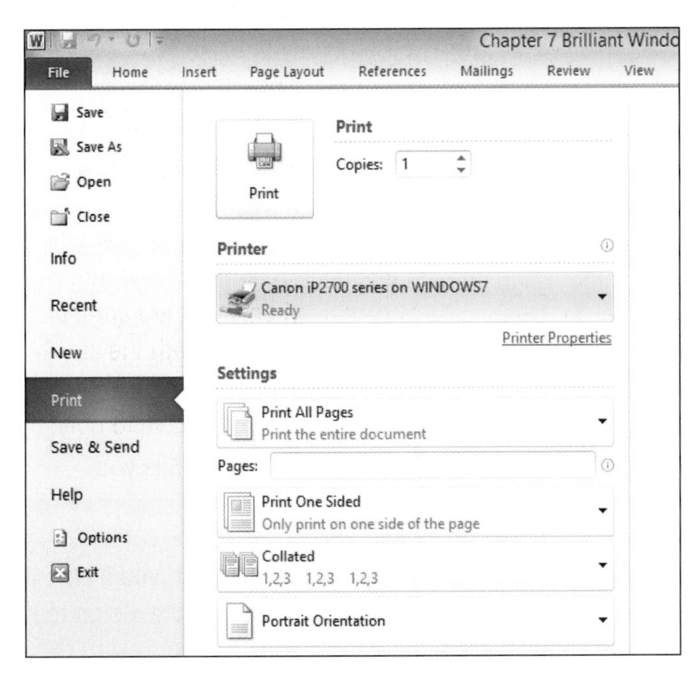

# Compose and send an email

To create a new email, you click the + sign. You'll see this button at the top of the Mail interface. Next to that is the Send/Reply/Reply All/Forward button, and next to that a trash can for deleting selected email.

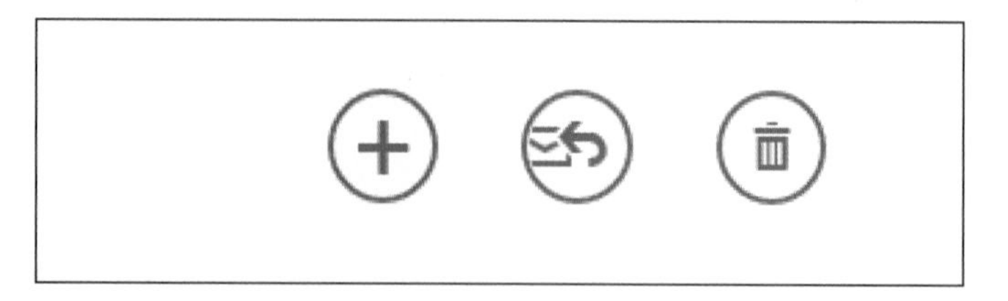

A new message is shown here, the result of clicking the + sign. Notice that all the available fields are empty. You will fill them in. Also notice the option to show more information. You click this if you need to access the Bcc (blind carbon copy, which is a secret copy) line or set a priority for the email (Normal, High or Low). Finally, notice the arrow beside Gmail. You'll see this arrow if you have multiple accounts configured in Mail. You click the arrow to switch accounts to send from, if you wish.

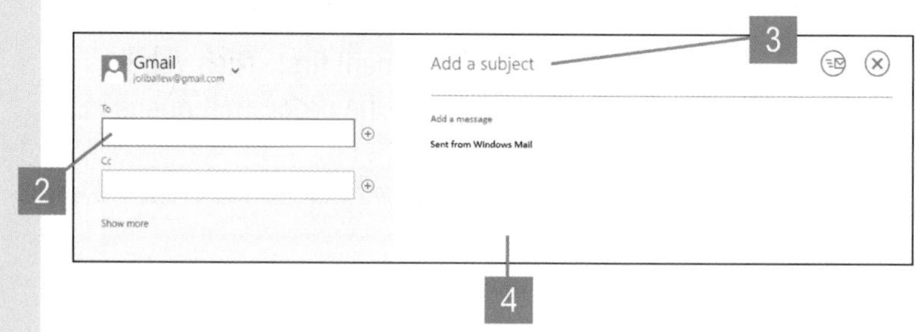


There are several other items to notice when composing a new email. The To line is where you input the recipients' names. You can click the + sign there to add them from the People app (refer to Chapter 2). There's also a Cc line and Bcc line if you click Show more. The subject line is where you input the subject or reason for the email. The body is where you type the message.

Here are some things to consider before and while you compose an email:

- You'll need the email address of the recipient; you'll type this into the To field. Alternatively, you can click the + sign to choose contacts from the People app.

## Send an email

1. Click the + sign.
2. Type the recipient's email address in the To line; press Enter on the keyboard. You can type multiple addresses.
3. Type a subject in the Add a subject field.
4. Type the message in the body pane.
5. Click the Send icon.

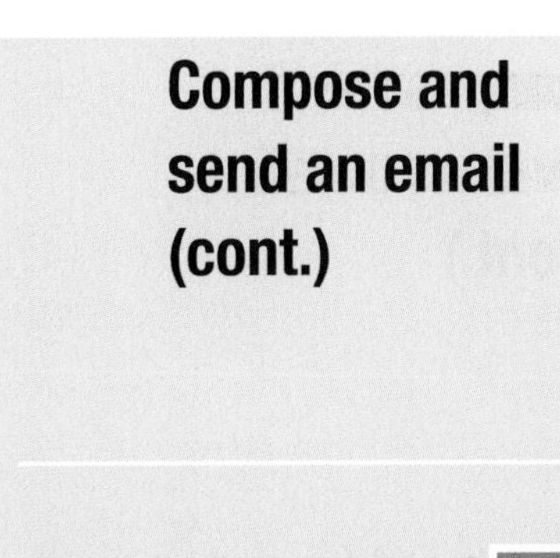

# Compose and send an email (cont.)

- To send the email to more than one person, simply continue typing email addresses and press Enter on the keyboard after each one. The addresses will be separated automatically, thus there is no need to input semicolons or commas.
- If you want to send the email to someone and you don't need them to respond, you can put them in the Cc line. Cc stands for carbon copy.
- If you want to send the email to someone and you don't want other recipients to know you've included them in the email, add them to the Bcc line (click on Show more).
- Type the subject of the message in the Add a subject field. Make sure the subject adequately describes the reason for your email. Your recipients should be able to review the subject line later and be able to recall what the email was regarding.
- Type the message in the body of the email. You can edit the data as you would in any word-processing program: you can cut, copy and paste, change the font, and more. These options are hidden until you select data or right-click to choose a font and other font characteristics.

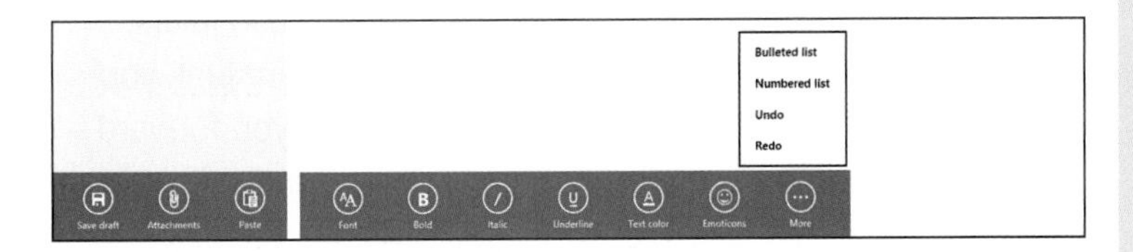


If you'd like to spice up your email with a different font, font colour, text colour and so on, or make selected text bold, italic or underlined, or if you want to create a bulleted or numbered list, you'll need to right-click. When you do, options appear across the bottom of the screen. If text is selected when you choose an editing option, the changes you make using these options will be applied only to the selected text. If you make changes when no text is selected, the options will be applied until you send the email or change the options.

**Important**

You apply changes to the font, font size, colour and so on using the same techniques you'd use when editing a Word document.

# Compose and send an email (cont.)

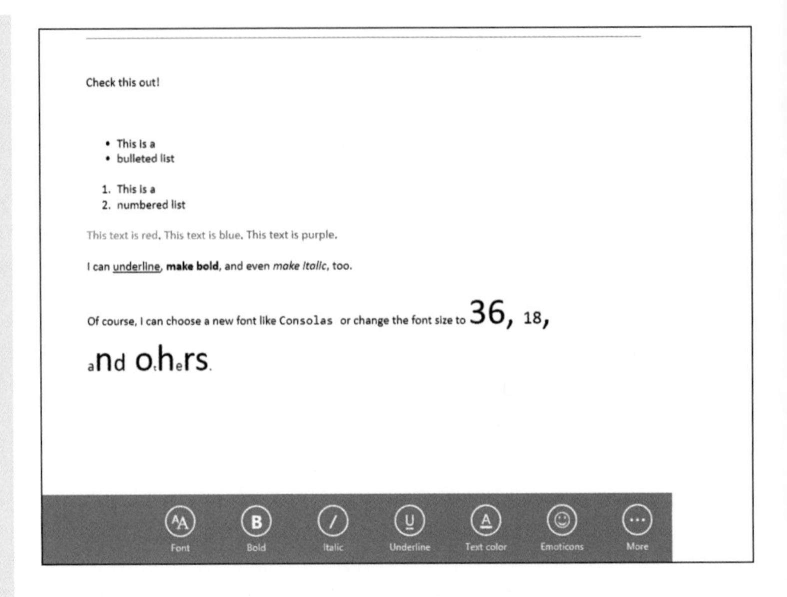


## Reply to and forward an email

1. Select the email you want to reply to or forward.
2. Click the Reply button and select the desired option.
3. If you wish, change the subject, then type the message in the body pane.
4. Right-click in the body of the email to access options to change the font, use bold or italic, and more.
5. Click the Send icon.

Beyond sending a 'new' email, you can reply to an email or forward an email. Replying lets you send a response to the sender (you can reply to everyone if there are multiple recipients in the email). Forwarding lets you send the entire email to another person, which is generally used to send an email to someone not included in the email you received. People spend a lot of time forwarding emails, and even though it's common practice, beware. Most forwarded emails contain bad jokes, untrue information (hoaxes), or simply unnecessary junk you don't want to read. Do your part by limiting what you forward – just because you think it's true or funny doesn't make it so.

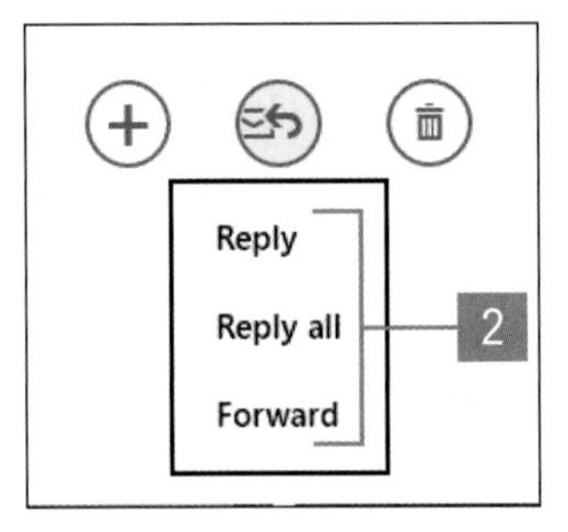


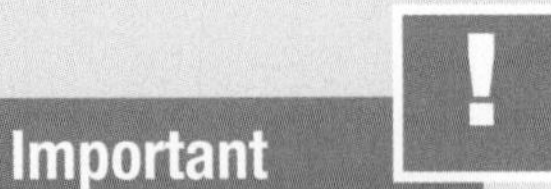

### Important

If the email you are replying to was sent to you along with other people, clicking Reply will send a reply to the person who composed the message. Clicking Reply all will send the reply to everyone who received the email as well as the person who sent it.

### Did you know?

When you select text, the formatting options become available automatically.

## Compose and send an email (cont.)

### Attach data to an email

Although email that contains only a message serves its purpose quite a bit of the time, often you'll want to send a photograph, short video, sound recording, document or other data. When you want to add something other than text to your message, it's called adding an attachment.

To add an attachment to an email, start the email, then right-click. One of the options that appears across the bottom of the screen is Attachments. You'll use this option to locate the file(s) you want to attach. As with selecting and deleting multiple files in other scenarios, you can hold down the Ctrl key to select non-contiguous files or the Shift key to select contiguous ones. Select the files you require and click Attach.

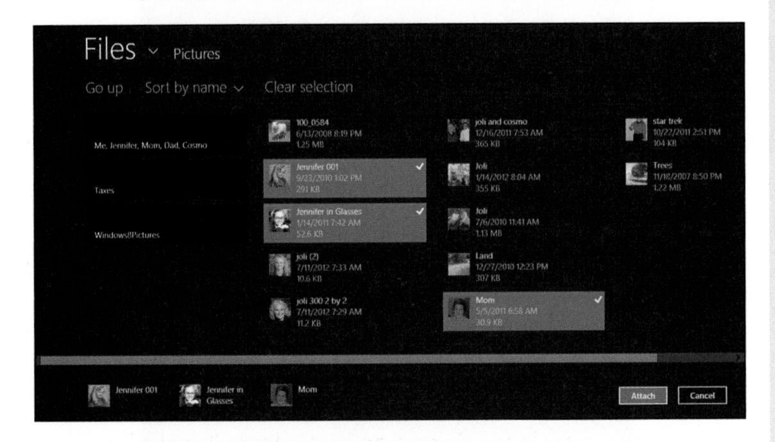


You can also email from within apps, such as Photos. Open the item to send using the appropriate app, access the Charms and click the Share charm. (You can use Ctrl + C to access the charms.) Then choose Mail from the results. Beyond apps like Photos, you may be surprised to learn you can share from apps you might not expect. For instance, you can share the current weather with the Weather app.

?

**Did you know?**

If you want to save an email to complete later, click the X icon and click Save draft. You'll be able to access the email later in the Drafts folder when you're ready to complete it.

# Compose and send an email (cont.)

## Attach a picture

1. Click the + sign to create a new mail message. Select the recipients, type a subject and compose the email.
2. Right-click and click Attachments.
3. Locate the file to attach and click it. Hold down Ctrl or Shift while selecting to choose multiple files.
4. Click Attach.
5. Complete the email and click the Send icon.

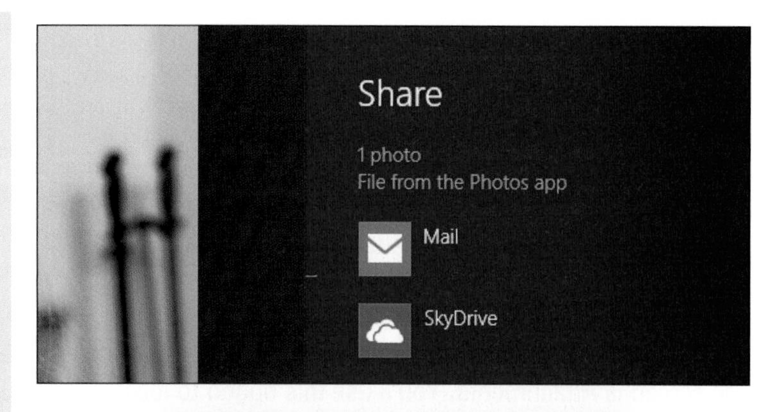


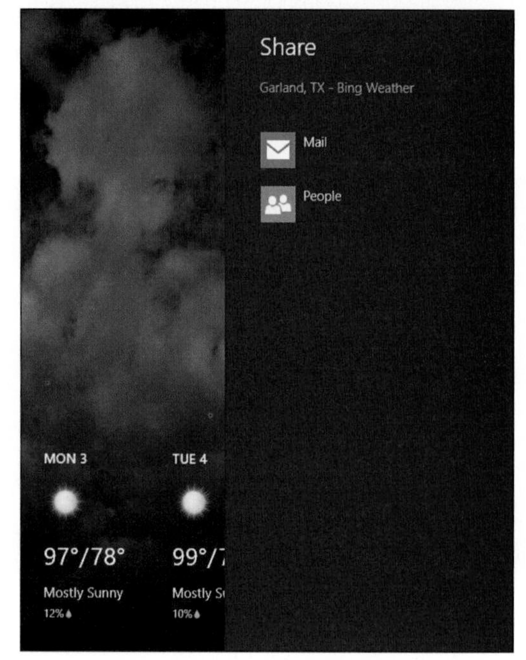


**Important**

Avoid sending large attachments, especially to people you know have a dial-up modem or those who get email only on a small device like a BlackBerry, iPhone or Mobile PC. A video of your grandkids, cats or children might take you only 8 seconds to send, but it can bog down a dial-up connection for hours.

## Compose and send an email (cont.)

Finally, a signature is automatically input for every email you send. If you want to change the default signature that appears on each outgoing message, in Mail, use the Windows key + I to access the Settings charm. Click Accounts. From there, choose the account to change. Note you can change Sent from Windows Mail to anything you like, and you can change what syncs with your account automatically. There are other options – use the scroll bar to access them.

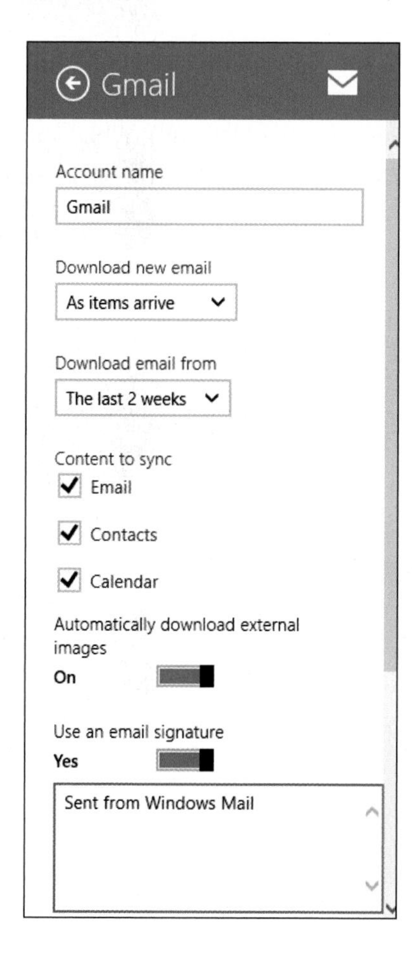


### Did you know?

Anything you attach won't be removed from your computer; instead, a copy will be created for the attachment.

## Manage contacts

You use the People app to organise and make available information about your contacts. Contacts will automatically appear when you add social networking sites, connect with Messaging contacts, and log on with your own Microsoft account. What you see depends on how you've used your Windows 8 computer so far. You learned about the People app in Chapter 2. If you haven't connected the People app with your contacts from Hotmail, Gmail, Twitter and the like, do so before continuing here.

Once the People app is populated with contacts, you can add them to the To, Cc or Bcc lines of an email by clicking the + sign there (while inside the Mail app). When you do this, you don't have to type the email addresses manually. Here is how it looks when you do this. You click the recipients and when you've finished you click Add.

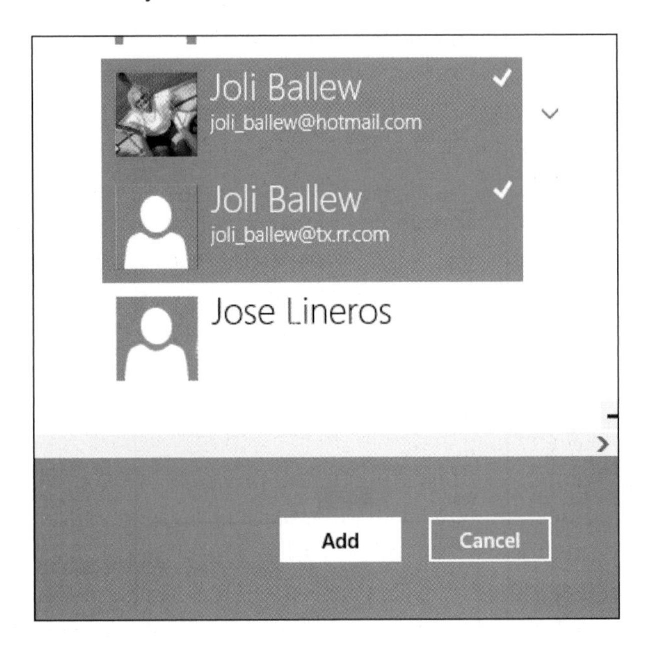


You can also send an email to a contact from inside the People app. Click the contact name inside the People app, then choose the Send email option. Note you can also opt to send a message, or even call their mobile or map their address, if applicable.

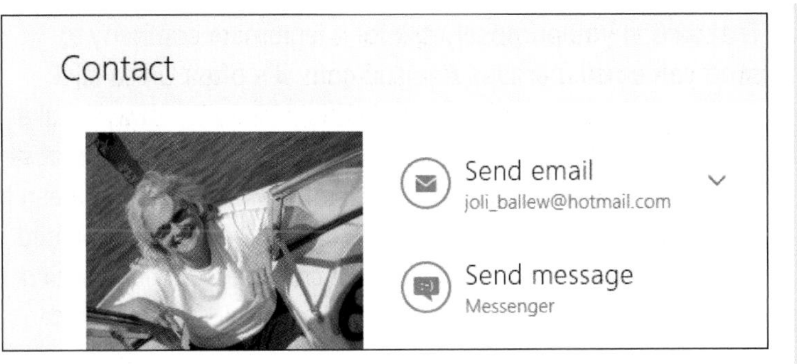


## Manage unwanted email

Just as you receive unwanted information from phone solicitors, radio stations, billboards, television ads and in the post, you're going to get advertisements in emails. This is referred to as junk email or spam. Unfortunately for you, there's no governing agency placing rules on what can and cannot be sent in an email as there is with television, radio and other transmission media. This means not only are most of the advertisements scams and rip-offs, they may contain pornographic images. Even if you were to purchase something via a spam email, it's not guaranteed that the item will arrive or that it will meet any governmental quality requirements. And you can be sure that someone is more interested in having your credit card numbers than sending you an actual product.

Before you read any further, take note: never, and I mean never, buy anything in a junk email, send money to a sick or dying Nigerian, send money for your portion of a lottery ticket, order medication, reply with bank account numbers, social security numbers or any other personal information, believe that Bill Gates himself will pay you for forwarding an email to friends, believe you'll have good luck (or bad) if you don't forward a message to friends, or otherwise do anything but delete the email. Do not attempt to unsubscribe from a mailing list that you do not recognise, do not click Reply and do not perpetuate hoaxes.

## Manage contacts (cont.)

### Did you know?

You can add contacts manually from the People app.

# Manage contacts (cont.)

That said, if you purposely ask for a legitimate company to send you email, perhaps Amazon.com, it's often OK to click on the link in the email to visit the site. However, always make sure you check the web address once connected. Just because you click on a link in an email to visit *www.amazon.com* doesn't mean you're going to get there. You might get to a site named *www.1234.amazon.com/validate your credit card number*, which would indeed be a scam. It's best to delete all spam. Period.

There are a lot of options for reducing the amount of junk email you receive, or might receive in the future. First, don't give your email address to any website or company, or include it in any registration card, unless you're willing to receive junk email from them and their constituents. Understand that companies collect and sell email addresses for profit. Don't get involved in that. Second, every now and then, check the junk or spam folders available to you.

### Check junk email folders for legitimate mail

1. From each account configured, click the Junk, Junk E-mail or Spam folder.
2. Use the scroll bars if necessary to browse through the email in the folder.
3. If you see an email that is legitimate, click it once.
4. Right-click to access the charms and click Move (not shown).
5. Click Inbox.

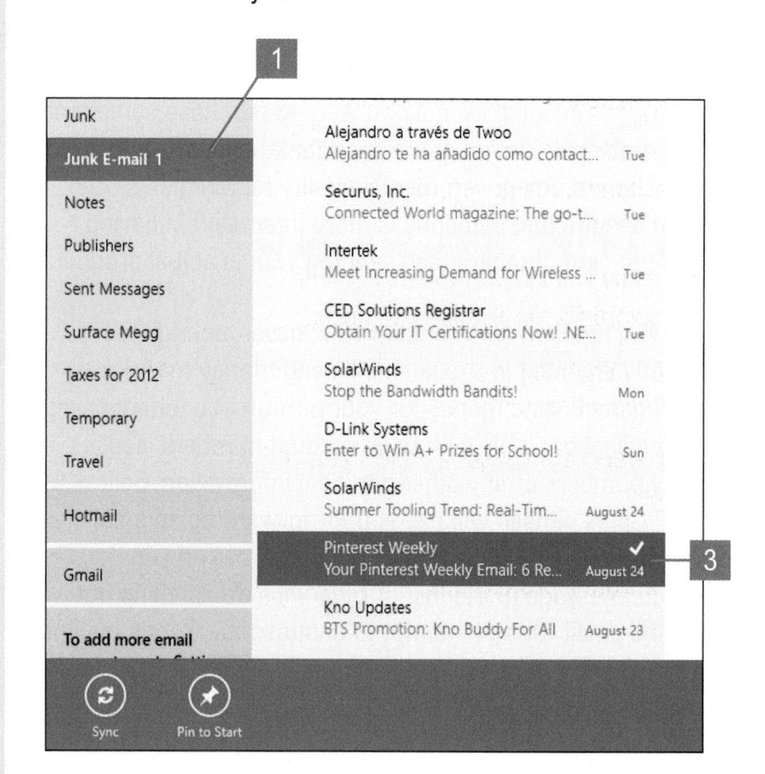


### Did you know?

Email from contacts you've input yourself is never sent to the junk or spam folder.

Spammers often create official-looking correspondence from financial institutions and shopping websites to lure you to a fake website, often one that looks much like the official one, to try to trick you into entering your personal information. Once you do, the spammers steal that information. This is called phishing. There's one sure way to avoid this: don't click links offered in an email, instead type the address yourself using your web browser.

Beyond phishing emails, you'll get junk email. A lot of this email will resemble the junk mail that you get in the post. It will claim you've won a prize, for instance. Of course, there is always spam that informs you that you are the recipient of an inheritance, or asks you to reply with personal information, such as your bank account numbers. Here's a list of things to watch out for:

- Banks and financial institutions, the government and investment houses never ask you to send personal information or account numbers via email.
- Your mortgage company will not ask you to send or verify an account number, ask for your date of birth or want you to verify your password.
- No entity will ask you to reply with your user name and/or password for verification purposes.
- If you inherit some money or win the lottery, you'll get a certified letter, not an email.
- No person from Nigeria knows you and wants to give you money.
- If an email has a typographical error in it and it's supposed to be from a professional institution, it's a fraud.

**Important**

When in doubt about the legitimacy of a website, open your web browser and type the web address yourself.

## Be safe with Mail

# Surf the web with Internet Explorer

8

## Introduction

You use Internet Explorer (IE) to access the Internet and browse websites. This is why it's called a *web browser*. You'll learn how to use Internet Explorer in this chapter. Before we start though, it's important to understand that there are two versions of IE available. The IE *app* is available from the Start screen. It offers limited functionality, but is streamlined to offer a clean and efficient web browsing experience. The IE *Desktop app* is available from the Desktop. It's the fully functional version of IE you may already be used to. You'll use this version if and when the IE app doesn't offer everything you need (or if you simply prefer it).

## What you'll do

**Visit a website with the IE app**

**Set a Home page**

**Mark a Favorite**

**Zoom in or out**

**Clear History**

**Print a web page**

**Create strong passwords for websites**

**Configure the IE Desktop app as the default**

## Understand the versions of IE

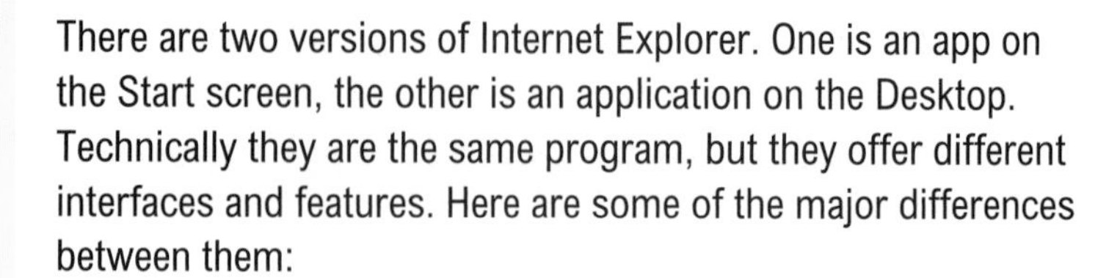

There are two versions of Internet Explorer. One is an app on the Start screen, the other is an application on the Desktop. Technically they are the same program, but they offer different interfaces and features. Here are some of the major differences between them:

- Whenever you click a link in an email, message, document and so on, the IE app will open. It is the default.
- The IE app is available from the Start screen but the Desktop version is not (although you can add it there). This is the IE tile.

- The IE app is a better option on tablets and computers with small screens than its full-version counterpart because the IE app was built to offer a full-screen browsing experience in a limited space.

The IE Desktop app is a traditional application that looks and acts much like its predecessor. It is fully extensible with third-party add-ons.

## Understand the versions of IE (cont.)

- You will have to switch from the IE app to the Desktop version whenever a web page won't function properly, such as when an add-on, Java or other unsupported technologies are required.
- You can use the IE app until you need the Desktop version and then switch to it easily.

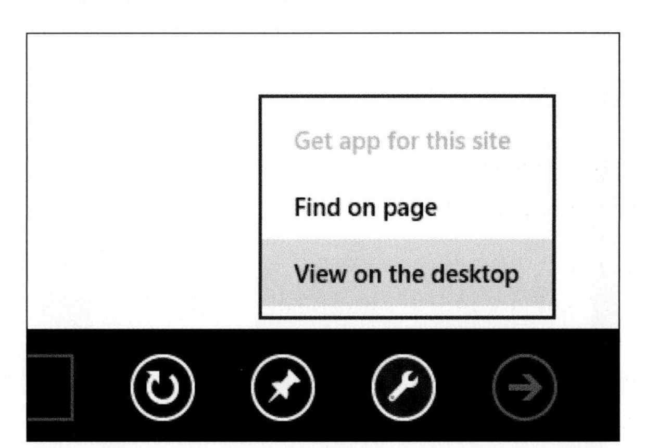


**For your information**

You can quickly pin any website to the Start screen from inside the IE app.

8

## Use the Internet Explorer app

You open the Internet Explorer app by clicking or tapping its tile on the Start screen. When the app opens, move your mouse over each icon to locate the various features. You must right-click or flick upwards from the bottom or downwards from the top with a touch screen to access these features. By default, nothing shows on the screen but the website itself. When you've finished, click any area of the screen to hide these charms and options.

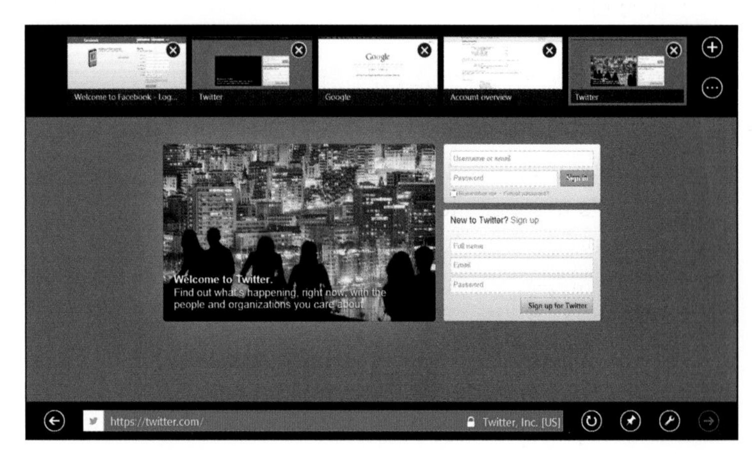


See if you can locate these options in the screen shot here, and on your own computer, from the IE Start screen app:

- Address bar – here we've navigated to https://twitter.com.
- Back – use to return to the previously visited web page. It's a back arrow.
- Refresh – use to reload the web page. It's a counter-clockwise circular arrow.
- Pin to Start – click to create a tile for the webpage on the Start screen. This charm looks like a thumbtack.
- Page Tools – click to find something on a page, view the website in the Desktop app, and more. This icon looks like a wrench.

### Did you know?

If you position your cursor in the middle of the left or right side of the page, transparent Back and Forward arrows appear.

- Forward– click to move to a previously visited page. This is available only after clicking the Back button.
- Tabs – click any thumbnail to return to a previously tabbed website. Note the option to remove the thumbnail (X) and the options to open and close tabs (+ and. . .). This is located at the top of the page.
- Content – this is the web page content. It is located in the middle of the page.

### Visit a website and access the available charms

There are several ways to visit a website, including clicking links on other web pages, in emails and in messages. You can also navigate to a website by typing its name in the address bar. After you've navigated to a few websites using the address bar, explore the Back and Forward arrows (which you can access by right-clicking if they aren't visible). After a while, the IE app will determine which websites you visit most. Then, when you click inside the address bar, thumbnails will be available to quickly access those sites.

While you're surfing the web with the IE app, new tabs will open automatically. Tabs enable you to keep multiple web pages open at the same time and switch among them easily. To access the tabs and see whether you have any open right now, right-click the screen. At the top of the page you'll see your open tabs as well as two other options, the + sign and the three dots.

## Use the Internet Explorer app (cont.)

### Visit a website with the IE app

1. From the Start screen, click the Internet Explorer tile.
2. Click once in the address bar. (Right-click if it's not visible.)
3. Type the web address you require.
4. If you've visited the page before, it may appear above the address bar and you can click it. If not, simply press Enter on the keyboard or click the right-facing arrow.

# Use the Internet Explorer app (cont.)

### Did you know?

If you opt to open a new tab using the InPrivate option (available from the Tab tools), IE won't remember the website in its History list and won't save anything else related to your visit either.

From the options at the top of the page you can:

- Click the X by any tab to close it.
- Click the + sign to open a new, blank page and type the desired address or choose from the thumbnails that appear.
- Click the three dots to open a new InPrivate tab, which enables you to surf the web without leaving traces of your Internet browsing session on the computer.
- Click the three dots to close all open tabs.

From the options at the bottom of the page you can:

- Refresh the page to view new content.
- Pin a Favorite website to the Start screen.

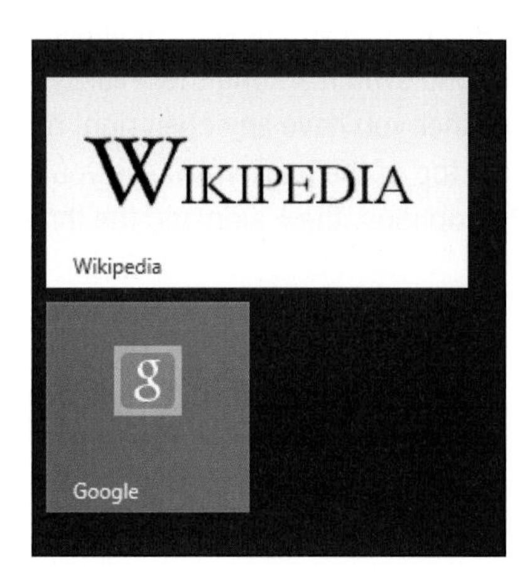

- View the page using the Desktop version of IE. Do this when features of the page aren't available to you in the IE app.

### Explore Settings

You can configure settings for IE from the Settings charm. These include the ability to delete your browsing history, enable or disable a website from asking for permission to ask for your physical location, and more. To access the available settings:

- Open the IE app and using any method, bring up the charms.
- Click Settings.
- Click Internet Options.

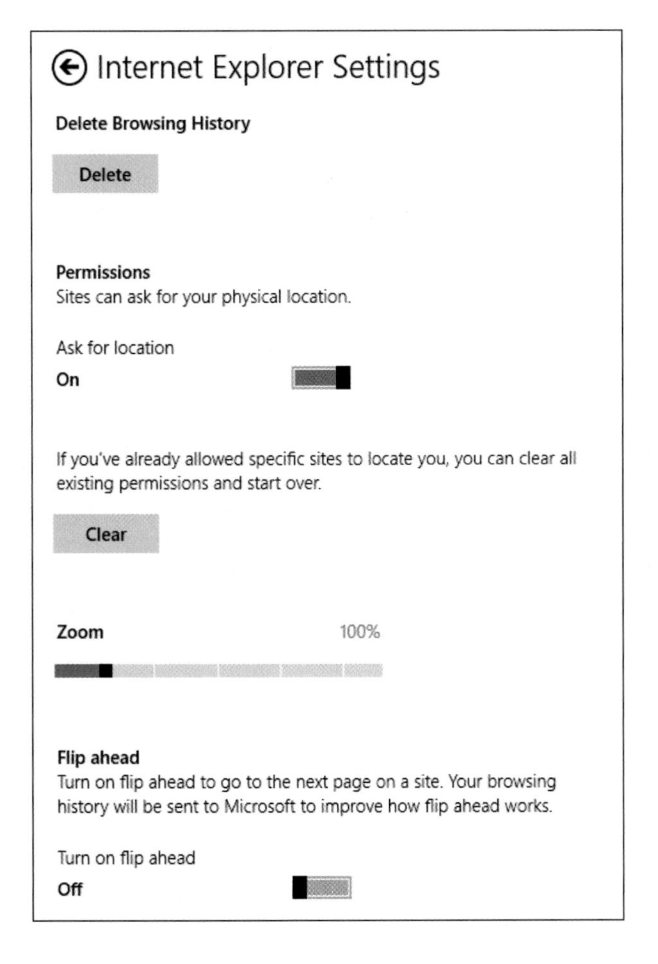




**Did you know?**

If you use a Microsoft account to log in to Windows 8, when you log in to another Windows 8 machine your Start screen configuration will be available there too.

**Did you know?**

Permissions let you enable or disable notifications about your current location.

# Use the Internet Explorer app (cont.)

## Explore the other charms

Speaking of charms and the IE app, the Devices charm offers access to any printers or compatible programs you can use to print the web page. Compatible programs are those like Microsoft OneNote and various 'document writers'. Generally, though, you'll choose to print using an available printer.

You can also access the Search charm. This opens the familiar search pane you've seen many times before. Type your search query and choose Internet Explorer from the options. Search results will appear in the app.

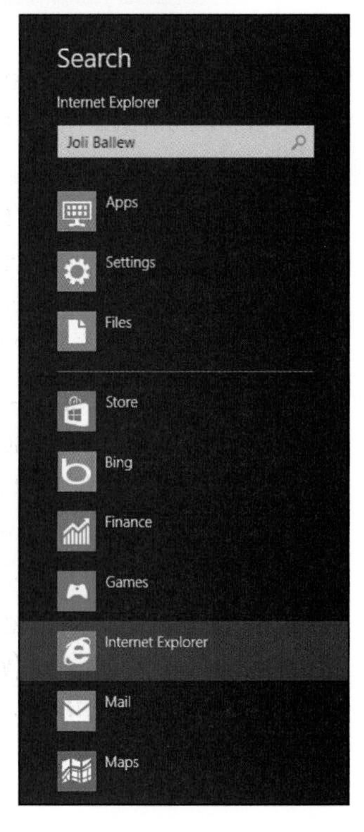

## Use the Internet Explorer Desktop app

As you know, Windows 8 comes with another version of IE, the Desktop version. If you've ever used IE on another computer, the IE you'll find on the Desktop is quite similar. To get started, access the Desktop and once there click the big blue E on the Taskbar, which represents Internet Explorer.

### Explore the interface

The Desktop version of Internet Explorer offers all the tools you'll need to surf the Internet. As with other Desktop applications, it has toolbars and icons where you can access everything you need to perform Internet-related tasks. You can save links to your most often accessed websites, use tabs to open multiple websites at the same time, and more. Here are some of the items to explore as you learn about IE on the Desktop:

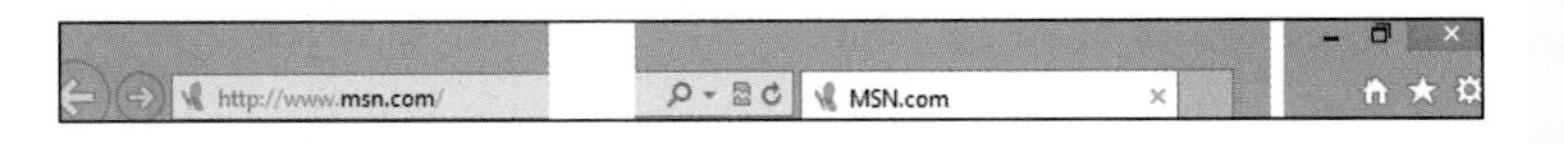


- Address bar – used to type in Internet addresses, also known as URLs (universal resource locators). Generally, an Internet address takes the form of *http://www.companyname.com*.
- Tabs – used to access other open websites or navigate to one. You'll always find a blank tab at the far right of the open ones.
- Home icon (the home) – to go to your Home page(s). A Home page opens each time you start a new browsing session with Internet Explorer. If you right-click here you can opt to add or change your Home page(s).
- Favorites icon (the star) – to access web pages you've marked as Favorites, generally sites you visit often or want to save for later. You can also view your history here, as well as RSS feeds, if you use them.
- Tools icon (the circle) – to access options to print the page, set safety features, view downloads, manage add-ons, access Internet Options (where you make configuration changes to IE) and more.

# Use the Internet Explorer Desktop app (cont.)

## Did you know?

If you ever come across a website that does not look or 'act' the way you think it should, you can click the Compatibility View icon located at the end of the address bar. It looks like a torn page.

## Did you know?

When a website name starts with https://, it means it's secure. When purchasing items online, make sure the payment pages have this prefix.

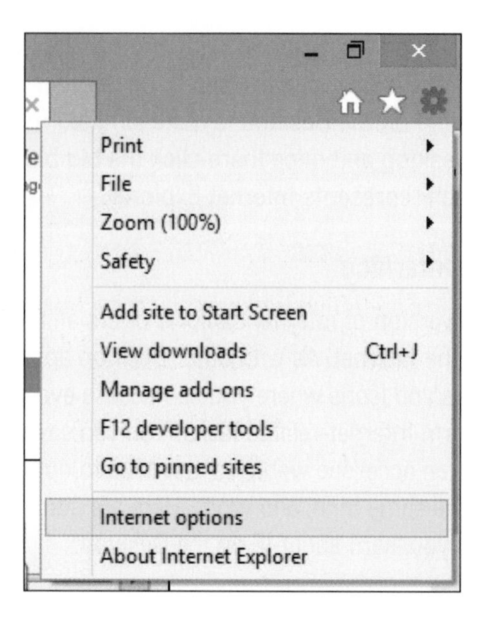


You can also enable various toolbars. These toolbars take up space but do offer access to the various tools and settings you may need regularly, especially if you're used to the older versions of IE. These include:

- Command bar – used to access icons such as the Home and Print icons, and various menus such as Page, Safety, Tools and Help.

- Favorites bar – used to access your list of saved websites, called Favorites, that you've saved here specifically.
- Menu bar – enable this to access the familiar menus including File, Edit, View, Favorites, Tools and Help.

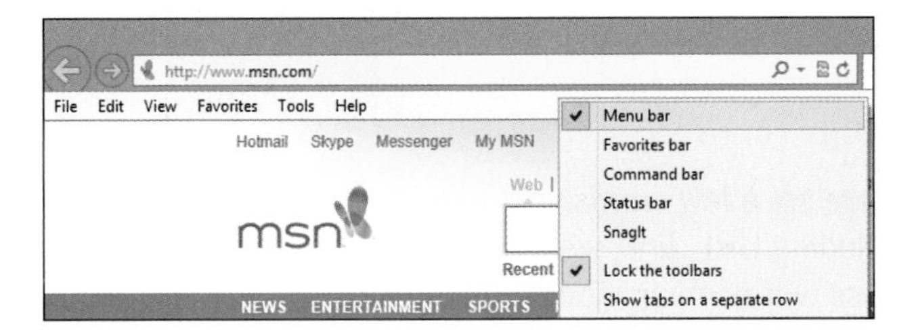


- Status bar – used to find information about the current activity. The Status bar also offers a place to change the zoom level quickly.

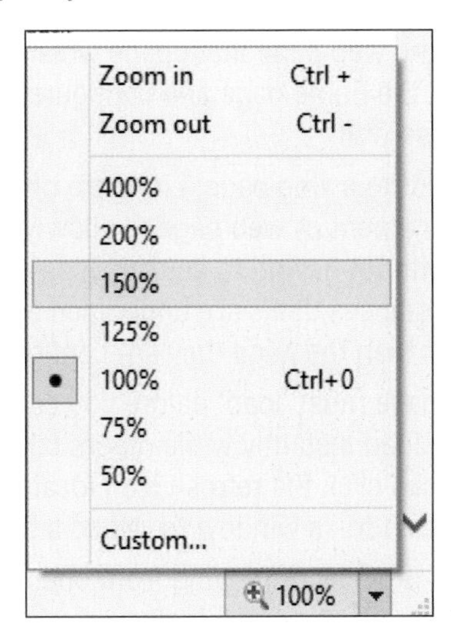


Just like the IE app on the start screen, you can also keep multiple websites open and available using tabs. A blank tab is available to the right of the last open tab. While practising how to use these, consider these websites you can type into the address bar after clicking the empty tab:

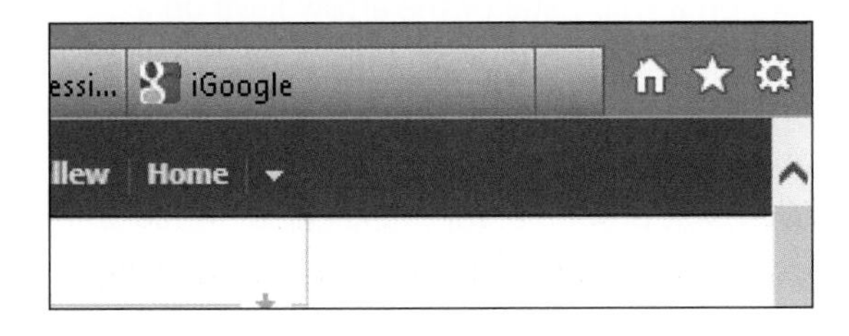


*http://www.microsoft.com/uk*
*http://www.amazon.com*
*http://www.greatbritain.com*

# Use the Internet Explorer Desktop app (cont.)

## Use tabs in the IE Desktop app

1. Open Internet Explorer on the Desktop.
2. Click an empty tab.
3. Type the name of the website you'd like to visit in the address bar.
4. Press Enter on the keyboard.

8

### Did you know?

.com is the most popular ending for website names and it means the website is a company, business or personal website. .edu is used for educational institutions, .gov for government entities, .org for non-profit organisations (mostly) and .net for miscellaneous businesses and companies, or personal websites. There are others though, including .info, .biz, .tv and .uk.com.

# Use the Internet Explorer Desktop app (cont.)

### Jargon buster

There are a few words you're going to see often, including URL, link, website and others. Here's what these words mean along with others:

**Domain name** – for our use here, a domain name is synonymous with a website name.

**Favorite** – a web page that you've chosen to maintain a shortcut for in the Favorites Center.

**Home page** – the web page that opens when you open IE. You can set the home page and configure additional pages to open as well.

**Link** – a shortcut to a web page. Links are often offered in an email, document or web page to allow you to access a site without having to actually type in its name. In almost all instances, links are underlined and in a different colour than the page they are configured on.

**Load** – a web page must 'load' before you can access it. Some pages load instantly while others take a few seconds. You can click the refresh icon located at the far right end of the address window to reload a page.

**Navigate** – the process of moving from one web page to another or viewing items on a single web page. Often the term is used as follows: 'Click the link to navigate to the new web page.'

**Search** – a term used when you type a word or group of words into a Search window. Searching for data produces results.

**Scroll Up and Scroll Down** – a process of using the scroll bars on a web page or the arrow keys on a keyboard to move up and down the pages of a website.

**Website** – a group of web pages that contains related information. Microsoft's website contains information about Microsoft products, for instance.

**URL** – the information you type to access a website, such as http://www.microsoft.com.

## Personalise the IE Desktop app

There are many ways to personalise Internet Explorer. You can configure a Home page or a set of Home pages to open each time you open IE, for instance. You can save and organise Favorites and set zoom levels. There's not enough room here to explain all the options, but once you learn how to access these features the rest will be intuitive.

### Designate Home pages

To assign web pages as home pages, you should always navigate to the pages first. Once you've opened all the web pages you want to add as a home page or home page group, right-click the Home button and choose Add or change home page. You can then choose from three options:

- Use this webpage as your only home page – select this option if you want only one page to serve as your Home page.
- Add this webpage to your home page tabs – select this option if you want this page to be one of several Home pages.
- Use the current tab set as your home page – select this option if you've opened multiple tabs and you want all of them to be Home pages.

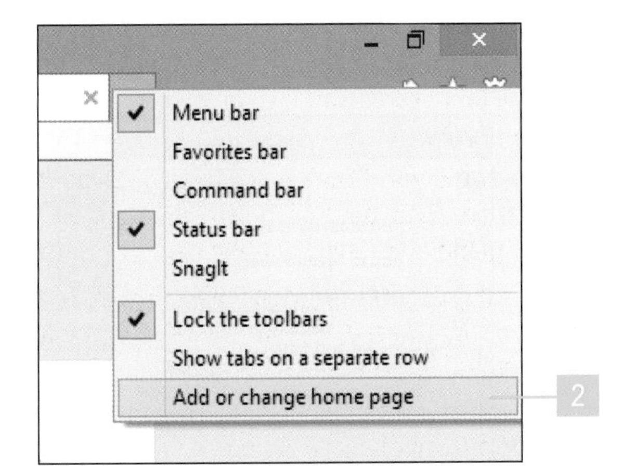


### Set a Home page

1. From the IE Desktop app, use the address bar to locate a web page (and use the empty Tab button to repeat to open additional web pages).
2. Right-click the Home icon and click Add or change home page. (Note you have additional choices, including showing various toolbars.)
3. Make a selection using the information provided regarding each option.
4. Click Yes.

**Did you know?**

To open your home pages, click the Home icon.

**For your information**

Look at how to open a website in Internet Explorer, earlier in this chapter.

# Personalise the IE Desktop app (cont.)

## Mark a Favorite

1. Go to the web page (or web pages) you want to configure as a Favorite (or group of Favorites).
2. Click the star to the right of the address bar.
3. Click the arrow by Add to favorites.
4. Make the desired choice.
5. When prompted, note you can name the website whatever you want, and save it to the desired Favorites folder. (Favorites is the default but you might want to choose Favorites bar.)

?

### Did you know?

You can also access Favorites from the Favorites menu (which you can access by pressing Alt on the keyboard) if you're a fan of menus.

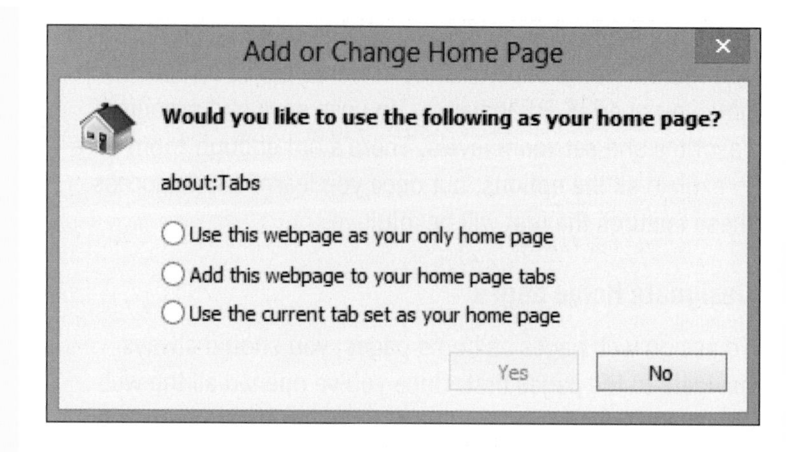


## Save and organise Favorites

Favorites are websites you save links to for accessing more easily at a later time. They differ from Home pages because by default they do not open when you start IE. The Favorites you save appear in the Favorites Center, which you can access by clicking the yellow star you learned about earlier. You can use the Favorites Center to quickly access your Favorites list, places you've recently visited, and any RSS feeds you've subscribed to.

When adding Favorites, you have several options. You can add a single web page as a Favorite, or add a group of web pages to create a Tab Group of Favorites. You can also add the Favorite to the Favorites bar, which you can enable by right-clicking just above the address bar.

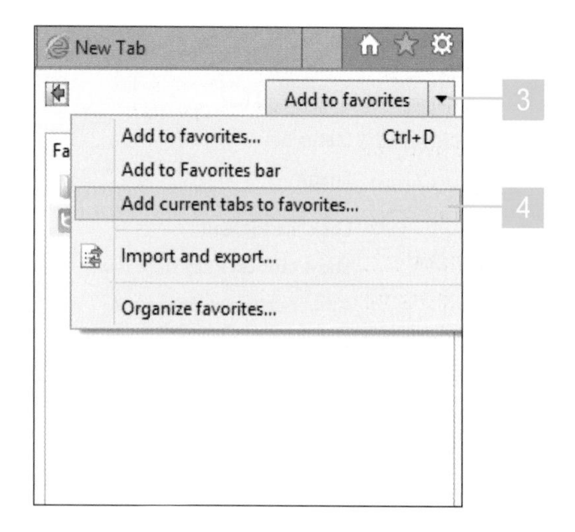

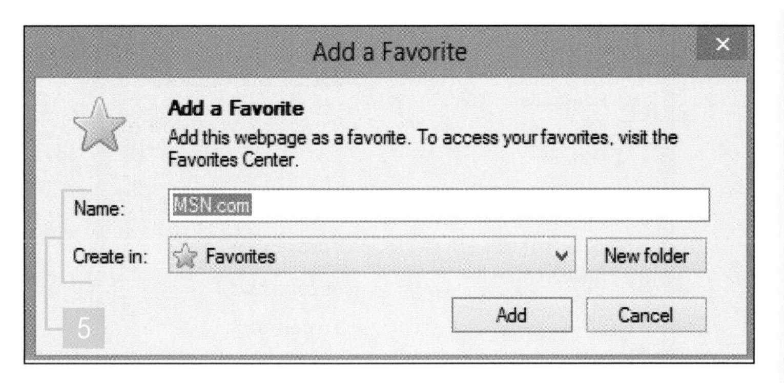


There will probably come a time when your Favorites Center becomes unwieldy. Perhaps you haphazardly saved Favorites and now need to organise them into folders you create, or maybe you have Favorites you want to delete. You can do this inside the Favorites Center. Here is an example of what a chaotic Favorites list looks like.

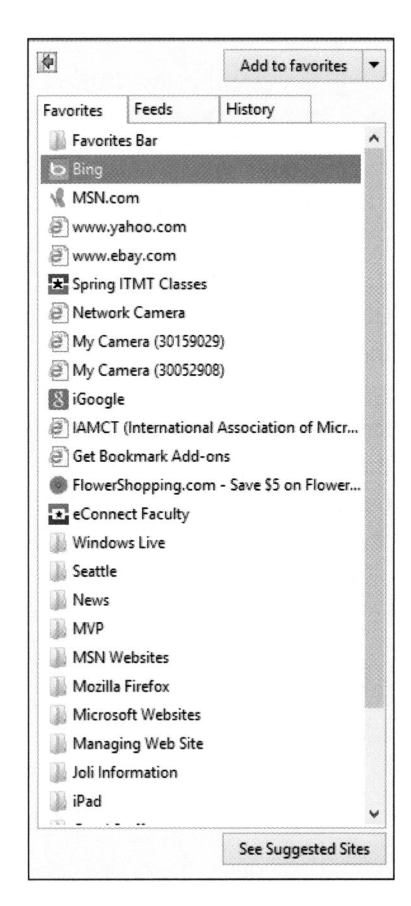


To organise a list of Favorites like this one, click the star and the arrow next to Add to favorites and choose Organize Favorites. In the Organize Favorites dialogue box you can create new folders, select Favorites to move into those folders, rename Favorites and delete them.

## Personalise the IE Desktop app (cont.)

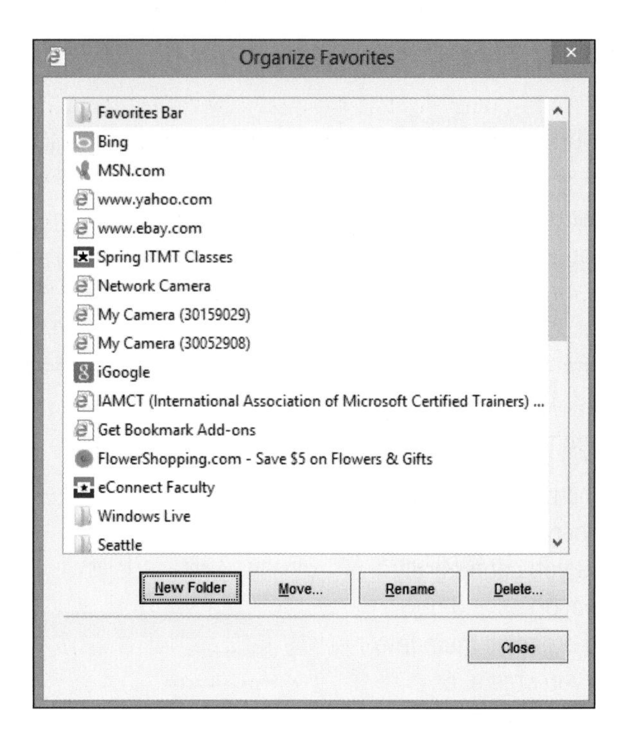


Obviously, it's best to create folders for Favorites as you save them. You can. In the Add a Favorite dialogue box, where you type the name for a Favorite and choose where to save it, you'll see an option to create a new folder. Click that and then save the new Favorite in it. This way you can stay organised from the beginning. From then on, each time you save a Favorite, choose the desired folder to save it to, or create a new folder to hold it.

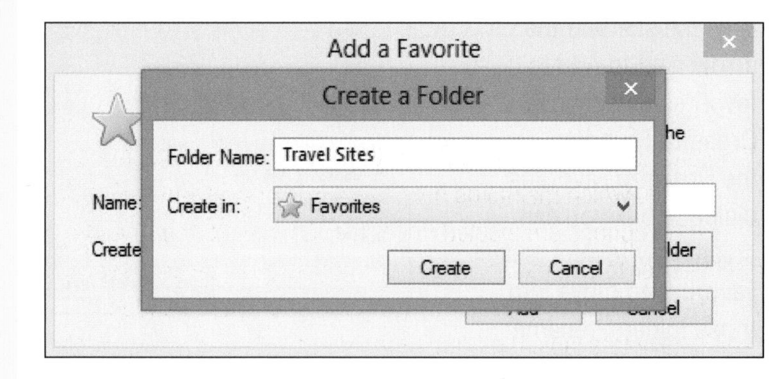

## Use Text size and Page Zoom

If you have trouble reading what's on a web page because the text is too small, you can make it larger in two specific ways. First, you can access the Text size options from the View menu (which you can access by clicking the Alt key on the keyboard) and choose from Largest, Larger, Medium (the default), Smaller and Smallest. This option works pretty well, but it can change the layout of the web page if it causes the text to become so large that it runs over images or other text on the page. Although most web pages have this problem solved, some don't, and thus there's a better way to zoom in on a page.

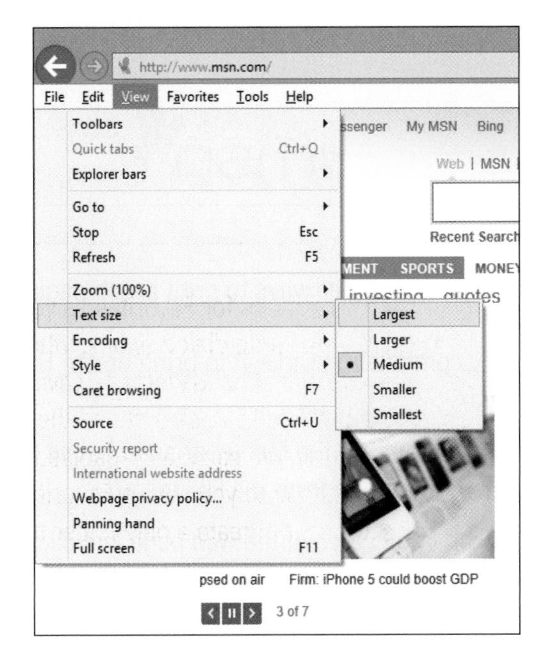


We prefer the Zoom feature. Zoom intelligently zooms in on the entire page, which maintains the page's integrity, layout and look. The Zoom options are located under the View menu too, but it's much easier to use the link at the bottom right of the browser window, on the Status bar. Just click it to show zoom options. (You'll have to enable the Status bar, which requires you to right-click just above the address bar.) You can also use keyboard shortcuts and touch gestures, as outlined in the panel here.

# Personalise the IE Desktop app (cont.)

### Zoom in or out

1. Open Internet Explorer and browse to a web page.
2. If you have a physical keyboard, use the Ctrl + = and the Ctrl + – combinations to zoom in and out.
3. If you have a touch screen, pinch in and out with two or more fingers.
4. Alternatively you can:
   - **a** Right-click the area above the tabs and address bar and place a tick by Status bar.
   - **b** Then click the arrow on the right end of the Status bar to zoom to a specific size.

?

### Did you know?

The term browse is used to describe both locating a file on your hard drive and locating something on the Internet.

# Print a web page

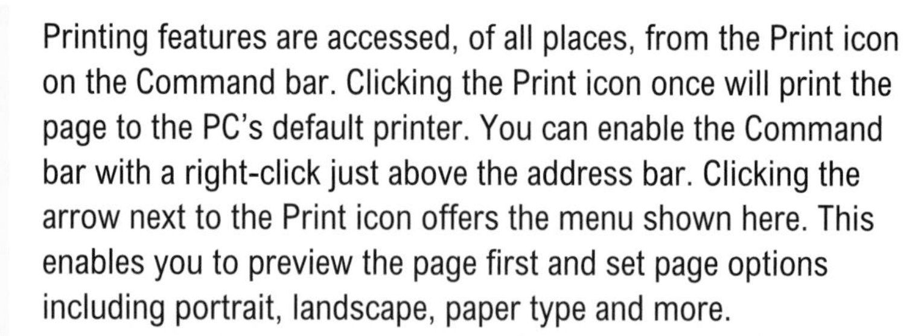

Printing features are accessed, of all places, from the Print icon on the Command bar. Clicking the Print icon once will print the page to the PC's default printer. You can enable the Command bar with a right-click just above the address bar. Clicking the arrow next to the Print icon offers the menu shown here. This enables you to preview the page first and set page options including portrait, landscape, paper type and more.

Beyond this, there are other ways to print a web page:

- Use the key combination Ctrl + P to bring up the Print dialogue box.
- Tap the Alt key to show the Menu bar and choose the appropriate print option from the File menu.
- Right-click an empty area of the web page and click Print from the resulting contextual menu. A long tap on a touch screen works, too.

**Did you know?**

You can search from the address bar. Simply type your keywords there and press Enter on the keyboard.

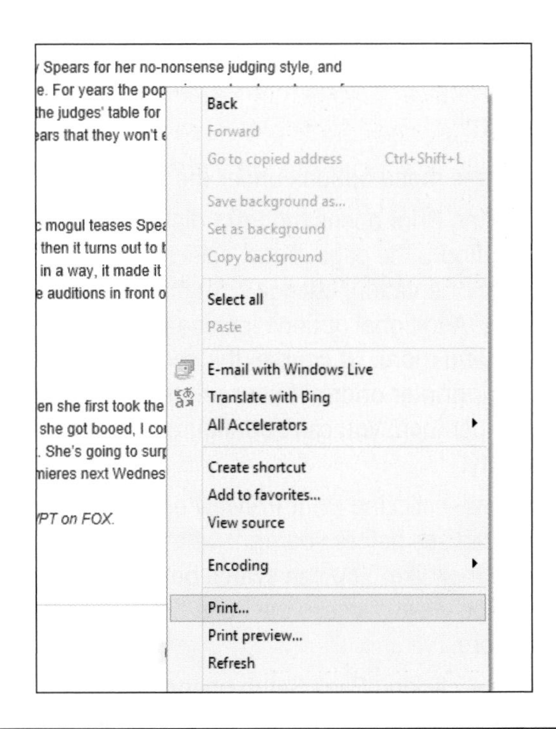


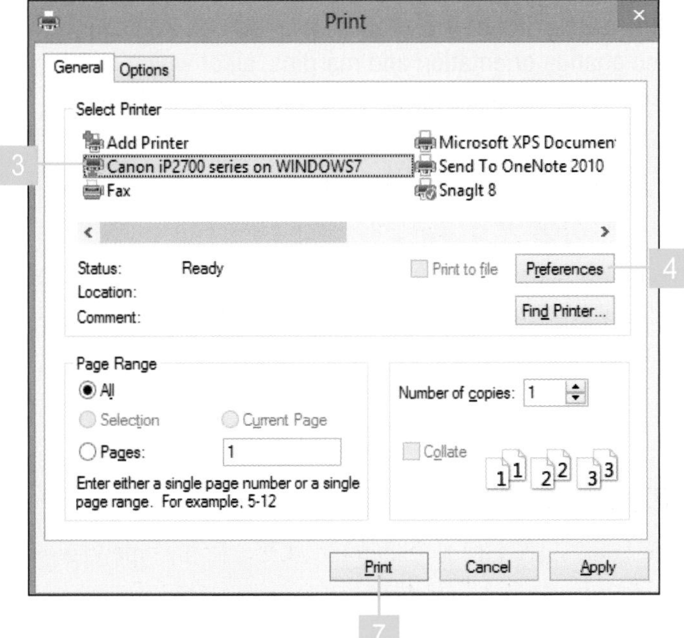


# Print a web page (cont.)

## Print a web page

1. Locate a page on the Internet you'd like to print.
2. On the keyboard, press the Ctrl key + P.
3. In the Print dialogue box, choose a printer.
4. Click Preferences.
5. As applicable to your printer and preferences, configure the desired options.
6. Click OK.
7. Click Print.

8

### For your information

If you want to print from the IE app, access the charms and click Devices. You'll see the printer in the list.

# Print a web page (cont.)

## Jargon buster

There are three menu options under the Print icon:

**Print** – clicking Print opens the Print dialogue box where you can configure the page range, select a printer, change page orientation, change print order and choose a paper type. Additional options include print quality, output bins and more. Of course, the choices depend on what your printer offers. If your printer can print only at 300 dots per inch, you can't configure it to print at a higher quality.

**Print Preview** – clicking Print Preview opens a window where you can see before you print what the printout will actually look like. You can switch between portrait and landscape views, access the Page Setup dialogue box, and more.

**Page Setup** – clicking Page Setup opens the Page Setup dialogue box. Here you can select a paper size and source, and create headers and footers. You can also change orientation and margins, all of which is dependent on which features your printer supports.

There's a lot going on behind the scenes in IE, and a lot of it is security related. There's a pop-up blocker to keep unwanted ads from appearing when you visit web pages configured with them, and there are Security Zones and Privacy Settings to help protect against any other threats you may run across while surfing the web. Since much of this is preconfigured, we won't go into much detail here. It is important to know they exist though.

However, there are a few things to discuss, specifically, cleaning up IE by deleting files that can be used to trace where you've been on the Internet. If your grandkids use your computer and do not have their own user account, you'll want to do this before they start surfing the web. You may also want to configure accessibility options. You can also take advantage of accelerators. These are quick access lists that allow you to perform tasks with selected data, such as emailing it, mapping it or even blogging about it.

## Be secure

### Delete your web footprint

If you don't want people to be able to snoop around on your computer and find out which sites you've been visiting you'll need to delete your 'browsing history'. Deleting your browsing history lets you remove the information stored on your computer related to your Internet activities.

- Open Internet Explorer on the Desktop.
- Click the Tools icon.
- Click Internet Options.
- From the General tab, under Browsing history, click Delete.
- Select what to delete and click Delete. (You may want to keep Preserve Favorites and website data selected.)
- Explore the other tabs and options in the Internet Explorer dialogue box. Click OK to close.

# Be secure (cont.)

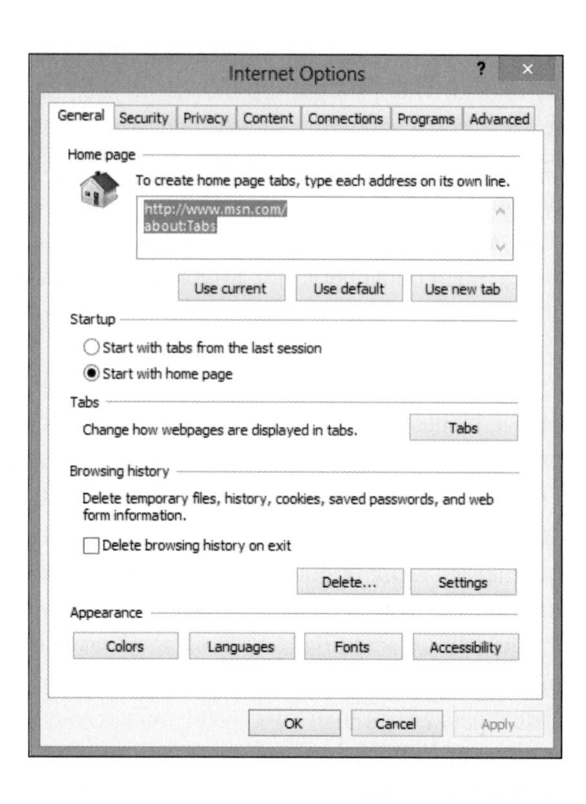


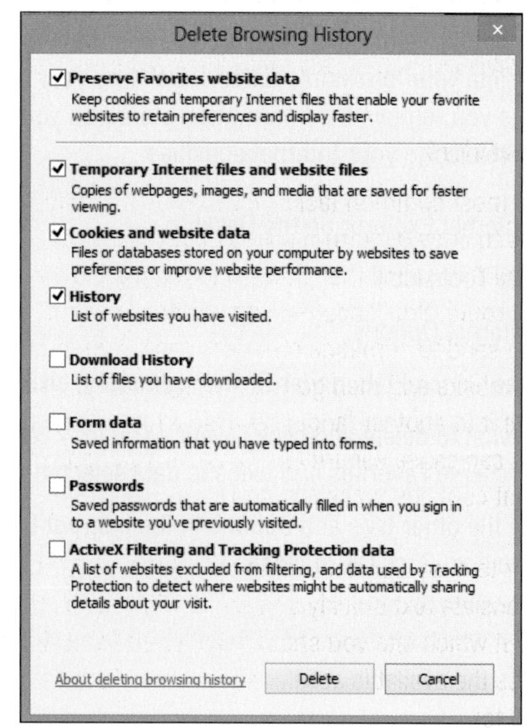

### Jargon buster

**Temporary Internet Files** – files that have been downloaded and saved in your Temporary Internet Files folder. A nosy, computer-literate person could go through these files to see what you've been doing online.

**Cookies** – small text files that include data that identifies your preferences when you visit particular websites. Cookies are what allow you to visit, say, www.amazon.com and be greeted with 'Hello <your name>, We have recommendations for you!'. Cookies help a site offer you a personalised web experience.

**Form data** – information that's been saved using Internet Explorer's autocomplete form data functionality. If you don't want forms to be filled out automatically by you or someone else who has access to your PC and user account, delete this.

**Passwords** – passwords that were saved using Internet Explorer autocomplete password prompts.

**InPrivate Blocking data** – data that was saved by InPrivate Blocking to detect where websites may be automatically sharing details about your visit.

## Use accelerators

One of the most common tasks you'll do in IE (besides surfing the web) is to copy data from a web page. You'll copy an address and then paste that address into a mapping website to obtain a route. You'll copy a map and then paste it into an email to send to someone else. You may even copy data from one website and then go to another to find its meaning or translate it to another language. This takes quite a bit of time and it can cause security problems if you happen upon a website that contains malicious code.

If you want to copy and paste data quickly, get information quickly, translate text quickly and so on without having to worry about which site you should visit to perform the task, you can use the available accelerators. These include but are not limited to:

## Be secure (cont.)

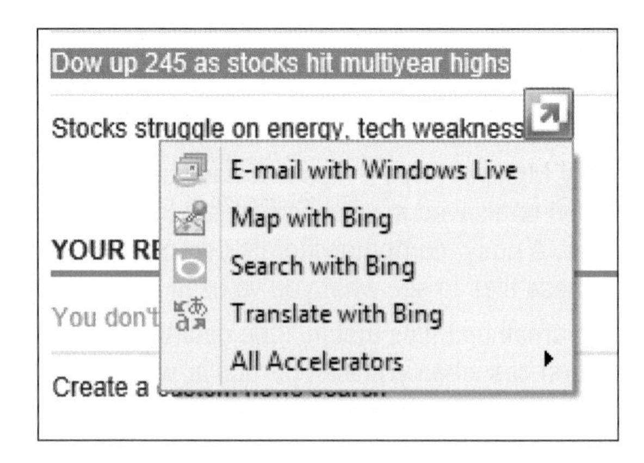


- E-mail with Windows Live
- Map with Bing
- Search with Bing
- Translate with Bing.

You can also opt for All Accelerators from the drop-down list, where you can find more accelerators and manage the accelerators you have. To use an accelerator, highlight any data on a web page and then click the accelerator icon – it's a blue arrow in a box. If you don't see it, right-click the selected data to access the menu you see here.

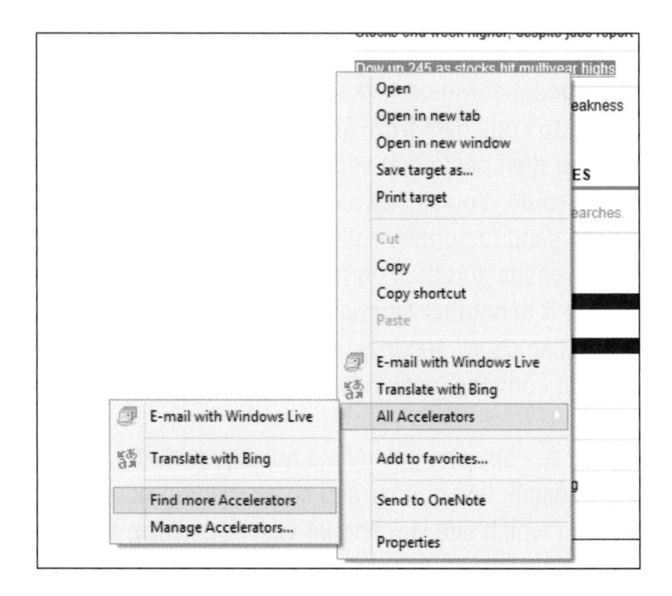

## Be secure (cont.)

After you select the desired accelerator from the list, results will appear. Here we've searched for a pub we'd like to visit on our trip to the United States and opted to Map with Bing. A map appears on the screen and we don't have to go to another website for the information. This is not only easier but more secure.

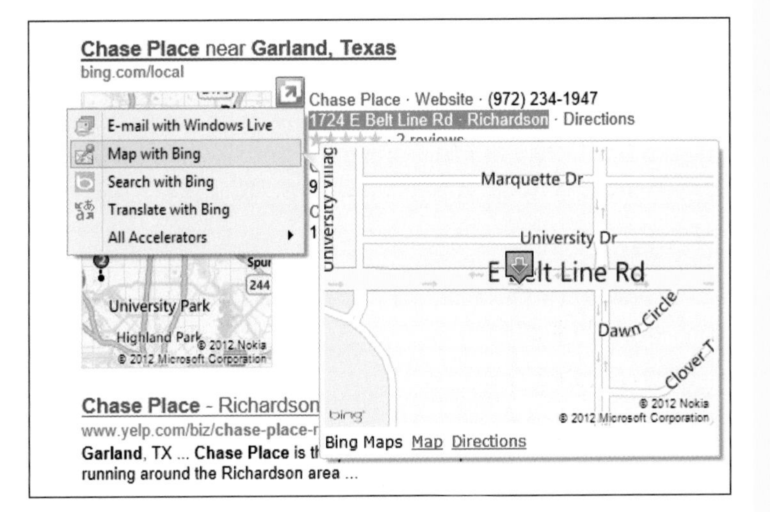

## Be safe online

Internet Explorer can only do so much to keep you safe on the Internet – the rest is up to you. Here are some tips for protecting your data, your identity and more.

### Important

If someone learns the password you set for, say, a savings and loan account, they'll try that same password at other places, too, like investing websites, shopping websites and others. That's why it's important to use a different password for every website (and a different user name, if possible).

### Create strong passwords for websites

1. Create passwords that are at least six characters long.
2. Include upper- and lower-case letters.
3. Include at least one number.
4. Include one or more special symbols.
5. Create passwords that you can remember with a little effort, such as MyAccountAtAmazOn74.
6. Don't opt to let websites keep you logged in.

## Create strong passwords

You must create user names and passwords for many of the websites you visit, including social networking sites, banking institutions, shopping websites and others. Those passwords should be hard to guess, and they should be different for each site you log in to.

You'll have to keep your passwords written down in a list. You'll also have to keep that list safe. Consider the damage a person could do with a list of user names and passwords. Here are some tips for protecting that list.

- Keep user names in one list and passwords in another, and keep the two lists in separate places.
- Put the list in a folder that is amid others, and name the folder something like Pet Health Records or My Favourite Recipes.
- When writing down your passwords, don't write down the entire password. For instance, if your password is MyDogHasFleez#, only write down MyDogHasFleez. This will work provided you always add a # to the end of every password.
- Consider storing passwords in a secure folder on the Internet. SkyDrive is an option. Then, should you need to access that list you only need to remember one password, the one that takes you to this folder.

?

### Did you know?

No matter how well you protect your passwords or how difficult they are to guess, your user name and password can still be stolen if there's a security breach at the institution that stores them.

i

### For your information

People whose business it is to steal passwords will try passwords like this first: password, 12345, abcde and letmein. They may also try your birthday, children's names and pets' names.

# Create strong passwords (cont.)

Important

If your house is ever burgled or your computer stolen, change all of your internet user names and passwords. Thieves don't just want your physical valuables any more, they want your virtual valuables, too.

## Know how to perform web searches

There are a lot of places you can search for information on the web. You can search from *www.google.com*, *www.bing.com*, *www.yahoo.com* and more. It is best to search with established search providers. Once you're ready to search, keep the following things in mind to obtain effective results:

- Avoid using words in your search that can be, in another context, sexual.
- Don't click the results listed first – those are ads. Scroll down a bit to the actual results.
- Note the source of the information in the result you like and make sure it's from a trusted source.
- Before clicking, try to get a preview of the information. Some search engines offer a right-facing arrow that will show you a preview of the page and you won't have to click it.

## Look for the 's' before making an online purchase

Before you make purchases from any website, make sure that the site can be trusted with your credit card information and other personal data. You can check easily by looking for https:// in the address bar. If you don't see the 's', don't enter any personal data. In addition, many websites now let you pay with PayPal, a secure way to perform online transactions. Setting up a PayPal account takes a little doing, but you only have to do it once!

For your information

If you've never tried Google Documents, visit www.google.com and under More, click Documents to get started. You can store documents there, too.

## Create strong passwords (cont.)

**For your information**

Common and trusted results pages can be from Microsoft, CNN, Apple, Wikipedia, Amazon, Google, Yahoo, WebMD and similar well-known entities, although results you'll find in user-submitted 'answers' and 'forums' can't always be trusted.

**Important**

Before you make purchases from a person on eBay or a similar website, make sure that person has good reviews and has been doing business at the site for a good length of time.

**Did you know?**

The 's' after https means the website has taken steps to get a 'certificate' from a certificate authority, and that authority has deemed the site safe for handling your personal information.

# Choose a default application

If you would prefer the IE Desktop app to open when you click a link in an email, message, document and so on instead of the simpler IE app, you can configure it in Internet Explorer's settings. Doing so will make the Desktop app the default.

## Configure the IE Desktop app as the default

1. Open Internet Explorer on the Desktop.
2. Click the Settings icon, then Internet Options.
3. Click the Programs tab.
4. Click the arrow beside Let Internet Explorer decide.
5. Click Always in Internet Explorer in the desktop.
6. Click OK.

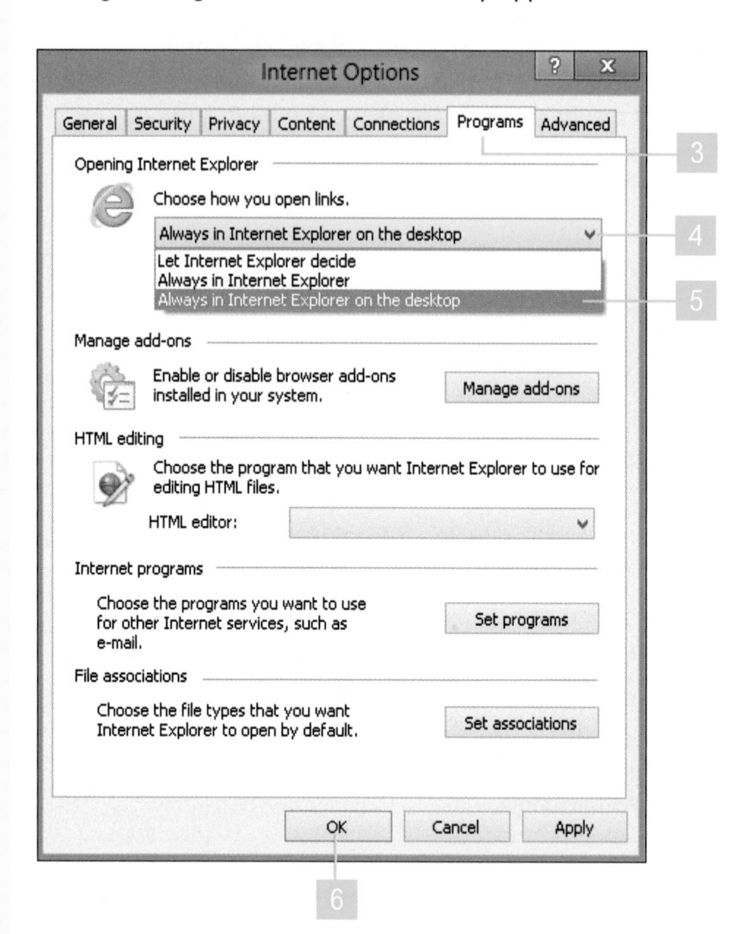


### For your information

While you have the Internet Options dialogue box open, explore the other options available. From the General tab, for instance, you can configure IE to start each time with tabs from the last session (instead of your configured Home page(s)).

# Play and manage media

9

## Introduction

Media apps are available from the Start screen. These apps let you view pictures, play videos and listen to music. These are the basic apps you'll use when you want to see and hear your media. There are also Desktop counterparts, or at least ways to access the same media in a different way while on the Desktop. These Desktop counterparts offer more features than the apps do, such as grouping and regrouping pictures in folders, renaming videos and creating your own music playlists and saving them, to name a few. Let's look at each of these items in more depth before we begin.

The Photos app is a basic app available from the Start screen. From there you can access all your pictures in a single place, and you can view, print and share them easily. You can also access pictures you've made available online such as those stored on Facebook, Flickr and SkyDrive.

If you'd like to do something a bit more complex, perhaps create folders to organise your photos, rotate them or open them in an editing program, you'll want to do so from the Desktop, specifically, using File Explorer. There you can access your Pictures library, move and organise pictures easily, and use the File Explorer ribbon to share photos in lots of different ways (including burning them to a CD or DVD). You can even sort photos by date, rating, and more.

You've probably seen the Music and Video apps on the Start screen, too. These apps are similar to other apps you've explored. Both offer a streamlined interface with limited functionality, making it easy to listen to music and watch videos. It's equally easy to purchase media there. When you need to do more than purchase or play media, you can use the Desktop app, Windows Media Player. Like other Desktop apps you've explored, Media Player offers much more functionality, many more features and more ways to manage media than either of its app counterparts.

## What you'll do

# Import, view and manage photos

You probably have a lot of digital photos, and you may have even more physical ones. If you want to put those physical photos on your computer, you'll need a scanner to do so, or someone who can do the scanning for you and save the images to a CD, DVD or thumb drive. Digital photos are easier to acquire – you only need to import them from whatever device they are stored on.

Once pictures are on your computer, you can manage them. You can place them in folders, edit them, rename them and so on. There are many ways to do this, but for the most part you'll use the Photos app, Windows Photo Viewer, Paint and File Explorer. These are all included with Windows 8. You can also install your own programs, such as Photoshop Elements or something similar.

**Important**

When you save pictures to your computer, make sure you save them to the Pictures library. You can save them specifically to the My Pictures or the Public Pictures folders if you prefer. Saving to the Pictures library or a specific pictures folder will make them easy to find in the Photos app.

## Import pictures

There are lots of different hardware options for taking digital pictures, including mobile phones, smartphones, digital cameras, web cams and video cameras. And there are even more ways to store and carry pictures with you, including USB drives, music players, digital cameras and iPads, among others. Finally, there are multiple ways to get pictures onto a PC, including using digital cameras, media cards and even scanners. In this section we'll talk about the latter – importing pictures from a device to the PC. Remember, the device doesn't necessarily have to be something that takes the pictures; it can be a scanner, USB drive, media card, CD or music player.

You can put photos on your computer in lots of ways, but the easiest method is to use the Photos app. The landing page offers an option to add a device to *see* photos that are on them, but if you right-click while on that page, the option to *Import* those photos appears.

**Jargon buster**

When you import photos, you copy them to your computer.

## View and manage photos with the Photos app

The Photos app, available from the Start screen, is the easiest place to view your photos. The app separates your photos by what's stored on your computer and what is stored in various places on the Internet. If you've created subfolders to organise your photos, those subfolders will appear, too. To get started, from the Start screen, click Photos.

# Import, view and manage photos (cont.)

### Import pictures from an external source

1. Connect your camera, insert a memory card or connect an external drive that contains photos.
2. Open the Photos app and click any back buttons as necessary to access the landing page. (You might have to right-click to access the back arrow.)
3. Right-click the landing page to access the toolbar.
4. Click Import.
5. By default, all the photos are selected, provided they have not already been imported. Right-click to deselect photos.
6. Type a name for the folder these pictures will be imported to, then click Import.
7. Click Open album (not shown) to view the photos.

**Important**

Create a descriptive name for the folder that will hold the imported photos; don't just accept the default name.

## Import, view and manage photos (cont.)

Note the folders that already appear. This is the landing page. (If you see something else, locate and click the applicable back arrows to navigate to this page.) If you have already associated your Windows 8 computer with your Microsoft account, Facebook, SkyDrive and so on, you'll already have access to pictures here. If not, you'll see tiles that prompt you to log in with the required account to add it. If you don't have the associated account and would like to hide the tile, click it once and click Hide.

When you click one of the folder tiles, that folder opens. You may then see subfolders, or a group of photos. Here you can see that if you open the Pictures library, you'll have access to the pictures already stored on your computer. The tiles here are 'live' and will automatically flip through the available photos in each folder.

As you navigate the Photos app, clicking folders and subfolders, you'll see the available media. While in folders in subfolders, the photos are in preview mode; they are not full screen. You can view them this way or click them once to view them in full screen mode. When you're ready to return to the previous screen or view, click the available back arrow. You might have to right-click to access a back arrow or position your mouse in the applicable hot corner.

You can also view a slide show of the photos stored in any folder. Once it starts to play, you can stop it in many ways. You can click Esc on the keyboard, right-click with a mouse, touch the screen and more.

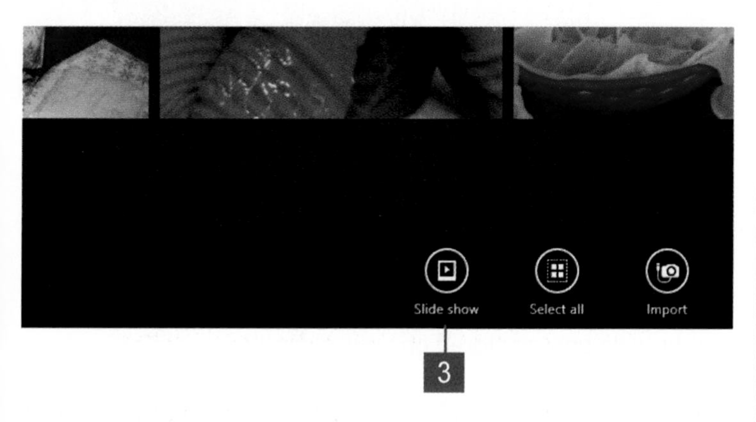


It's best to delete photos you don't want. Unwanted photos not only make the Photos app harder to navigate, the photos also take up valuable hard drive space on your computer. You can delete photos that are stored on your own computer from the Photos app. You cannot delete photos that are stored on Facebook and the like – you have to access that website to delete photos stored there.

To delete a photo stored on your computer using the Photos app, right-click it and click Delete from the available charms. You can select more than one photo at a time and delete photos in groups if you prefer. If you change your mind about the photos you've selected for deletion, either right-click a single photo to remove the tick (and deselect it), or click Clear selection to clear all selections.

## Import, view and manage photos (cont.)

### Play a picture slide show

1. Open the Photos app from the Start screen.
2. Navigate to any folder that contains photos.
3. Right-click and choose Slide show. (Remember, on a tablet you can swipe up.)
4. Stop the show by pressing the Esc key on the keyboard.

?

**Did you know?**

You can pause a slide show by tapping a key on the keyboard, and start it again with a right-click of the mouse (you'll have to click Slide show again).

9

# Import, view and manage photos (cont.)

## Connect social accounts from the Photos app

1. From the Photos app, on the landing page, click Facebook or Flickr.
2. Click Connect.
3. If prompted, type your email or user name and your password.
4. If you decide later you don't want to connect to a specific social network from Photos:
   - a Access the Settings charm and click Options.
   - b Choose which sites to disable or configure options for those sites.

The options that appear when you right-click a photo in the Photos app include more than Clear selection and Delete. You can also opt to browse the photos by date, start a slide show, select all photos in a folder or import more.

Finally, you can view the pictures stored on SkyDrive, Facebook or Flickr from the Photos app. These are all free, online storage spaces. You'll have to click their respective tiles and log in with your account first (if prompted) to use those areas. Once you've logged on, you can browse those photos the same way you browse photos stored on your computer.

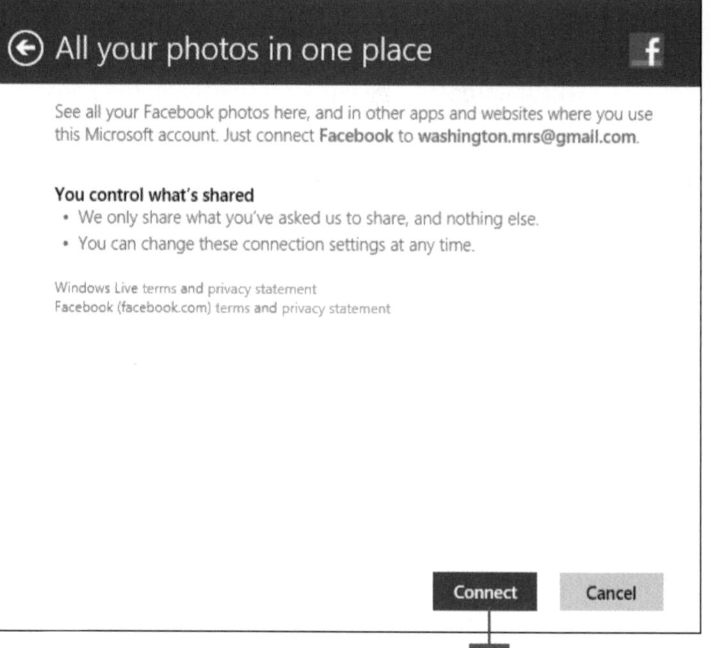

# Import, view and manage photos (cont.)

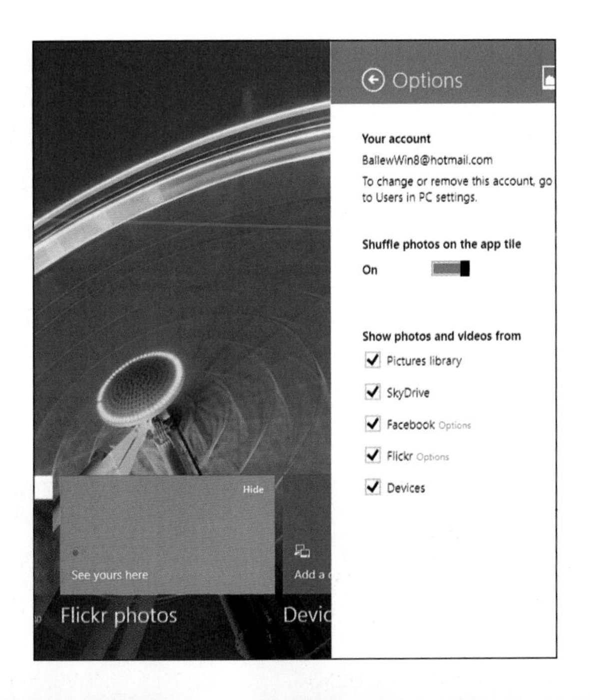

You can do a lot more with the Photos app than you've learned specifically about here. You can:

- Select a photo, click the Share charm, and share the photo with others using Mail, People or SkyDrive, as applicable.

## Import, view and manage photos (cont.)

- Select a photo, click the Devices charm and show the device on a second screen, print it, and so on.
- Right-click and choose Browse by Date to view all your pictures by month.
- Position your cursor in the middle left or right edge to access back arrows, or in the top left corner.
- When in a folder, position your cursor in the bottom right corner and click the – sign to show thumbnails of the photos in the folder. Repeat and click the + sign to return to the normal view.

# Play and purchase media with the Music app

The Music app, available from the Start screen, offers access to the music you have on your computer. You can use this app to play and control music, and to view information about an artist, among other things. While a song is playing you'll have access to various view options too – you can view the track list, album art, visualisations provided by Windows 8, and more. You can also access the Xbox Music Store, where you can browse, preview and purchase songs and albums.

## Find your music in the Music app

1. From the Start screen, click the Music tile.
2. Scroll left.
3. If you have music in your Music library, you'll see it under My Music.
4. If you click the My Music heading, you'll have access to all your music.
5. If you accessed My Music, click the Back button to return to the Music app's landing page.

While browsing the My Music option, you may see more than music. If you've obtained audiobooks and saved them to your computer in a compatible file format that the Music app recognises, you'll see those audiobooks listed in My Music, too. You may also see playlists you've previously created, and you can sort what is there by date added, alphabetically, release year, genre and artist. With that done, you can sort what's listed by albums, artists, songs and playlists.

# Play and purchase media with the Music app (cont.)

## Play a song or listen to an audiobook

1. Open the Music app and navigate to any album (or song or audiobook) to play.
2. Click Play album, Add to now playing, or Play as applicable.
3. Repeat. As you add songs, click Add to Now Playing.
4. Explore the playback options at the bottom of the screen. You will have to flick up or right-click to access these.
5. Click the album cover, located in the middle of the toolbar, to view the album cover, track list, artist information and more.

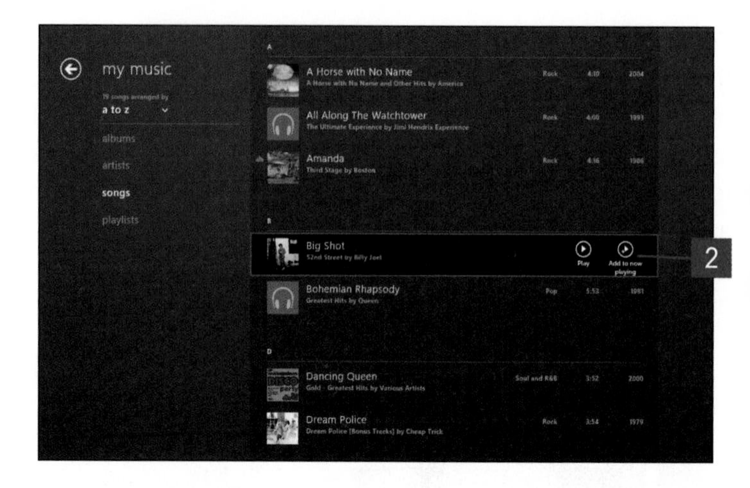


Once you've found the album or song you want to play, you simply click it and choose Play or Add to now playing.

## Play and control media

If you have music in your Music library, you can play it from the Music app. You need to navigate to the song to play first though, which may involve browsing My Music and sorting data as applicable. Once the song is playing, you'll have access to the controls required to manage it. These controls will appear for a few seconds and disappear if you don't access them. To bring them back, right-click the screen.

Depending on the view you are currently in, you'll have access to various controls, including but not limited to:

- Play the selected song again.
- Skip to the previous or next song.
- Pause the song.
- Add the song to a playlist you've already created.
- Delete the song from your Music library.
- Shuffle the songs on the album or in the playlist so they play in random order.
- Explore the artist.

## Play and purchase media with the Music app (cont.)

- Open a new music file from the Music library.
- Access the visualisation view that shows your album covers in the background and enables you to control the media from the foreground controls. You can also view the songs on the album or return to the Music app's landing page by clicking the appropriate icon.

- Access the default charms:
  - Use Settings to change the volume.
  - Use Search to search for songs. Choose an option underneath to choose a place to search.

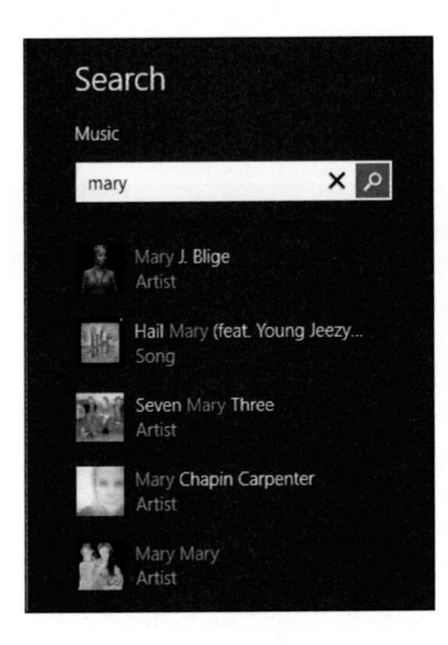


  - Use Share to share as applicable.
  - Use Devices to access devices as applicable.

### ? Did you know?

If you don't have any music on your computer, you can copy songs from CDs you own. This is called ripping and you do this using the Desktop application, Windows Media Player. You'll learn about this later in the chapter.

### ? Did you know?

As you add music to your Music library, the songs and albums will appear in the Music app automatically.

# Play and purchase media with the Music app (cont.)

## Explore the Music Store

1. Open the Music app and click the back arrow as necessary to access the Music app's landing page.
2. Use the scroll bar at the bottom of the screen, the wheel on your mouse, or use your finger to scroll to the right.
3. Click xbox music store.
4. Choose your preferred sorting options.
5. Continue browsing, then click an album or song you like to see the related details page.
6. Note you can select and preview a song, buy the song, buy the album and explore the artist.
7. If you opt to buy the song, you'll need to work through the process to set up an account to purchase media.

## Use the Music Store

If you have a Microsoft account, you can access the Store where you can buy music online. You can also preview the media before you buy it. To purchase music from the Store, you'll have to set up an account. You then use this account to make your purchases. Alternatively, you can buy a monthly music pass. To get started, from the Music app's landing page, scroll left and click xbox music store.

You'll notice that the interface for the Store looks much like the interface under My Music. There are various ways to sort what's available, such as by what's featured, new releases and popular. Once you've selected one of these options you can then sort what's left by genre. You can view all genres, or a specific one such as Latin, Classical, Jazz, Soundtracks, Kids, Christian/Gospel and so on.

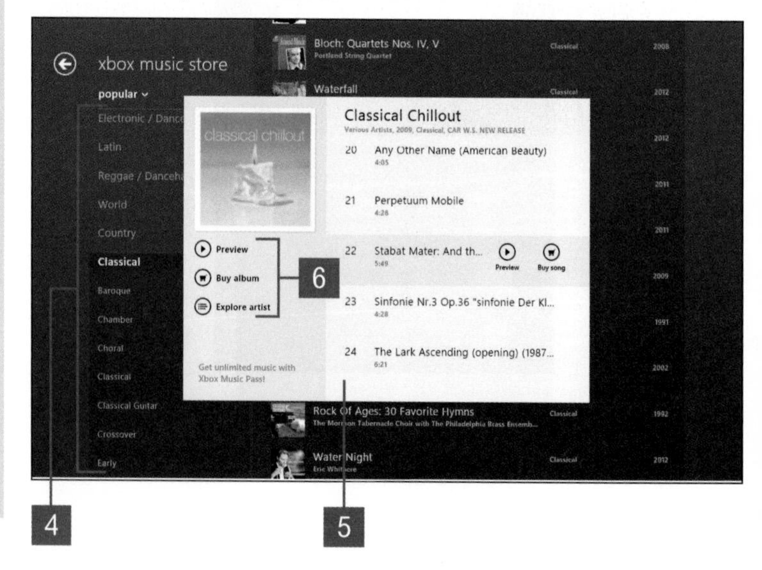

## Play, purchase and manage video with the Video app

The Video app is very similar to the Music app. It contains a My Videos section. If you have video, perhaps something you've purchased or something you've taken yourself with a video camera, you'll probably see it under My Videos. Like the Music app you'll also have access to the Store, where you can purchase movies and TV shows.

The Xbox Video Store works in the same way as the Xbox Music Store. You browse the available media and you make purchases. For movies, you can often play a movie trailer, learn more about the movie, and rent it as well as buy it, if this is an option for the media you've selected. For TV shows, you can often view the various seasons, learn more about the show or series, select a particular show, or buy the entire season.

!

**Important**

As with the Music app, you can use the default Settings charm to access the app's options. You can also explore the Search, Share and Devices charms to see what's available.

### Navigate the Video app and watch a video

1. From the Start screen, open the Video app.
2. If you have video in your Video library, you'll see it under My Videos.
3. Use the scroll bar, the scroll wheel on your mouse, or flick with your finger to see the other video options, including options to purchase media.
4. To play a video (perhaps your personal video), click it once.
5. The video will play and controls will become available on the screen. Right-click to see additional controls.

**Did you know?**

If the controls disappear while you're watching a video or movie, move your mouse on the screen to show them. You can also right-click.

# Work with pictures on the Desktop

Music, pictures, documents, videos and other data are stored on your computer's hard drive, and are organised in folders and libraries. You can navigate to that data with File Explorer. You will want to do this when you need to perform tasks you can't achieve in the Photos app, such as burning a group of photos to a CD or DVD or editing a picture, among other things.

As you know, you can access the tabs while in File Explorer to perform tasks on selected data. Working with pictures is no different. You can select a picture in File Explorer and click the various tabs to see those options. You can print a photo, for instance, rotate it, move or copy it, and so on.

## Access your pictures library on the Desktop

1. From the Start screen, click Desktop.
2. On the Taskbar, click the folder icon.
3. In the left pane, click Pictures.
4. What you see in the resulting window are the pictures available to you from your Pictures library. You may see subfolders you've already created.
5. Note the tabs and explore them as desired.

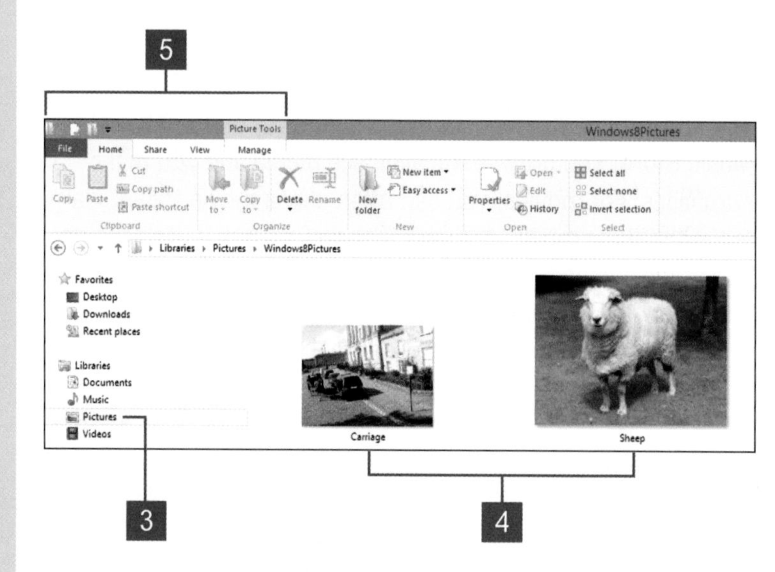


### Did you know?

From the View tab you can choose how to show the items in a folder. We prefer Large icons, but you can also choose Extra large icons, Medium icons, List, Small icons and others.

## Explore the File Explorer ribbon

File Explorer has three main features. The Navigation pane is the vertical pane on the left, the Content pane is the larger area on the right, and the ribbon is the area just above both, near the top of the screen. When you select a folder in the Navigation pane and/or content in the Content pane, what appears on the ribbon changes.

Here are some of the items you'll have access to from the ribbon, when Pictures is selected in the left pane:

- Home tab:
  - Copy – to copy the photo for pasting elsewhere.
  - Move to – to move the photo to a different folder.
  - Delete – to delete the photo.
  - Rename – to rename the photo.
- Share tab:
  - Email – to email a photo. (You'll need a compatible email client configured for this to be available.)
  - Burn to disc – to copy selected photos to a CD or DVD.
  - Print – to print a photo.
- View tab:
  - Extra large icons – to view very large thumbnails of the pictures in a folder.
  - Sort by – to sort the pictures in a folder by their name, date, size, type and so on.
  - Options – to change folder and search options.
- Manage tab:
  - Rotate left or Rotate right – to rotate the selected image.

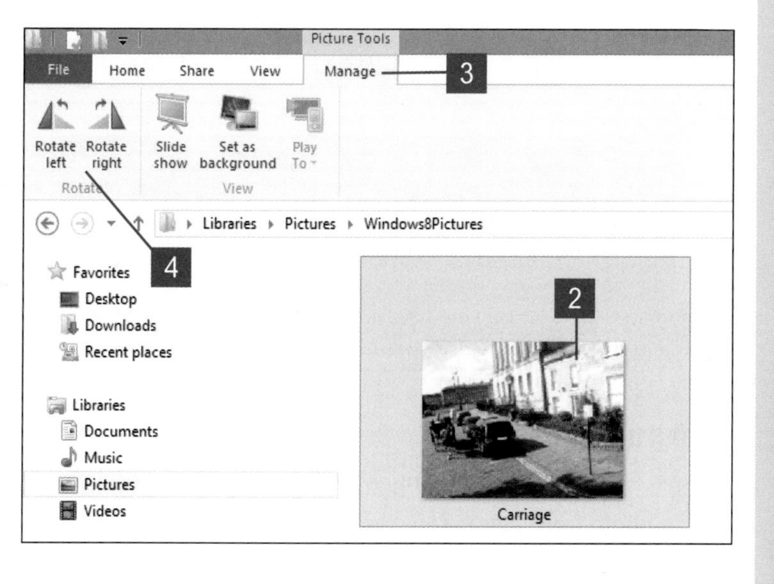


  - Slide show – to play a slide show using the images in the folder (or the selected images).
  - Set as background – to use the selected image(s) as background on the Desktop.

# Work with pictures on the Desktop (cont.)

## Rotate a photo

1. Open File Explorer and navigate to a photo that needs to be rotated.
2. Click the photo once.
3. Click the Manage tab.
4. Click the desired rotate option.

### Important

If the ribbon appears only when you click a tab title but does not appear all the time, click the down facing arrow located in the top right corner of the File Explorer window.

### Important

If you can't see the Navigation pane, click the View tab. Then click Navigation pane and click Navigation pane from the drop-down list.

# Work with pictures on the Desktop (cont.)

### View pictures with the Windows Photo Viewer

1 While in File Explorer, right-click the photo to view.

2 Position your mouse over Open with and click Windows Photo Viewer.

**Did you know?**

You can right-click any picture to access its contextual menu. You'll see familiar options there, including Rotate right and Rotate left, Delete, Rename, and Share with, among others.

**For your information**

See Chapter 6 for how to manage files, folders and libraries.

## View pictures with the Windows Photo Viewer

By default, if you double-click a picture while in File Explorer (in order to view it in full screen mode), the Photos app opens to show it. If you don't want to use the app and would rather view the picture on the Desktop, you'll want to opt for Windows Photo Viewer.

When you open a photo in Windows Photo Viewer you can, among other things:

- Delete the photo.
- Copy or make a copy of the photo.
- View the properties of the photo.
- Print, email and burn photos to a data disk.
- Open the photo in another program such as Paint, perhaps to edit it.

## Print a photo

If you've explored Windows Photo Viewer, you know you can print a photo from there. You can also access the print command from inside File Explorer. Here is one way to print a photo:

1 Navigate to a single photo to print.

2 Click the photo and then click the Share tab on the ribbon.

3 Click Print.

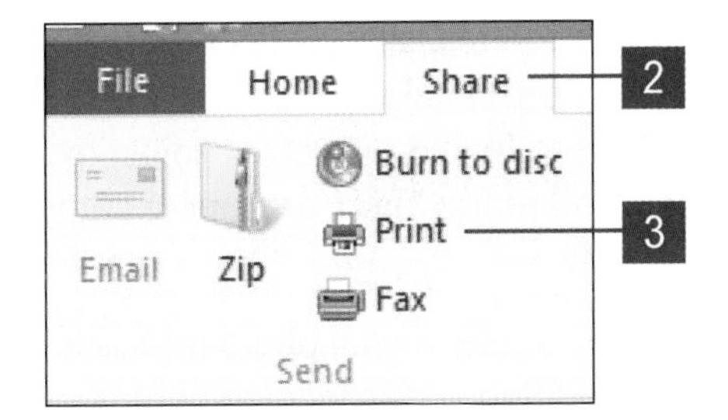


4 Use the drop-down lists to choose a printer, a paper size, quality settings and paper type.

5 Depending on your selections in step 4, you may also be able to choose how many prints to include on a single page.

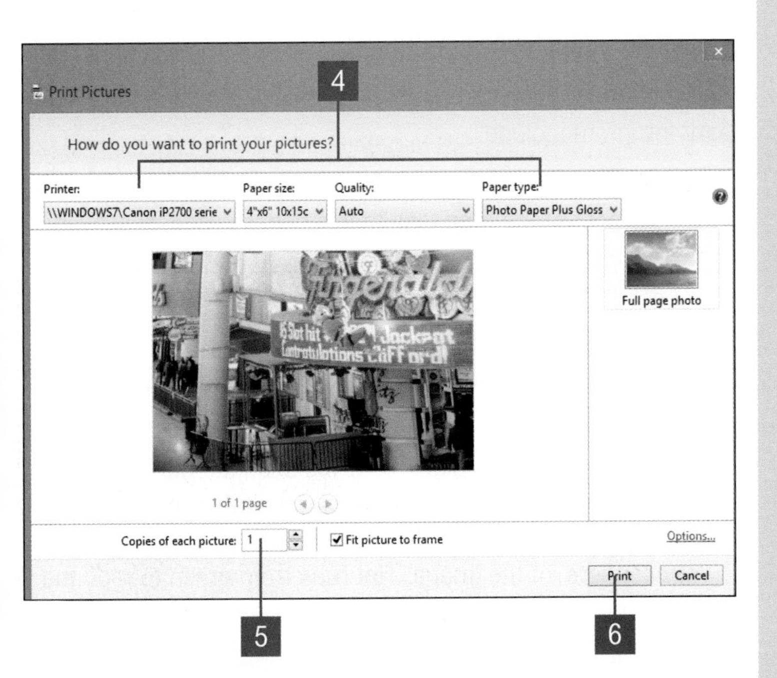


6 Configure additional options if applicable and click Print.

## Explore third party editing options

You can edit photos, but you'll need to use an editing program. To find out what your editing options are, right-click any photo while inside File Explorer and choose Edit. Paint may open. Paint is a Desktop application included with Windows 8. Paint isn't a very good editing tool though. Consider the following instead:

## Work with pictures on the Desktop (cont.)

3 Note the available options:

- **a** File – to delete, make a copy, view the image properties or exit the program.
- **b** Print – to print using your own printer or to order prints online.
- **c** E-mail – to email the photo.
- **d** Burn – to burn the image to a data disk.
- **e** Open – to open the image in another program.
- **f** Zoom options – to zoom in and then out of an image. This icon is a magnifying glass. There's also a square to the right of this you can use.
- **g** Previous – to view the previous image in the folder.
- **h** Slide Show – to start a slide show of the images in the folder (click Esc to exit). This is the large middle button.
- **i** Next – to view the next image in the folder.
- **j** Rotate options – to rotate the photo.
- **k** Delete – to delete the photo.

## Work with pictures on the Desktop (cont.)

- Windows Live Photo Gallery. This is part of the free Windows Live Essentials suite. Like most editing programs, it enables you to fix red-eye, crop, adjust exposure and sharpness, and more. There are lots of automatic fixes to make it easy.
- Picasa. This is a free, digital photo *organiser*, so it might complicate locating and managing photos, but the editing tools that come with the program enable you to edit photos quickly and easily. Picasa offers the usual editing tools, including crop and various auto adjustments.
- Photoshop Elements. You'll have to pay for this program, but for what you get, it's well worth the cost if you want to do some serious editing. The interface is user friendly and enables you to edit your photos in ways you never imagined.

Some of the options you might see while editing in a third-party program include:

- Auto Adjust – automatically assesses the image and alters it, which most of the time results in a better image. However, there's always the Undo button, and you'll probably use it occasionally.
- Adjust Exposure – offers slider controls for Brightness and Contrast. You often move these sliders to the left and right to adjust as desired.
- Adjust Color – offers slider controls to adjust the temperature, tint and saturation of the photo. Temperature runs from blue to yellow, allowing you to change the 'atmosphere' of the image. Tint runs from green to red, and saturation moves from black and white to colour.
- Straighten Photo – automatically straightens photos and offers a slider you can use as well.
- Crop Picture – removes parts of a picture you don't want.
- Adjust Detail – allows you to sharpen the image and reduce 'noise'. This can help bring a fuzzy or blurry picture into focus. You can apply changes automatically or manually.
- Fix Red Eye – lets you draw a rectangle around any eye that has a red dot in it and the red dot is automatically removed.
- Black and White Effects – lets you apply effects to the image, to change the 'tone' (colour) of the image.

## Use Windows Media Player on the Desktop

Windows Media Player is a Desktop app. You open Media Player the same way you open other programs, from the Start screen. Just type *Media* and select Windows Media Player from the results. Once opened, you'll need to know where the Library button is so that you can access different kinds of media.

Windows Media Player has more features than the Pictures, Music and Video apps put together. You can listen to and manage music; view, rate and sort pictures and videos; and create personal playlists of music or set criteria to create automatic playlists. You can also access media stored on shared drives and in other libraries on your home network, or share the media on your computer with others. You can even access the music stored on your computer from a compatible computer over the Internet.

Before we get started with Windows Media Player though, let's review some terms you'll see throughout this part of the chapter:

- Playlist – a group of songs that you can save and then listen to as a group, burn to a CD, copy to a portable music player, and more. To get started, click Playlists and follow the prompts. You can also click Create Playlist from the Media Player interface.
- Rip – a term used to describe the process of copying files from a physical CD to your hard drive, and thus your music library.
- Burn – a term used to describe the process of copying music from a computer to a CD or DVD. Generally music is burned to a CD, since CDs can be played in cars and generic DVD players, and videos are burned to DVDs since they require much more space than a CD can offer and can be played on DVD players.

If you've never used Windows Media Player, the first time you open it you'll have to work through a wizard to tell Windows Media Player how you want it to perform. You'll have two options, Express or Custom. If you're new to Media Player it's OK to select Express and accept the defaults. You can always change any options you decide you don't like after you've worked with it for a while.

# Use Windows Media Player on the Desktop (cont.)

After completing setup, you may be able to watch Windows Media Player add the music stored in your Music library, if that library is large. As the music becomes available, look for familiar attributes, such as the Back and Forward buttons, and menus. You'll also see tab titles: Play, Burn and Sync, on the right side of the window. Look deeper and you'll see the media controls at the bottom. As with File Explorer, you can change the view in lots of ways. Here we're sorting by Music, Album and have chosen Icon view, but you might want to try Tile or Details.

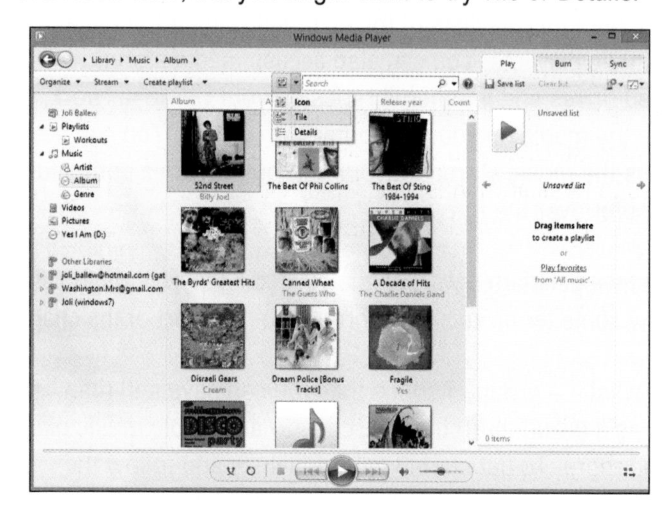


## Choosing a category and the resulting view

To change the available media, locate the Library button. If you click the arrow to the right of this button, you can navigate to all the media on your PC, including music, pictures, videos, recorded TV and other media, including radio stations you like. When you make a selection from the Library menu options, what you see in the left pane will change. This is how you navigate to other types of media in Windows Media Player.

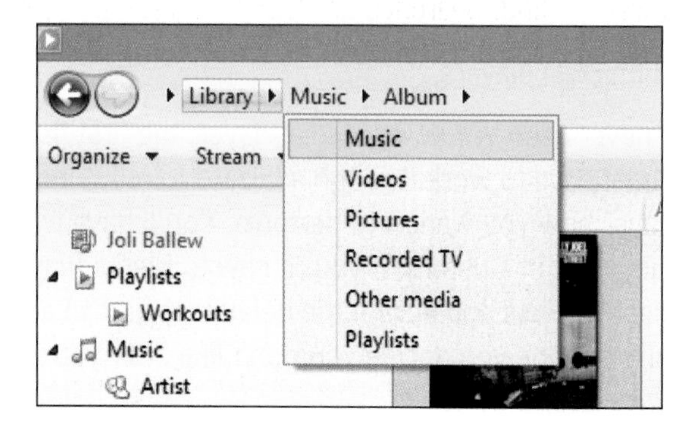

The Music view is the default, because almost everyone will use Media Player for music and something else for other media. Most of the time, for simple listening and viewing, the Start screen apps will suffice and they open automatically by default when media is played.

### Use Media Player features

The Organize button offers several options you'll want to explore, including Manage libraries, Customize navigation pane, Layout and Options. If you choose Layout, you can also opt to show the Menu bar. We believe it's best to enable the Menu bar, so that you have access to menus you may be more familiar with. Once you've enabled this option, you'll have access to familiar menus: File, View, Play, Tools and Help. Both the enabled option and the Menu bar are shown here.

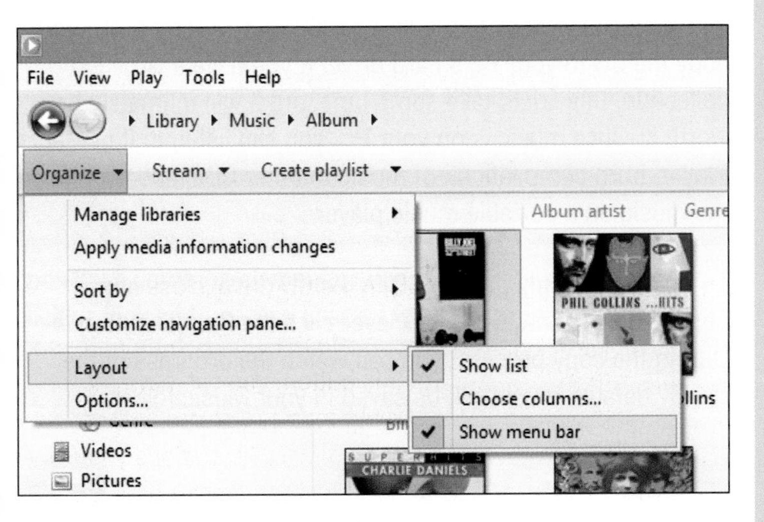


You can also search for media using the Search box. Just type in what you want to find. Searches produce 'live' results, so results show as you type and are culled down the more you type.

**Important**

If time allows, explore the options under each menu title. This will help you get a feel for the depth of the application and how it can be used.

## Use Windows Media Player on the Desktop (cont.)

9

# Use Windows Media Player on the Desktop (cont.)

### Play a song in Media Player

1. Open Media Player and click Music in the Navigation pane. (Note you can also click Artist, Album or Genre to locate a song.)
2. Double-click any song to play it.
3. Use these media controls located at the bottom of the Media Player interface:
   - **a** Shuffle – to let Windows Media Player choose what order to play the selected songs. This icon looks like two criss-crossing arrows.
   - **b** Repeat – to play the current song again. This icon is a counter-clockwise circular arrow.
   - **c** Stop – to stop playback. This is the solid square.
   - **d** Previous – to play the previous song in the list, on the album, and so on. This is the left double-facing arrow.
   - **e** Play/Pause – to play and pause the song (and playlist). This is in the middle.

### Play media

Now that you're somewhat familiar with the Media Player interface, let's play some music. To play any music track (or view any picture, watch any video, or view other media), simply navigate to it and double-click it. (After you've played some music, try to view pictures and videos – it's almost the same process.)

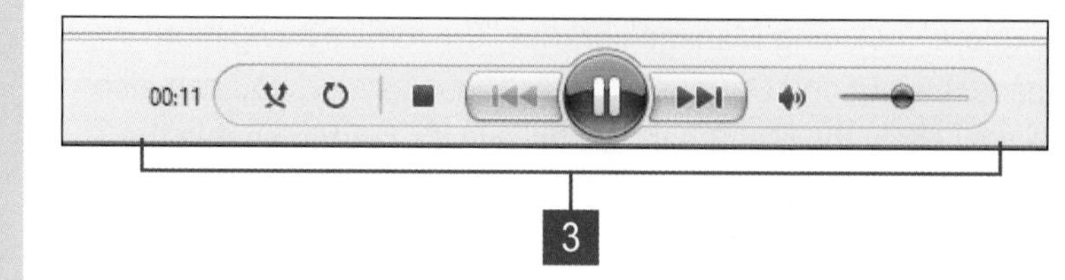


### Rip a CD

To rip means to copy in media-speak. When you rip a CD, you copy the CD to your PC's hard drive. If you have a large CD collection, this could take some time, but it will ultimately be worth it. Once music is on your PC, you can listen to it in Media Player, burn compilations of music to other CDs, and even put the music on a portable music player.

To rip a CD, simply put the CD in the CD drive, close any pop-up boxes, and in Media Player click the Rip CD button. During the copy process, you can watch the progress of the rip. By default, music will be saved in your Music folder.

?

**Did you know?**

Media Player has Back and Forward buttons you can use to navigate it.

!

**Important**

If Windows Media Player seems to disappear, check your Taskbar. To bring it back to the Desktop, click the Media Player button.

## Use Windows Media Player on the Desktop (cont.)

- **f** Next – to play the next song in the list, on the album, and so on. This icon is a right double-facing arrow
- **g** Mute – to quickly mute the song. This icon is a speaker.
- **h** Volume – to change the volume of the song. This is a slider.

### Copy a CD to your computer

1. With Media Player running, insert the CD to copy into the CD drive.
2. If any pop-up boxes appear, click the X to close out of them.
3. Deselect any songs you do not want to copy to your PC. (All songs are selected by default.)
4. In Windows Media Player, click the Rip CD button.
5. Watch as the CD is copied – you can view the Rip status.
6. The ripped music will now appear in your music library.

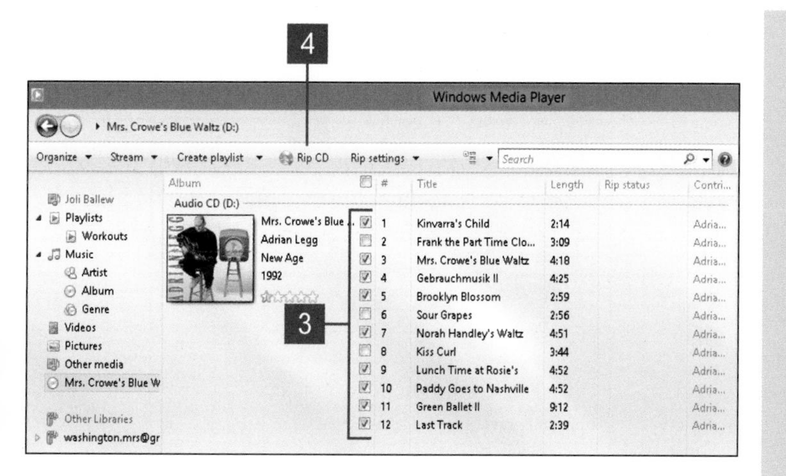


?

### Did you know?

You can deselect songs during the rip process if you decide you don't want to wait for them to be copied.

### Burn a CD

There are two ways to take music with you when you are on the road or on the go. You can copy the music to a portable device like a mobile phone or compatible music player (and keep it synchronised using Media Player), or you can create your own CDs, choosing the songs to copy and placing them on the CD in the desired order. CDs you create can be played in car stereos and portable CD players, as well as on lots of other CD devices. A typical CD can hold about 80 minutes of music, but don't worry, Media Player will keep track of the songs you select and will let you know when you're running out of space on the CD you are creating.

The Burn tab can assist you in creating a CD. Burn is media-speak for copying music from your PC to a CD. Clicking Burn brings up the List pane, where Media Player will tell you to insert a blank CD if one is not in the drive already, and allow you to drag and drop songs into it to create a burn list. As music is added, the progress bar at the top of the List pane shows how much space you've used.

# Use Windows Media Player on the Desktop (cont.)

## Copy music files to a CD

1. Open Media Player.
2. Click the Burn tab.
3. Insert a blank, recordable CD into the CD drive.
4. Under Library, click Music.
5. Click any song title to add and drag it to the List pane.
6. Drop the song in the List pane to add it to the burn list. Continue as desired.
7. Look at the graphic in the List pane to verify there is room left on the CD. Continue to add songs until the CD is full or until you've finished.
8. When you've added the songs you want, click Start Burn.

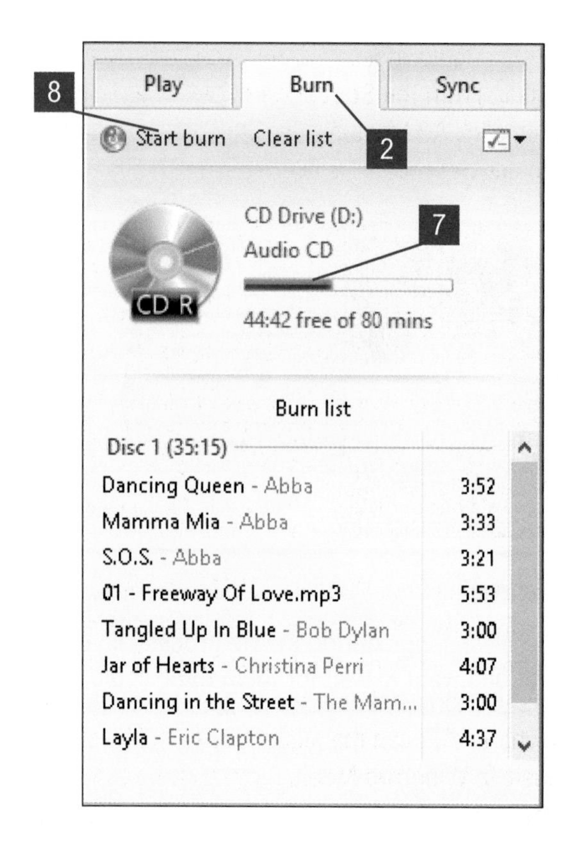


### Important

Once you've added music, the Start burn button becomes active.

### Did you know?

You do not need to fill the entire CD with songs if you don't want to.

### Did you know?

You can right-click any song in the Burn list to access additional options, including the option to delete the song from the list (not the PC), or to move up or move down in the list order.

## Acquire and explore Media Center

Windows Media Center doesn't come with Windows 8 but you can purchase it. From the Start screen, type Add Features, click Settings, then click Add features to Windows 8. Follow the directions to acquire Media Center.

Once installed and set up, Windows Media Center becomes a one-stop media application that lets you access and manage pictures, videos, movies, music, television, DVDs and CDs, and radio. As you already know though, you can do much of this elsewhere. You can manage pictures in File Explorer; manage music in Windows Media Player; and watch videos with the Videos app. Of course, for simple viewing and playing of media, the Start screen apps are the best. So where does Media Center fit in, and should you get it?

Media Center, although it can be used to listen to music and view other media, really stands out for viewing, recording, watching and managing television. Of course, if you acquire it you'll certainly use it for other things. Media Center has an online television guide to help you find out what's available to watch and when too, and you can record television programmes, pause live TV, then fast-forward or rewind through what you've paused. If you want to get Media Center to watch live TV, make sure your computer has a TV tuner installed. If it doesn't, you can buy an external tuner. This tuner is necessary for the TV feature to work.

Once Media Center is set up and you know how to navigate through it, it's simple to watch TV. Just browse to TV and click Live TV. If everything is set up and installed as it should be, you'll get a live TV signal. And once you have a live TV signal, it's almost as easy to get started recording TV.

## Acquire and explore Media Center (cont.)

Here are a few of the options you'll probably find in Windows Media Center, although features can and do change as time passes:

- Program Info/Program Guide – displays the Program Info screen where you can record the programme, the series, and acquire information about the show.
- Record – immediately starts recording the current television show.
- Record Series – immediately starts recording the current television show and schedules the television series to be recorded.
- Mini Guide – shows information about the show on the screen in a minimised format (at least compared with Program Info).
- Settings – opens Media Center settings.

There are also TV controls. These controls appear when you move your mouse to the bottom of the screen, if you press specific buttons on a remote control or keyboard, and in a few other instances. With these controls you can:

- Record the show you're watching by pressing the Record button.
- Change the channel using the Channel Up and Channel Down buttons.
- Stop watching TV using the Stop button.
- Rewind quickly or more slowly using the two Rewind buttons.
- Pause (and then Play) live TV using the Pause/Play button.
- Fast forward slowly or more quickly using the two Fast Forward buttons.
- Mute the TV by clicking the Mute button. (The x here means the volume is currently muted.)
- Decrease or increase the volume using the Volume Down and Volume Up buttons.

If you decide to acquire Media Center, make sure you explore every category and option. It's a feature-rich application and well worth the cost if you have a lot of media.

# Configure and manage a network

10

## Introduction

A home network consists of two or more computers connected together for the purpose of sharing things like music, photos, printers and a connection to the Internet. There's often a modem that connects to the Internet, a router for connecting those computers together, and a password for joining the network. If you have something like this at your house, you'll want to connect to it. Home networks are private and secure.

A free Wi-Fi hot spot is a different kind of network. This is generally offered by an establishment such as a library, pub, hotel or coffee shop and enables you and others to connect to the Internet for free while there. These networks also have a modem and router, and you connect wirelessly. This kind of network is public and is not secure.

In this chapter you'll learn how to join these two types of networks. You'll also learn how to enhance your home network with a homegroup, user accounts and strong passwords. Once your network is in good form, you can share personal data, enable a Guest account, and more.

## What you'll do

## Understand the types of networks

If you already have a network set up and you've joined your new Windows 8 computer to it, you can skip this section. This section and the following section are for those readers who do not yet have a network but would like to create one. That said, if you want to create a new network, read on. Otherwise, skip to 'Join networks'. You may want to change your previously configured network settings or connect to a different kind of network, which you'll learn to do there.

While there are many ways to connect two or more PCs, I'll suggest you choose from one of these three: direct connection, Ethernet or wireless. Let's look at each of these in more detail.

### Direct connection

If you have only two computers, do not want to purchase expensive equipment, and you trust everyone who has access to the two computers, you may want to consider a direct connection network. This is an older technology though, and thus the connection between the two computers will be much slower than newer alternatives. However, if you don't want to purchase expensive equipment, this is the way to go. Often you need to purchase only one thing: an Ethernet crossover cable.

For this method to work, both computers must be able to connect to an Ethernet cable. That means that each computer must either have a network interface card (NIC) or a USB port for attaching a USB-to-Ethernet converter. An Ethernet port looks much like the port you use to connect your telephone to a wall jack or a phone cord to a modem in the PC; the Ethernet port is just a bit larger. I will venture to say that all computers that come with Windows 8 preinstalled will have the required hardware, but it's possible they do not. If you want to use this method but don't have an Ethernet port in one of the PCs, purchase and install an external USB-to-Ethernet converter. Once connected, you can share an Internet connection and data, just as you can with any network.

Another option for connecting two PCs directly is to use a USB-to-USB direct link cable. Microsoft offers the Easy Transfer cable that can be used for this purpose. If both PCs have a USB port, consider this option.

## Jargon buster

**Router** – a piece of equipment used to send data from computer to computer on a network. A router 'routes' the data to the correct PC and also rejects data that is harmful or from unknown sources.

**Ethernet cable** – a cable that is used to connect PCs to routers and cable modems, among other things.

**Network Discovery** – a state where computers can find other computers on the network. Network Discovery must be on to locate and communicate with network devices.

**Network** – a group of computers, printers and other devices that communicate wirelessly or through wired connections.

**Permissions** – rules associated with a shared resource, such as a folder, file or printer.

## Ethernet

If you have more than two computers to network, consider an Ethernet network. Ethernet networks connect computers through a hardware device like a router. A router is a small piece of external hardware that offers multiple Ethernet ports for plugging in multiple computers and 'routes' the data flowing through the network from PC to PC. Routers come in 4-port, 6-port and similar varieties. Ethernet networks are fast too, and are a good option when sharing a broadband Internet connection.

The downside here is that you have to purchase a router and cables, and you have to set it up (or pay someone to do it). Often this entails adding a cable modem to the mix too, so you have to know how to position the equipment. While routers come with instructions, it can be a time-consuming and frustrating task, so if you're new to routers, cable modems and networking, have the network professionally installed or call on your children or neighbours to help. If you want to set it up yourself though, no worries – I'll include some generic instructions shortly.

## Understand the types of networks (cont.)

### Wireless

Wireless networks are the third option. Wireless networks use radio waves, just like mobile phones and walkie-talkies, and allow you to connect to your networked PCs without cables. If you have a laptop with a built-in wireless card, this is the way to go. If you have older computers that do not have wireless capabilities, you can still make it work. Just get a wireless router that offers a few Ethernet ports. Additionally, you could purchase a USB adapter or PCI card for any computer not wireless-ready. While this network is great once it's set up, like any new network, getting it up and running can be time-consuming and frustrating. Instructions that come with the hardware in my experience at least are clear, but if you've never done this type of thing before, consider having it professionally installed or getting help.

### Install the hardware

Because of the different types of routers, networking hardware and configurations, there's no way I can walk you through physically installing every type of network hardware here. The hardware you purchase will come with specific instructions anyway, and setup is not always the same from manufacturer to manufacturer. However, I can offer information that is generic to specific networks, and understanding this may make installing hardware easier.

### Direct connection networks

When creating a direct connection network, you first need to connect the two PCs using the desired cable (Easy Transfer or Ethernet Crossover). You may have to also install USB-to-Ethernet converters if your older PCs don't have Ethernet ports. Once you make the connection, Windows 8 will attempt to configure it, and you'll be prompted when a network is available. Once a network is available, you can tweak it using the Network and Sharing Center. There will be more on that later.

Computers that are in the same 'workgroup' can communicate more easily than those that are not. The most common workgroup name is WORKGROUP. If you can't see other computers on your older network, consider changing their workgroup names to WORKGROUP. (You can do this by right-clicking Computer on Windows 7, Windows Vista, or My Computer on Windows XP and choosing Properties.)

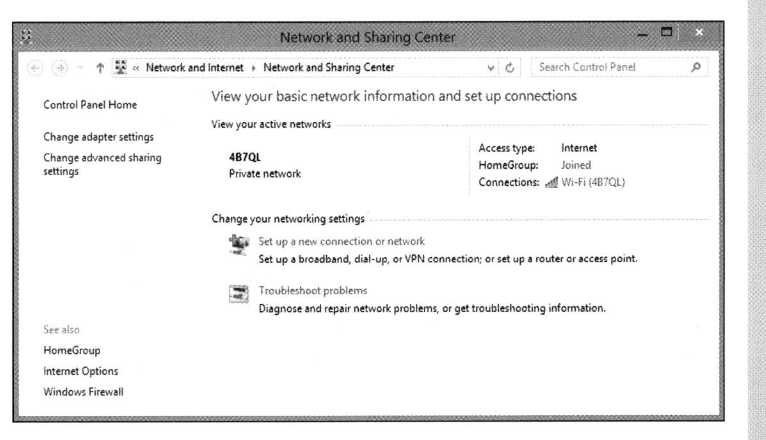


### Ethernet networks

Direct connection networks generally require the installation of only a single cable, but Ethernet networks require much more setup. Although there's no way to outline how to install the hardware for any Ethernet hardware, the steps offered here usually need to be performed in the order detailed here.

### Wireless networks

During the process of configuring your wireless router, you'll also set up your wireless network. You'll want to follow the directions that come with your wireless hardware, which often begin with the instruction to install the wireless router's software. As with Ethernet networks, you'll need to make sure you have a working, wired (not wireless) connection to the Internet before starting. Once software is installed, you'll be prompted to physically install the hardware.

The hardware you need to install a wireless network includes:

- a wireless router (also called an access point)
- a wireless network adapter for each computer on your network

## Understand the types of networks (cont.)

### Set up network hardware

1. Set up any satellite, cable or broadband modems and connect one of the PCs to the Internet. This may already be done.
2. Set up the router as detailed in the instructions that come with it. For the most part you'll need to:
   1. Install the router software.
   2. Connect the router to the external cable or satellite modem through the router's WAN port.
   3. Connect the PC to an available Ethernet port on the router.
   4. Run the setup wizard provided by the router manufacturer and work through the wizard and/or follow the written directions.
   5. During setup, if prompted regarding how your ISP obtains an IP address, choose *Obtain an IP Address Automatically*. If you have problems with this step, call your ISP.

## Understand the types of networks (cont.)

3 Once the router is configured, turn off the PC, cable or satellite modem, and router.

4 Turn on the modem and wait for all self-tests to complete.

5 Turn on the router and wait for all self-tests to complete.

6 Turn on each PC.

- an installation CD
- external cable, DSL or satellite modem.

During setup you'll be prompted to create a Wireless Network Name (SSID), passphrase or password, and security settings. Don't worry, there's almost always a wizard to guide you through this. However, just to be on the safe side, here are few terms you should be familiar with:

- SSID – the name you create and use for the wireless network during setup.
- Channel – denotes the operating frequency your wireless network will use. Don't worry, this will probably be configured automatically.
- Mode – where you'll tell setup what type of wireless hardware you are using (G, B, A, etc., but you can simply choose Auto to let the software configure all of that for you).
- Encryption – the security you'll apply to your network. You can choose:
  - None – no data encryption.
  - WEP – Wired Equivalent Privacy, 64-bit or 128-bit options. 64-bit WEP uses ten hexadecimal digits (0–9 and A–F) for a password. 128-bit uses 26 hexadecimal digits.
  - Security Encryption (WPA-PSK, WPA2-PSK, WPA-PSK+WPA2-PSK) – Wi-Fi Protected Access with Pre-Shared Key. The passphrase is 8–63 characters in length.

This isn't nearly as complicated as it sounds though – for the most part all of this will happen automatically. During setup you'll also be prompted to install the hardware. Again, instructions will be included, but generically, you'll perform the following steps:

1. Place the router near the centre of the area where all your PCs will operate. Make sure it's elevated so all PCs have access to its wireless signal. Keep the router away from microwaves and similar devices.
2. Verify that a cable modem is installed and connected to the Internet.

3 Connect an Ethernet cable from the Ethernet out jack on the modem to the WAN port on the wireless router.
4 Connect an Ethernet cable from the Windows 8 PC to the wireless router.
5 Complete any additional instructions.

Once the network is set up, all you have to do is wait for Windows 8 to discover the network and prompt you to join. You'll probably be prompted to create (or join) a homegroup; if so, go ahead and follow the prompts to do so. If you are prompted to enable Network Discovery, do that, too.

# Join networks

Windows 8 offers plenty of ways to network (connect) multiple computers. With all your computers networked, you can share data, printers and an Internet connection. You also have access to various tools you can use to set up, join or manage the network, or connect to networks such as virtual private networks. Here are a few of those tools:

- Settings charm – no matter where you access the Settings charm (Windows key + I), the network option is available. Click that icon to view your current network status, join networks and change basic network settings. This is the option you'll use most of the time.

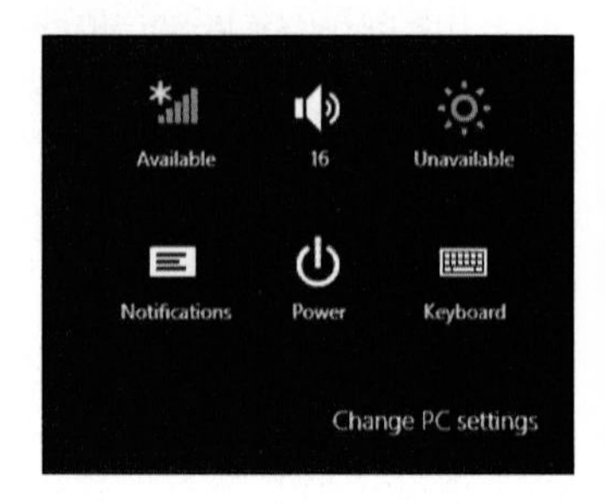


- Network and Sharing Center – a collection of features, available only on the Desktop, where you can easily access network connections, sharing options, networked computers and devices, and diagnose and repair features.
- Network – the Network window, available from the Desktop, offers links to computers on your network and the Network and Sharing Center. You can also add printers and wireless devices here.

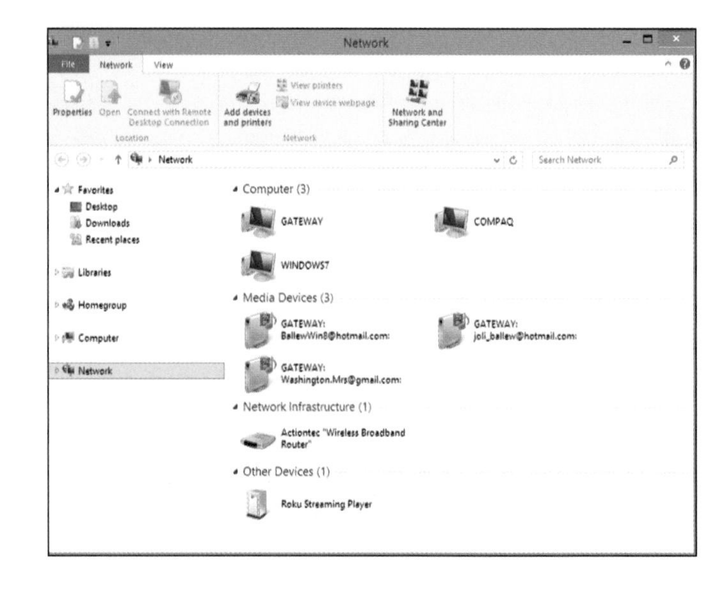

- Network Setup Wizard – use this wizard to create a new network. New networks can include dial-up connections, virtual private networks, and more. Again, this is available only on the Desktop.

**Important**

Try the Settings charm to access basic network settings first. Use the Desktop options only if you need to create a new network or troubleshoot network settings.

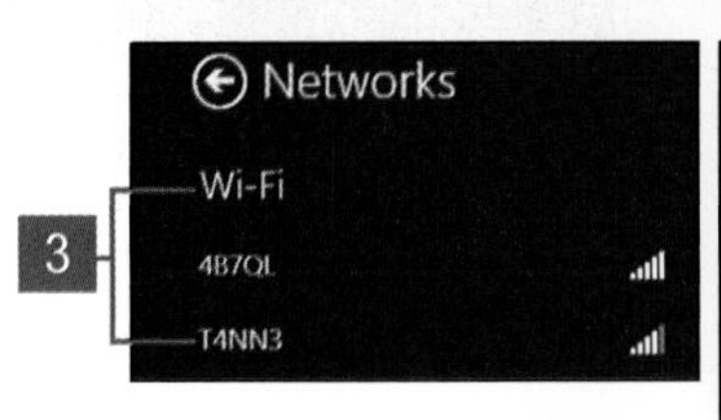


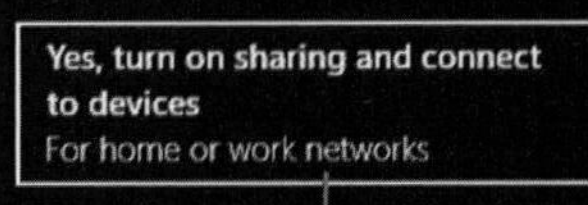


**Did you know?**

The network name and the password or passcode are created when you or a technician install a modem and/or router.

**Jargon buster**

**Private** – this is a network you trust (such as a network at a friend's house, at your house, or at work). This connection type lets your computer discover other computers, printers and devices on the network, and they can discover you. This is why you select Yes, turn on sharing and connect to devices. You want this to happen.

**Public** – this is a network that is not secure and that you cannot trust, such as networks in coffee shops, airports and libraries. Choose No, don't turn on sharing or connect to devices before connecting to these kinds of networks. You do not want to share anything here.

# Join networks (cont.)

## Join your home network

1. Connect physically to a wired network using an Ethernet cable, or if you have a wireless device, get within range of your wireless network.
2. Use the keyboard shortcut Windows key + I to access the Settings charm, then click the Network icon.
3. Click the desired network in the resulting list.
4. Place a tick in the Connect automatically box if you plan to connect to this network again, then click Connect.
5. Type the required passcode, passphrase or other credentials as prompted. Click Next.
6. Click Yes, turn on sharing and connect to devices. This tells Windows 8 you trust this network and want to consider it a private network (rather than a public one).

# Join networks (cont.)

## Connect to a free wireless hot spot

1 Get within range of the public wireless network.

2 Use the keyboard shortcut Windows key + I to access the Settings charm, then click the Network icon shown earlier.

3 Click the desired network.

4 Place a tick in Connect automatically box if you plan to connect to this network again, then click Connect.

5 Click No, don't turn on sharing and connect to devices. This tells Windows you do not trust this network and want to consider it a public network (rather than a private one).

## Connect to a free wireless hot spot

Wi-Fi hot spots are popping up all over the country in coffee houses, hotels, parks, libraries and more. Wi-Fi hot spots let you connect to the Internet without having to be tethered to an Ethernet cable or tied down with a high monthly wireless bill. These are public networks.

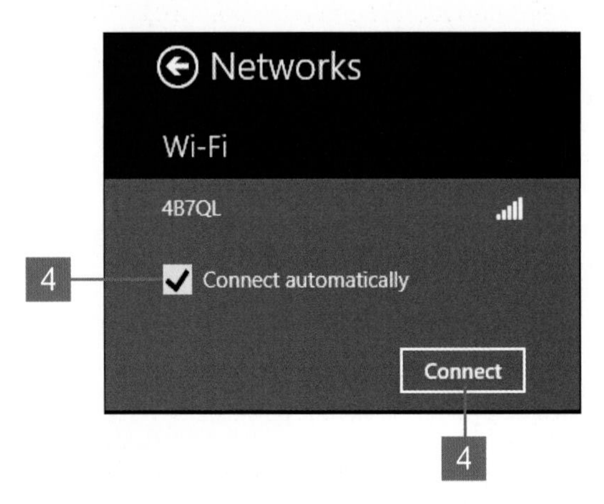


### For your information

You'll be prompted for a security key if you're logging on to a secure network. You should not be prompted when logging on to a free, public Wi-Fi hot spot.

### Important

You'll need a laptop or tablet with the required wireless hardware to use a free Wi-Fi hot spot.

### Did you know?

You can find Wi-Fi hot spots close to you at http://maps.google.com. Search for Wi-Fi hot spots.

### Change from public to private (or private to public)

If you made the wrong choice when deciding whether or not to turn on sharing and connect to devices the first time you connected to a network, you can change the setting. It's hidden away though, and is difficult to find if you don't know the trick. In the same area you can right-click any network connection and choose View connection properties to re-enter the passcode or change settings related to the network such as security and encryption type.

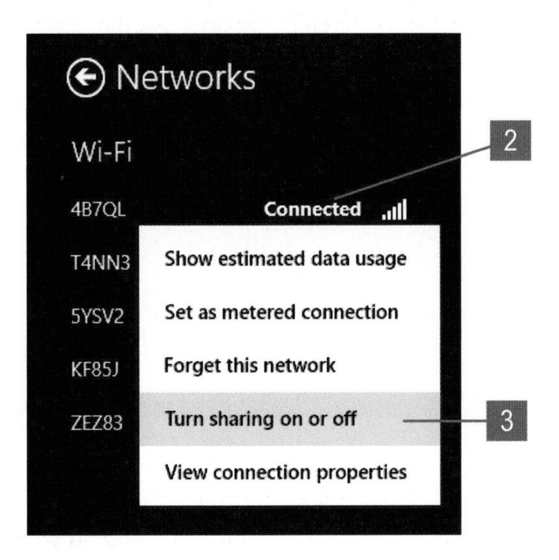


**For your information**

You can stop automatically connecting to a network by right-clicking it and choosing Forget this network.

## Join networks (cont.)

### Change the network type

1. From the Settings charm, click the Network icon.
2. Right-click the network you're connected to.
3. Choose Turn sharing on or off. Note the other options.
4. Select the proper setting:
   - **a** No, don't turn on sharing or connect to devices – for public networks.
   - **b** Yes, turn on sharing and connect to devices – for private networks.

10

# Use a homegroup

A homegroup is a feature that became available in Windows 7 that allows you to simplify the task of sharing media, documents, printers and other data on your home network. You may have created or joined a homegroup during the Windows 8 set up process. However, if you did not, or if you have now decided you'd like to, you can do so from the Network and Sharing Center.

If you recall, the Network and Sharing Center is a Desktop feature. Although you can type Network and Sharing at the Start screen to access it, it will only open on the Desktop and is part of Control Panel. Once this is open and available, you'll see one of three options. You can join an existing homegroup if one exists, create a new homegroup, or leave a homegroup.

## Set up a homegroup

1. Access the Desktop. The Windows key + D is one way.
2. Right-click the Network icon on the Taskbar, then click Open Network and Sharing Center.
3. If a homegroup exists on the network already, you'll see Available to join. Otherwise, you'll see Ready to create. Click the option you see.
4. Click Create a homegroup or Join now, as applicable.

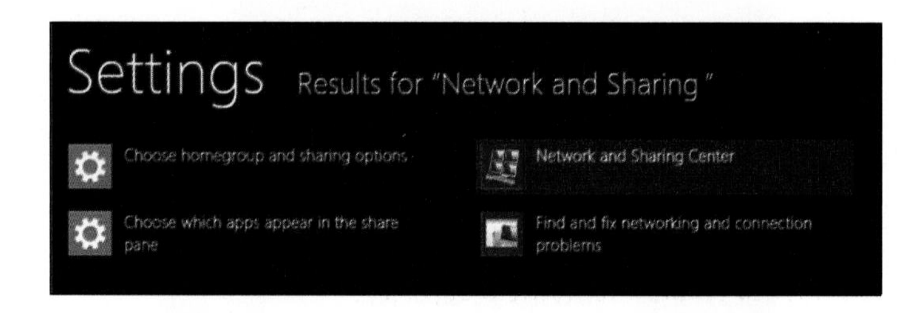

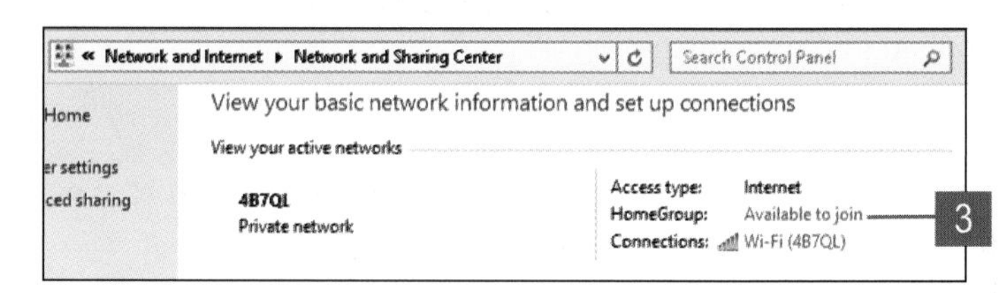

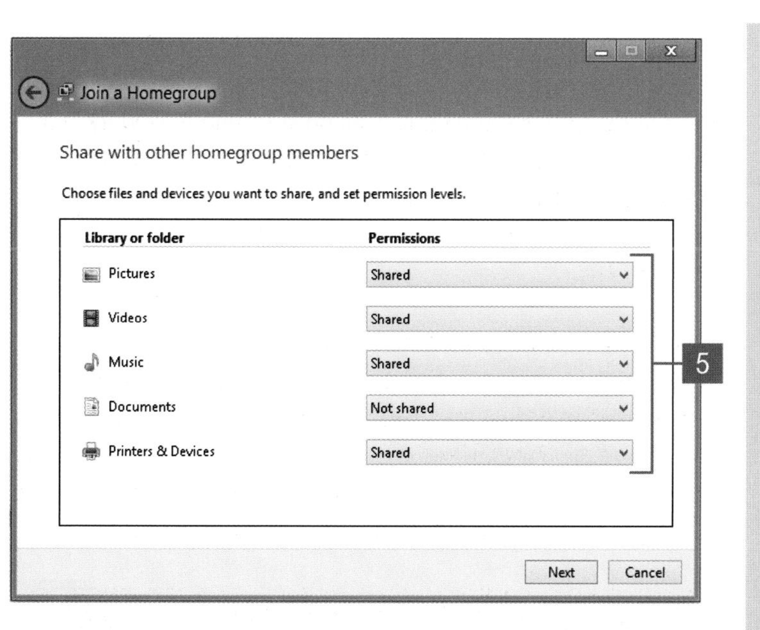


# Use a homegroup (cont.)

5. Click Next and choose what to share.
6. If you created a new homegroup, write down the password – you'll need it to allow other computers to join. If you're joining an existing group, locate the password on another computer.

**For your information**

See how to locate the homegroup password, next.

**For your information**

Even though only computers running Windows 7 or Windows 8 can participate in the homegroup, you can still create one even if you also have computers that run Vista or Windows XP. You can still share data using the public folders quite easily.

A homegroup password secures your homegroup. You'll need to know that password to connect another Windows 7 or Windows 8 computer to it.

# Use a homegroup (cont.)

## Locate the homegroup password

1. In the Network and Sharing Center, click Joined beside Homegroup.
2. Click View or print the homegroup password.

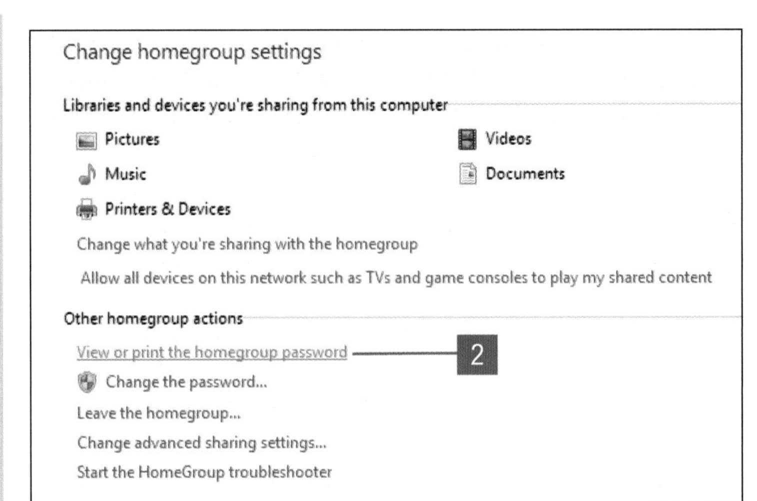


### Did you know?

You can leave a homegroup in the same manner as you join it.

# Add users and share data

If every person who accesses your PC has their own standard user account and password, and if every person logs on using that account and then logs off the PC each time they've finished using it, you'll never have to worry about anyone accessing anyone else's personal data. That's because when a user logs on with their own user account, they can only access their data (and any data other users have specifically elected to share).

Additionally, every user with their own user account is provided with a 'user profile' that tells Windows 8 what Desktop background to use, what screen saver, and preferences for mouse settings, sounds and more. Each user also has their own Favorites in Internet Explorer, and their own email settings, contacts and personal folders. User accounts help everyone who accesses the computer to keep their personal data, well, personal.

You created your user account when you first turned on and set up your new Windows 8 computer. However, if you now share your computer with another person, it's time to create a new account for them. You'll have to sign on with administrator credentials to do this.

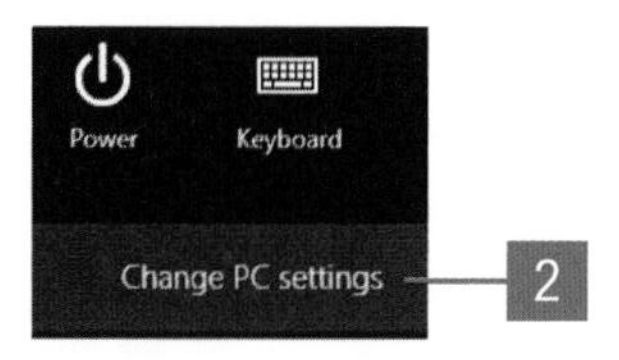


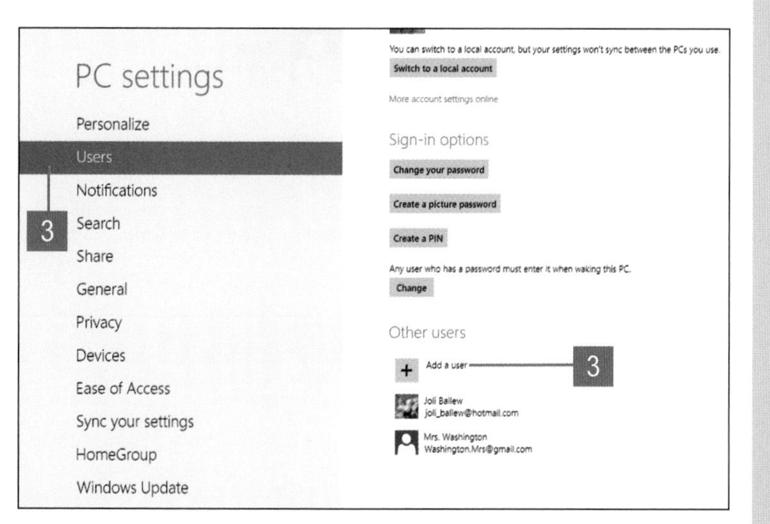


## Create a new user account

1. Click the Settings charm.
2. Click Change PC settings.
3. If applicable, click Users in the left pane. Then select Add a user in the right pane.
4. Work through the process to add a new user. It's the same process you worked through when you set up Windows 8.

# Add users and share data (cont.)

## Require passwords

1. From the Start screen, type Users.
2. Click Settings and from the results choose Make changes to accounts.
3. Verify each user account is password protected (and that the Guest account is off).
4. If you find there is a user without a password, take the necessary steps to apply one.

?

### Did you know?

The first account you created, probably your own, is an administrator account. Administrators have full access to the computer. Subsequent accounts you create are standard accounts. Standard users have limited access, permissions and rights on the computer for security reasons. You can change the account type in Control Panel.

## Secure user accounts

All user accounts should be password protected. If you logged in with a Microsoft account, a password is already configured. If you use a local account though, you may have opted not to apply a password. Whatever the case, every account should have a complex password applied to it. This protects the PC from unauthorised access. To see whether there are accounts that do not have passwords applied to them, view the users in the Manage Accounts window.

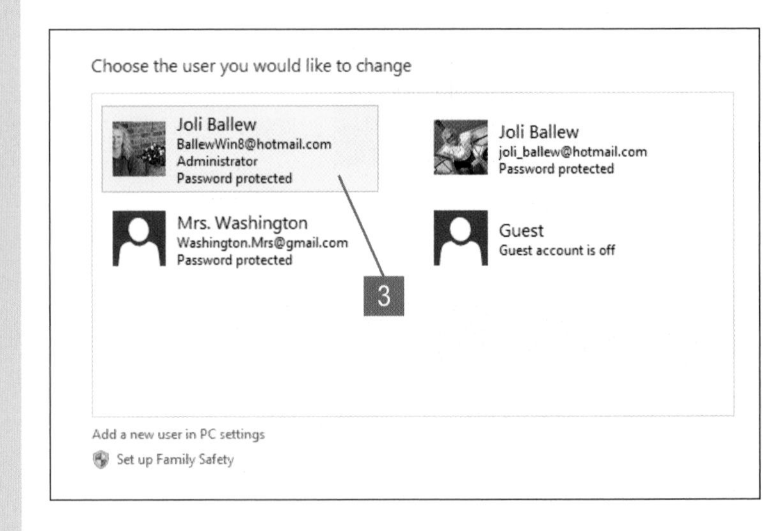

## Important

Make sure your password contains upper- and lower-case letters and a few numbers. This is a stronger password than, say, your dog's name. Write the password down and keep it somewhere safe and out of sight.

## Did you know?

When you need to make a system-wide change, you have to be logged on as an administrator or type an administrator's user name and password. In some instances, such as creating user accounts, you must be logged in as an administrator.

### Use the Guest account

If guests visit your home and bring their own laptop, you can give them the credentials required to access your network and connect to the Internet through it. If they don't bring their own computer and need to use yours, you can enable the Guest account. This account offers your guests access to the Internet and some access to the programs on your computer they might need, such as shared word-processing programs. Guests can't access your personal files, install software or hardware, change settings or create a password.

# Add users and share data (cont.)

### Enable the Guest account

1. At the Start screen, type Guest.
2. Click Settings.
3. Click Turn guest account on or off.
4. When prompted, type your administrator password.
5. Click the Guest account and click Turn On.

10

# Add users and share data (cont.)

## Important

The Guest account should be disabled immediately after your guest(s) leave.

## Share data and printers

The main reason people create networks is to share data, printers, media and an Internet connection. In this section, we'll talk about sharing data. There are two ways to share data: you can either put the data you want to share in the built-in public folders, or you can share data using personal folders. You can use a combination of the two as well. How do you know which to use and when? Here are some things to take into consideration.

### Public folder sharing

Public folders are already built into the Windows 8 folder structure. The Public folder contains several subfolders, including Public Downloads, Public Documents, Public Music, Public Pictures and Public Videos. You can create your own folders here, too. To share data using the folders, simply save or place the data there. Then anyone who has access to the computer or network can easily access what's in the folders.

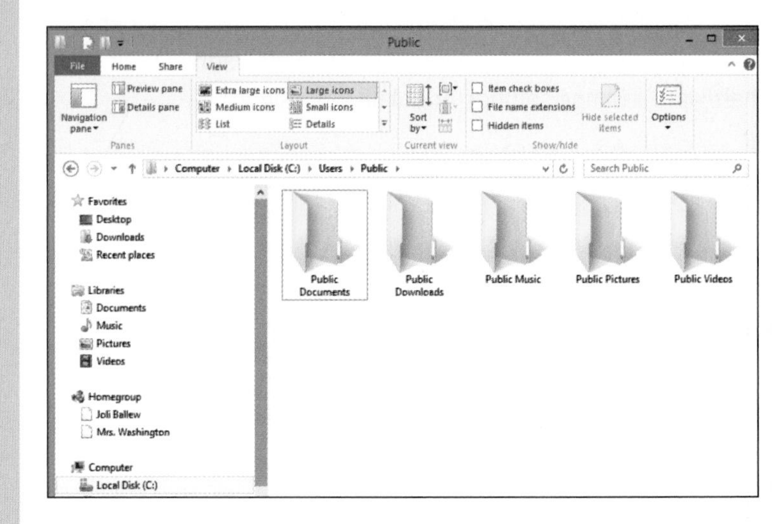

Use the Public folder for sharing if:

- You want every person with a user account on the computer to be able to access what's in the folder.
- You want to share files and folders from a single location on your PC. If you choose to use your personal folders, shared data will not all be stored in a central location.
- You want to be able to access, view and modify everything you have shared quickly.
- You want everything you are sharing kept separate from your data you do not want to share.
- You do not need to configure different sharing rules for different people who have access – you are OK with everyone having access to the data and everyone being able to do what they wish with the data.
- You prefer to use the default shared settings and do not want to manually share data.

One way to locate the public folders is to open File Explorer from the Desktop, click Computer in the left pane, double-click Local Disk in the right and then double-click Users. Once you locate these folders, right-click the Public Folders icon, as shown here, and choose Send To, then Desktop to create a shortcut to the folder on your PC's Desktop.

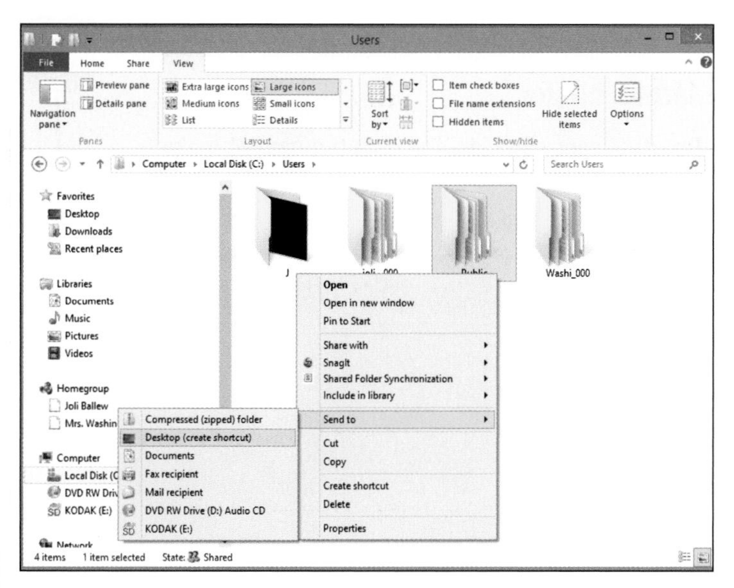


## Add users and share data (cont.)

10

# Add users and share data (cont.)

### Personal folder sharing

Your personal folders and any folders you create yourself can be shared. In contrast to using public folders for sharing, with personal folder sharing you have much more control over the shared data.

Use any folder for sharing if:

- You want to share data directly from your personal folders, such as My Documents, My Pictures, My Music and others, but do not want to have to re-save or move data you want to share to your Public folder.
- You want to allow some users the ability to change the data in the shared folders while at the same time only allowing others to view it. Additionally, you want to completely block others from accessing the data at all. (You can't do this with public folder sharing.)
- You share large files that would be burdensome to copy and manage in a separate shared folder.

When you share a folder, you can configure who can access the folder by right-clicking it. Click Share with to see your options. After selecting an option, you can configure other sharing details, if applicable.

**Jargon buster**

**Read** – users can view the data but cannot make changes to it.

**Read/Write** – users can view and change the shared data.

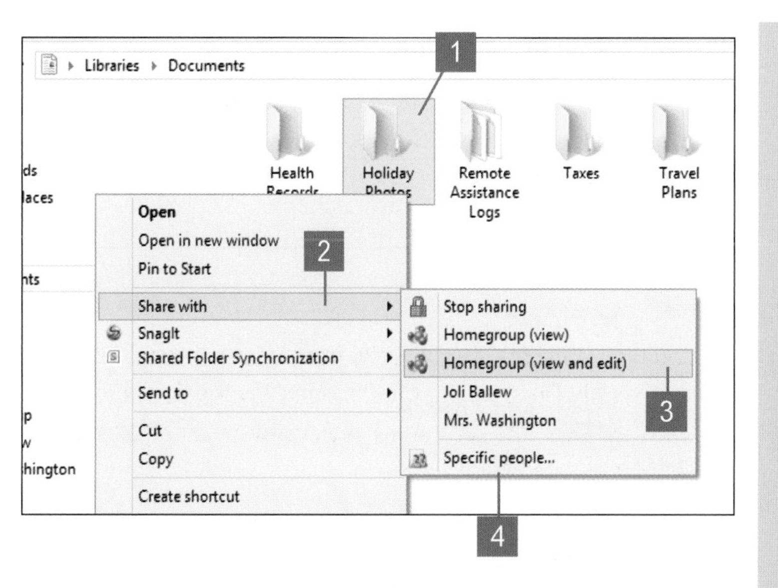


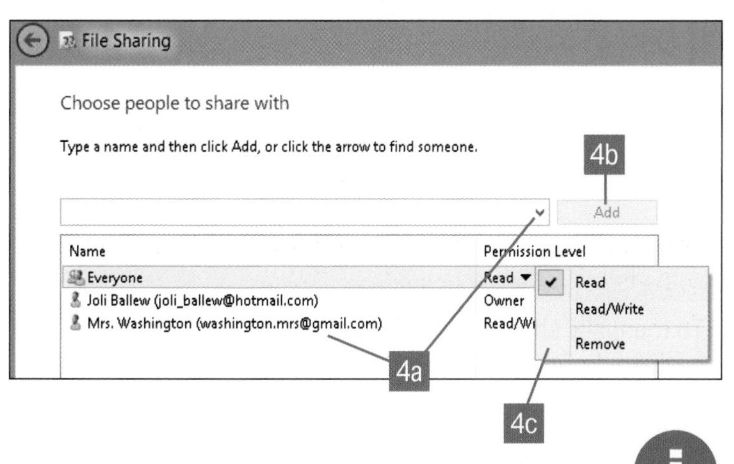


## For your information

If you use a specific Desktop folder often, right-click it and click Pin to Start. A tile for the folder will be added to the Start screen.

# Add users and share data (cont.)

## Share a personal folder

1. From File Explorer, locate the folder to share.
2. Right-click the folder and click Share with.
3. If you want to share with your homegroup or another user, select the appropriate option from the list. Follow any prompts to complete the process.
4. If you want to share with specific people who are not in a homegroup, choose Specific people, then:
   - **a** Click the arrow and choose with whom to share. (Everyone is an option.)
   - **b** Click Add.
   - **c** Click the arrow to set the permissions for the user.
   - **d** Click Share.

# Add users and share data (cont.)

## Share a printer

If you have a printer connected to your computer, you can share it. Likewise, you can access shared printers connected to other computers.

1. At the Start screen, type Printers. Click Settings.
2. In the results, click Share printers.
3. Verify Printers and devices is set to Shared.
4. To add a printer, repeat steps 1 and 2. This time, click Add printer.
5. Select the printer from the list.
6. The printer will appear under Devices.

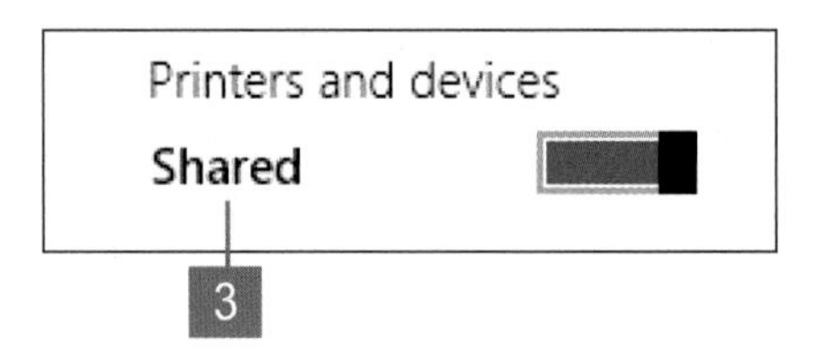


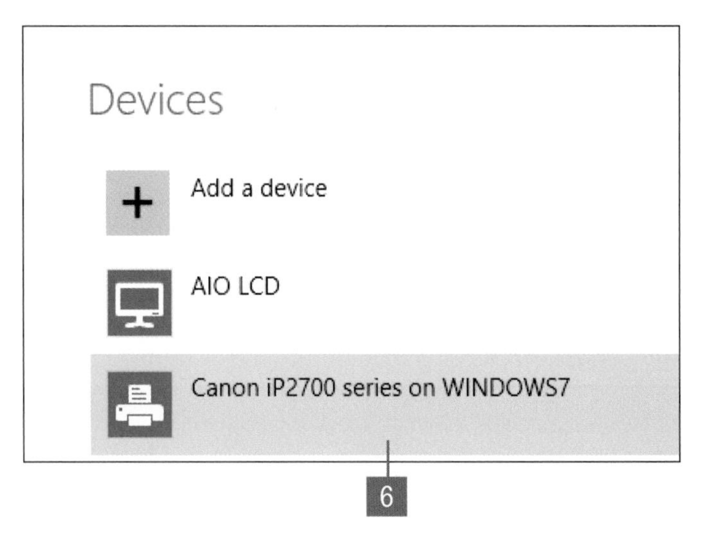


### For your information

To manually share a printer, open Control Panel and navigate to Devices and Printers. Right-click the printer to share and then choose Printer Properties. From the Sharing tab, select Share this printer.

### Important

When others on your network access the printer for the first time, they may be prompted to install a driver for it. This is OK and will be managed by the PC.

## Troubleshoot connection problems

You can see the active networks in the Network and Sharing Center. On a home computer, this is most likely a private network, as shown here. If you are having trouble connecting to the Internet and you don't see any network connections or you have limited connectivity, you can troubleshoot the problems with Windows Network Diagnostics.

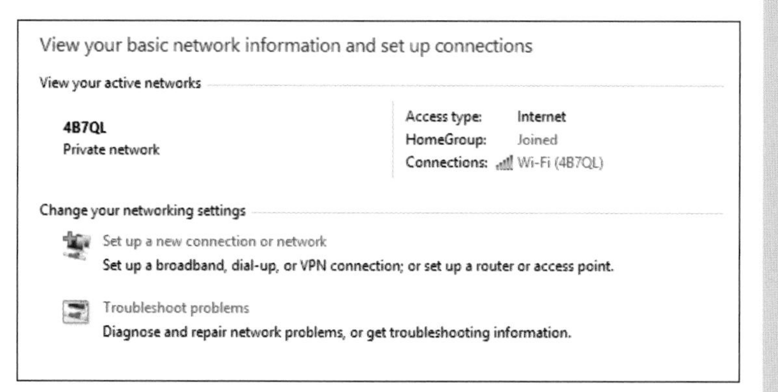


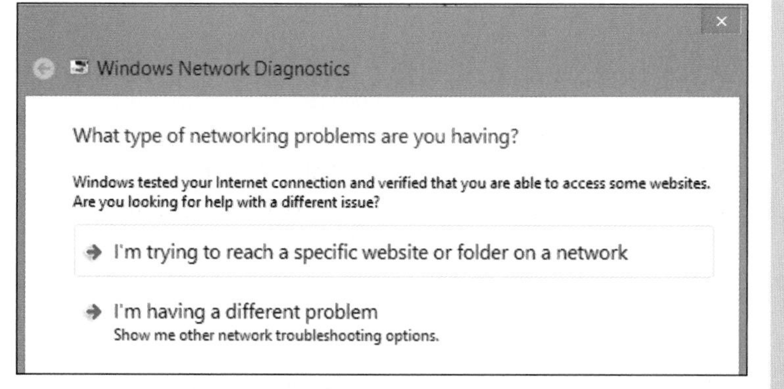


### Did you know?

There are additional troubleshooting tips in the Help and Support pages. From the Start screen, type Help and Support. Select Help and Support from the results.

## Diagnose connection problems

1. At the Desktop, right-click the Network icon on the Taskbar.
2. Click Troubleshoot problems.
3. Work through the troubleshooter to resolve the problem.

### Important

If you are prompted to restart your network, turn everything off first. Then start the modem that connects your network to the Internet, wait two minutes, then turn on the router. Wait another minute and then turn on each of the computers.

# Secure and troubleshoot Windows 8

11

## Introduction

Windows 8 comes with a lot of built-in features to keep you and your data safe. The security tools and features help you avoid email scams, harmful websites and hackers, and also help you protect your data and your computer from unscrupulous co-workers or nosy family members. If you know how to take advantage of the available safeguards, you'll be protected in almost all cases. You just need to be aware of the dangers, heed security warnings when they are given (and resolve them) and use all the available features in Windows 8 to protect yourself and your PC.

In this chapter you'll learn about many of the available safeguards. You'll learn how to further secure Internet Explorer, how to configure and use Windows Update, Windows Defender, the Firewall, File History and more. You'll also learn what you can do to stay safe, such as choosing your own anti-virus software, creating backups, and so on.

## What you'll do

**Choose anti-virus software**

**Verify security settings in Internet Explorer**

**Configure Windows Update**

**Use Windows Defender**

**Enable the firewall**

**Heed Action Center warnings**

**Use File History**

**Configure a password-protected screen saver**

**Configure System Restore**

**Create your first backup**

## Protect your computer

> **For your information**
>
> See Chapter 10 for instructions on how to create a new user account.

Your PC was not shipped to you with all the available safety measures in place. While many measures are enabled by default, which you'll learn about later, some require intervention from you.

Here's an example. If you have grandchildren who use your computer, they can probably access or delete your personal data, download harmful content, install applications or change settings that will affect the entire computer, all very easily. You can solve all of these problems by creating a computer account just for them. In conjunction, every account you create should be password protected, especially yours. It wouldn't do much good to create accounts and not assign passwords!

Beyond creating user accounts, here are some other ways to protect your PC, which we'll discuss in depth in this chapter:

- Windows Update – if enabled and configured properly, when you are online, Windows 8 will check for security updates automatically and install them. You don't have to do anything, and your PC is always updated with the latest security patches and features.
- Windows Firewall – if enabled and configured properly, the firewall will help prevent hackers (people whose job it is to get into your computer and do harm to it or steal information from it) from accessing your PC and data. The firewall blocks most programs from communicating outside the network (or outside your PC). If you want to allow a program to communicate outside your safety zone you can 'allow' a program by adding it to an 'exceptions' list. This is very easy to do.
- Windows Defender – you don't have to do much to Windows Defender except understand that it offers protection against Internet threats. It's enabled by default and it runs in the background. However, if you ever think your computer has been attacked by an Internet threat, you can run a manual scan here.
- Action Center Warnings – the Action Center is a talkative application. You can be sure you'll see a pop-up if your anti-virus software is out of date (or not installed), if you don't

have the proper security settings configured, or if Windows Update or the Firewall is disabled. You'll learn about warnings and what to do about them in this chapter.

- System Restore – if enabled, Windows 8 stores 'restore points' on your PC's hard drive. If something goes wrong you can run System Restore, choose one of these points and revert to a pre-problem date. Since System Restore deals only with 'system data', none of your personal data will be affected (not even your last email).
- Family Safety – if you have grandchildren, kids or even a forgetful or scatterbrained spouse who needs imposed computer limitations, you can apply them with built-in Family Safety controls. With these controls you are in charge of the hours a user can access the computer, which games they can play, and what programs they can run (among other things).
- File History – this feature lets you save copies of your files so you can get them back if they're lost or damaged. You'll need external storage for this to be effective. However, there are other backup options you'll also want to employ, including copying files to a CD or DVD, copying pictures and media to an external hard drive, USB drive or memory card, or storing them on an Internet server.

## Use anti-virus software

Windows 8 does not come with anti-virus software – you have to obtain and install this yourself. It's extremely important to do this if you haven't already: it will protect your computer from known threats, viruses, malware and so on.

### Choose anti-virus software

- You can purchase popular anti-virus software from well-known companies such as Kaspersky, Symantec, AVG and McAfee.
- You can obtain free and reliable anti-virus software from Microsoft – Microsoft Security Essentials. Visit www.microsoft.com from the Desktop version of Internet Explorer to learn more.
- Once you've installed the software, configure it to check for updates and install them daily.

**For your information**

Consider purchasing a book to help you learn more about staying safe, such as *Staying Safe Online* by Joli Ballew, from Pearson Education.

**Did you know?**

If a threat does get by your anti-virus software, theoretically it can do less damage if you're logged on with a standard user account than if you are logged on with an administrator account. Consider creating a standard user account for yourself if you access websites often that aren't 'mainstream', where these threats are more prolific.

### Jargon buster

**Adware** – Internet advertisements (which are also applications) that often include additional code that can be used to track a user's personal information and pass it on to third parties, without the user's authorisation or knowledge.

**Virus** – a self-replicating program that infects computers with intent to do harm. Viruses often come in the form of an attachment in an email.

**Worm** – a program that infects computers with intent to do harm. However, unlike a virus, it does not need to attach itself to a running program.

## Use anti-virus software (cont.)

## Lock down Internet Explorer

You can configure a few security settings in the Internet Explorer app available from the Start screen, as shown here. This doesn't consist of much, but does allow you to delete your browsing history and turn off the ability for websites to ask for your physical location. You can also clear existing permissions regarding your location settings and start afresh.

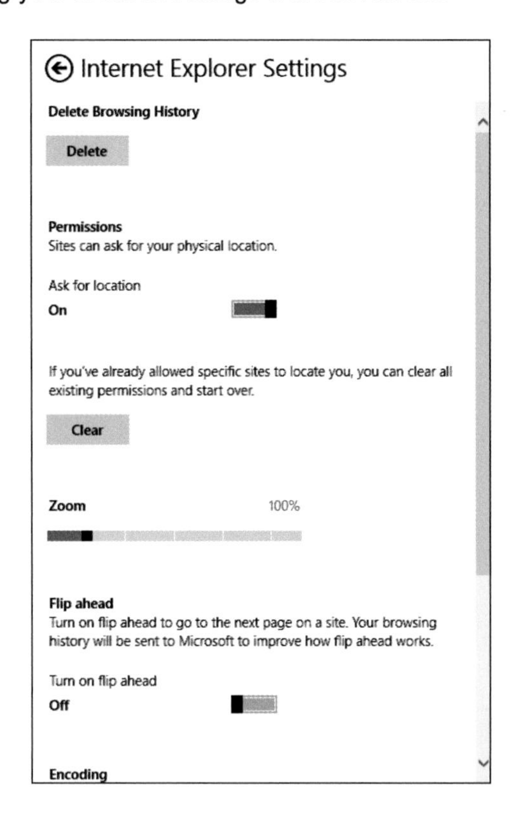


However, the full set of settings is available only from the Internet Explorer Desktop app, available from the Taskbar on the Desktop. You should explore what's available here, verify the settings are enabled, and consider raising the protection level if you often visit questionable websites or just want a little more security than is configured by default.

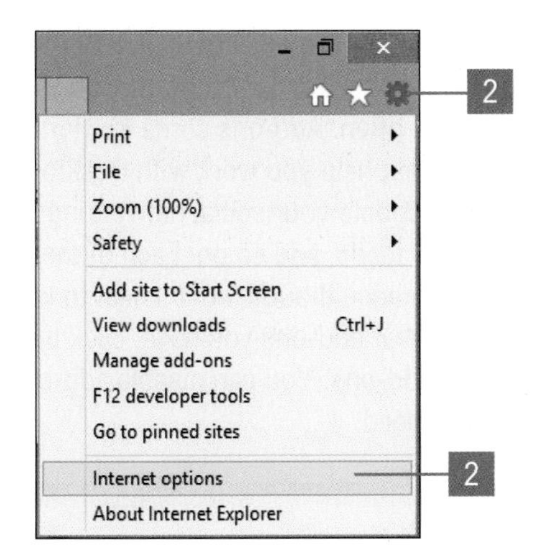


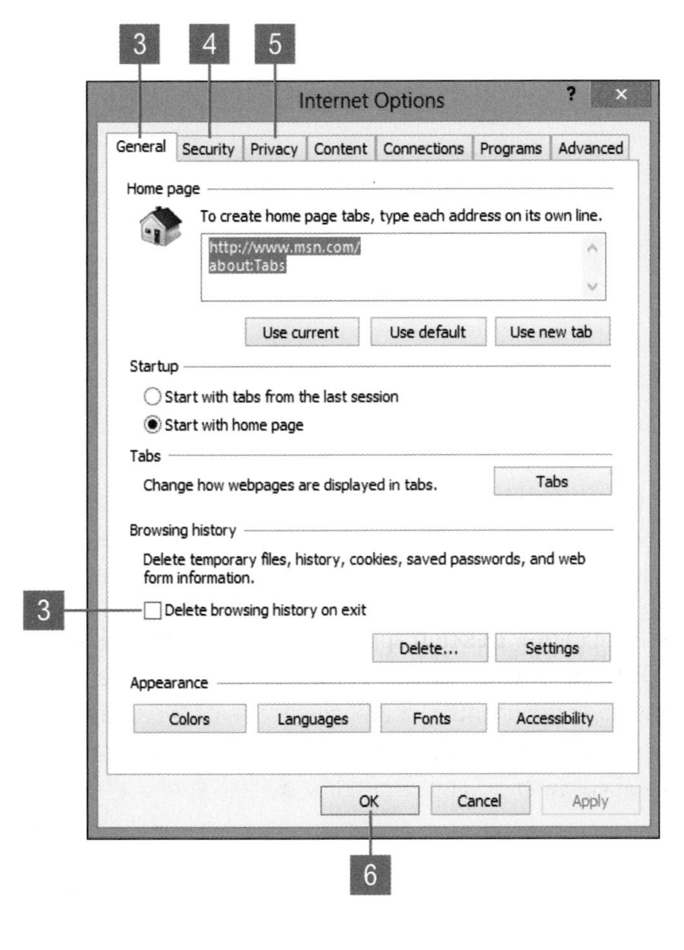


# Lock down Internet Explorer (cont.)



## Verify security settings in Internet Explorer

1. From the Desktop, open Internet Explorer.
2. Click the Tools icon and click Internet options.
3. From the General tab, note you can delete your browsing history.
4. From the Security tab, note you can configure security zones. Medium–high is best.
5. From the Privacy tab, note you can turn on the Pop-up Blocker or select a higher security setting.
6. If desired, make changes and click OK.

?

### Did you know?

Click the Tools icon and then Zoom (100%) to increase the size of the data on a web page.

# Lock down Internet Explorer (cont.)

You can improve the performance of Internet Explorer by reviewing your add-ons from the Programs tab and disable those you don't use often. Add-ons come from multiple places: there are add-ons that help you work with Desktop programs, add-ons to let you update your social networking status, view email and read RSS feeds, and so on. Each of these add-ons can hamper performance though, so it's best to keep them to a minimum. To see what add-ons you have, click the Tools icon and click Manage add-ons. You can disable add-ons you've acquired but don't need.

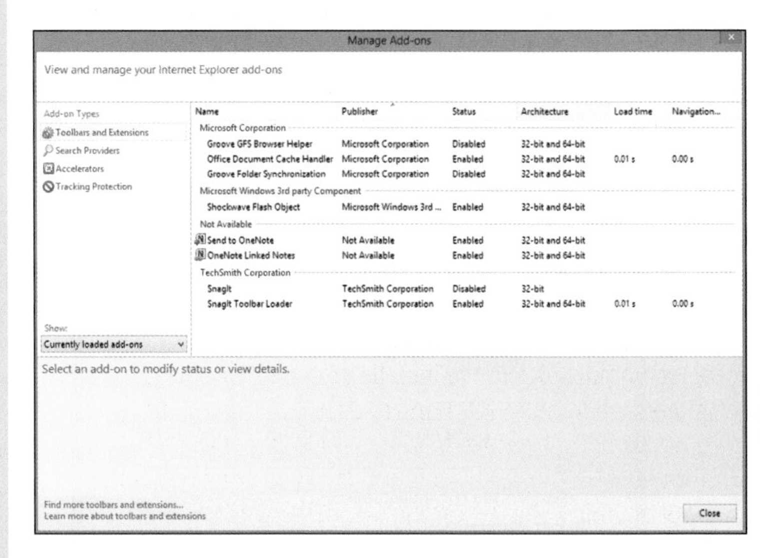


You can also add or change search providers and accelerators, and view information about and enable tracking protection. The latter can help you enhance your privacy by preventing the websites you visit from automatically sending details about your visit to other providers. Tracking Protection Lists are sort of like 'Do Not Call' lists for your telephone.

## Did you know?

You can enable the Family Safety feature from the Content tab. This enables you to control the Internet content that can be viewed by a user.

## Configure Windows Update

It's very important to configure Windows Update to get and install updates automatically. This is the easiest way to ensure your computer is as up to date as possible, at least as far as patching security flaws Microsoft uncovers, having access to the latest features and obtaining updates to the operating system itself. I propose you verify that the recommended settings are enabled as detailed here and occasionally check for optional updates manually.

When Windows Update is configured as recommended, updates will be downloaded automatically when you are online (on the Internet), installed, and if necessary your computer will be rebooted automatically. You can configure the time of day you want this to happen.

### Did you know?

The Windows Help and Support Center offers pages upon pages of information regarding Windows Update, including how to remove installed updates or select updates when more than one is available. I think the above paragraphs state all you need to know as an average 50+ computer user, and that you need not worry about anything else regarding Windows Update.

Windows Update

**You're set to automatically install updates**

No important updates are scheduled to be installed. We last checked yesterday
We'll continue to check for newer updates daily.

Check for updates now

### Configure Windows Update

1. From the Start screen, type Update.
2. Click Settings. Click Windows Update.
3. Verify that your computer is set to automatically install updates. If it is not, perform the required tasks to remedy this.

### For your information

If Windows Update is enabled and configured properly, when you are online Windows 8 will check for security updates automatically and install them. You don't have to do anything and your PC is always updated with the latest security patches and features.

# Enable Windows Firewall and Windows Defender

**Important**

Windows Defender and Windows Firewall will be disabled if you installed additional software to protect your computer that also offers these features or similar ones. This is OK!

There are two more security features to explore: Windows Firewall and Windows Defender. There isn't much you need to do with these features except to make sure they are both enabled and are protecting your PC. By default, both are enabled.

Windows Firewall is a software program that checks the data that comes in from the Internet (or a local network) and then decides whether it's good data or bad. If it deems the data harmless, it will allow it to come though the firewall; if not, it's blocked. You need a firewall to keep hackers from getting access to your PC, and to help prevent your computer from sending out malicious code if it is ever attacked by a virus or worm.

Some features are blocked by default, and the first time you try to use them you'll be prompted to unblock them. These include things like Media Center Extenders, remote Desktop features, remote shutdown and the Windows Media Player Network Sharing Service. There is reasoning behind this, and it has to do with protecting you from Internet ills. A hacker may try to come through the Internet to your PC using an application you don't normally use, such as Remote Desktop. However, it can't come through unless you 'allow' it to. Here you can see that the Mail, Calendar, People and Messaging apps are enabled for both private and public networks, but Media Center Extenders is not.

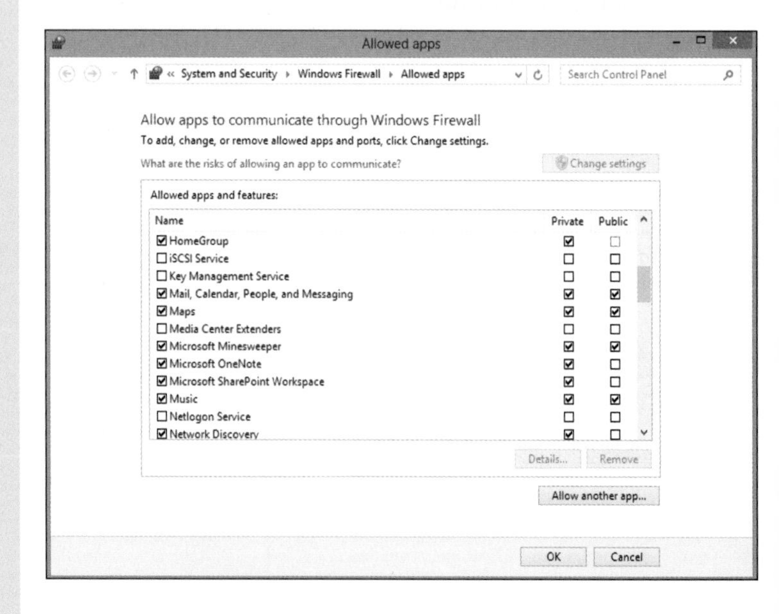

Windows Defender protects your PC against malicious and unwanted software. Generally this is a type of data called spyware, malware or adware. This can install itself on your PC without your knowledge and can wreak havoc by causing these types of problems:

- Adding toolbars to Internet Explorer.
- Changing Internet Explorer's Home page.
- Taking you to websites you do not want to visit.
- Showing pop-up advertisements.
- Causing the computer to perform slowly.

Windows Defender helps prevent this type of data from getting onto your PC and thus limits infection on PCs.

It's up to you to make sure that the firewall and Windows Defender are running and configured properly. That's what you'll learn in the next two panels. Additionally, you'll have the option of changing a few of the parameters, such as when scans are completed and what happens when potentially dangerous data is detected.

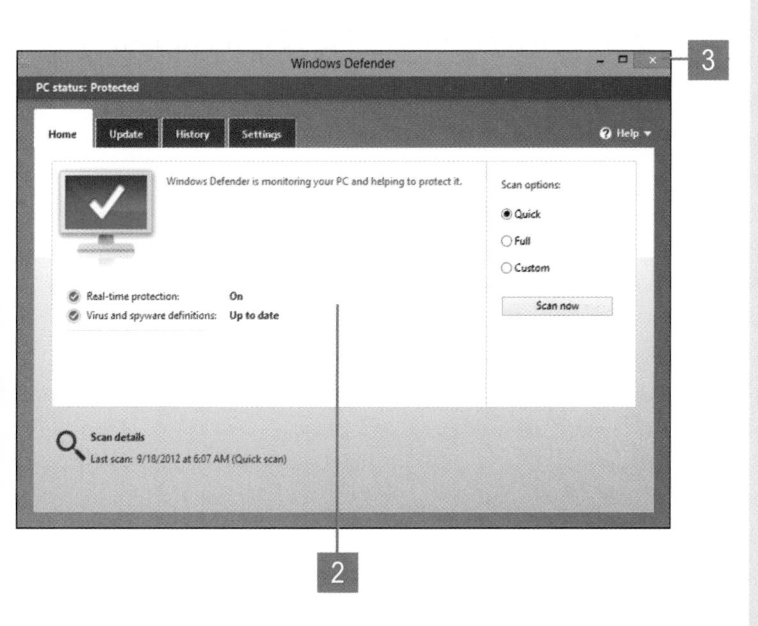


# Enable Windows Firewall and Windows Defender (cont.)

11

## Important

If you work through the steps for using Windows Firewall and it is turned off, this may be because you have a third-party firewall installed. If you aren't sure, go ahead and enable Windows Firewall. If you know you have a third-party firewall, don't enable it. Running two firewalls can cause problems for the PC.

### Use Windows Defender

1. Open Windows Defender. (You can search for it from the Start screen.)
2. Verify Windows Defender is enabled and note the option to run a scan if desired.
3. Click the X in the top right corner to close the Windows Defender window.

# Enable Windows Firewall and Windows Defender (cont.)

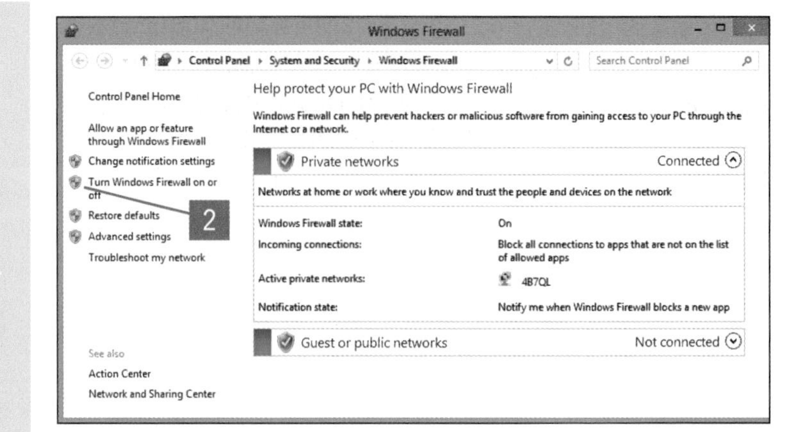


## Enable the firewall

1. Open Windows Firewall. (Type Firewall at the Start screen and click Settings to find it.)
2. Verify the firewall is on. If not, select Turn Windows Firewall on or off, enable it and click OK.
3. Review the other settings.

**Important**

Click each tab available from Windows Defender to explore all the options.

# Use the Action Center

Windows 8 tries hard to take care of your PC and your data. You'll be informed if your anti-virus software is out of date (or not installed), if you don't have the proper security settings configured or if Windows Update or the firewall is disabled. You can resolve these issues in the Action Center, a Desktop application.

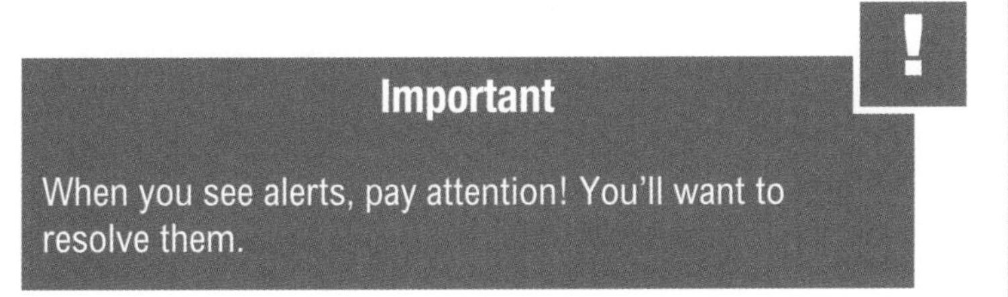

**Important**

When you see alerts, pay attention! You'll want to resolve them.

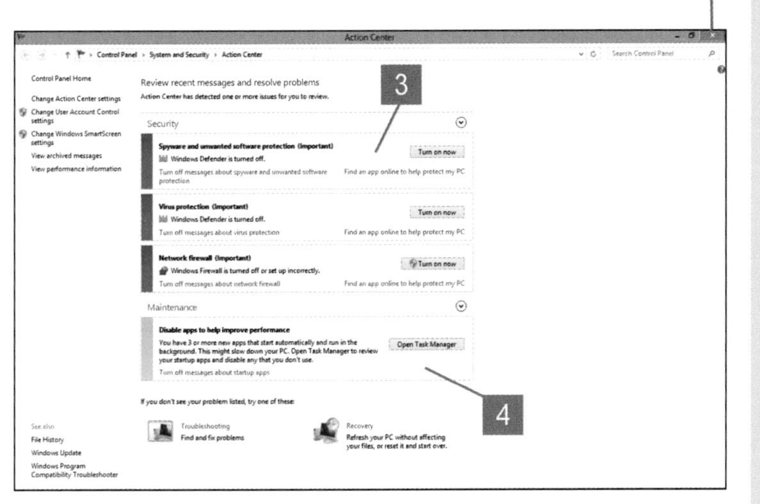


## Heed Action Center warnings

1. From the Desktop, on the Taskbar, locate the Action Center flag. (It looks like a flag!)
2. Right-click the flag icon and then click Open Action Center.
3. If there's anything in red, do what is necessary to resolve the problem. You may have to click the down arrow to see this.
4. If there's anything in yellow, review the problem and solution and take action if desired. You may have to click the down arrow to see this.
5. Close the Action Center when all problems have been resolved.

## Explore File History

Most of the security features in Windows 8 are enabled by default. File History is not. File History saves copies of your files so you can get them back if they're lost or damaged. You'll need an external drive for File History for it to be effective. Enabling File History offers another mechanism for protecting your data. When you combine File History technology with personal backups, you can have a backup of your backups!

### Use File History

1. Connect an external drive.
2. From the Start screen, type File History.
3. Click Settings, then click File History.
4. In the File History window, click Turn on.
5. If desired, click Run now.

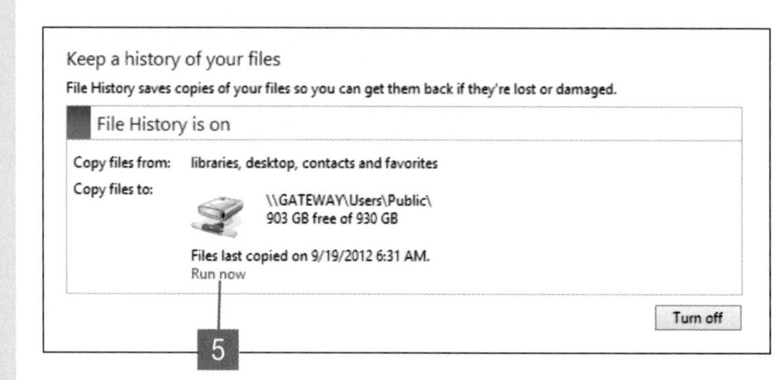


**Did you know?**

You can click Advanced Settings to change how often File History makes copies of files. Every hour is the default.

Your computer will automatically sleep after a specific amount of idle time (requiring you to input your password when you're ready to use the computer again), but you can configure a screen saver to engage after as little as one minute of inactivity. You can also configure your computer to display the Lock screen when you are ready to access the computer again. If you're concerned about co-workers, spouses, children or grandchildren accessing your computer when you step away from it, set the screen saver to engage after, say, three minutes of inactivity and set a password to wake it once it's applied. Make sure the password isn't something anyone can guess, such as a dog's name, your birth date or your middle name.

Finally, if you want to keep people from seeing what is on the screen when the screen saver is engaged, make sure you don't select a screen saver like Bubbles that is see-through. You configure a screen saver in the Personalization options of Control Panel.

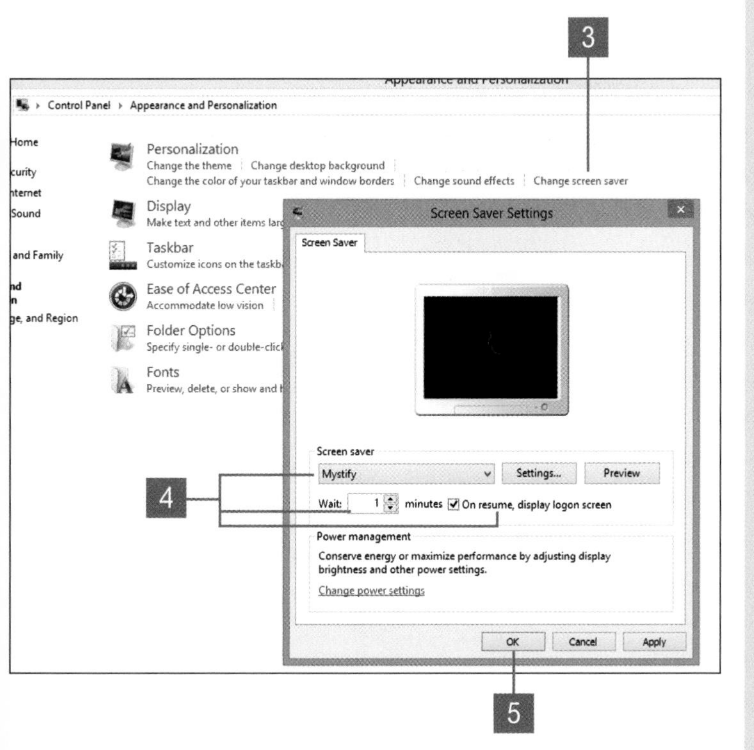

# Use a screen saver



## Configure a password-protected screen saver

1. Open Control Panel.
2. Click Appearance and Personalization.
3. Under Personalization, click Change screen saver.
4. Select a screen saver, choose how long to wait, and place a tick in On resume, display logon screen.
5. Click OK.

### Important

If you regularly work on sensitive data that you don't want anyone else to see, make sure you set a screen saver to engage after a very short amount of idle time.

# Use System Restore

System Restore lets you restore your computer to an earlier time without affecting your personal files, including documents, spreadsheets, email and photos, among other things. You'll generally use System Restore if and when you install a program or driver that ultimately produces error messages or causes problems for the computer, and uninstalling the problematic application or driver doesn't resolve the issue.

System Restore, by default, regularly creates and saves restore points that contain information about registry settings and deep down system information that Windows uses to work properly. It does this automatically and is configured by default. Because System Restore works only with its own system files, it can't recover a lost personal file, email or picture. In the same vein, it will not affect this data either.

## Configure System Restore

1. At the Start screen, type System.
2. Click Settings, then click System.
3. In the left pane, click System protection.
4. Verify that System protection is On. (To use System Restore, click System Restore here instead.)
5. Click Configure.
6. Choose how much space to devote to System Restore. What you choose depends on how much free hard drive space you'd like to devote.
7. Click OK and OK again.

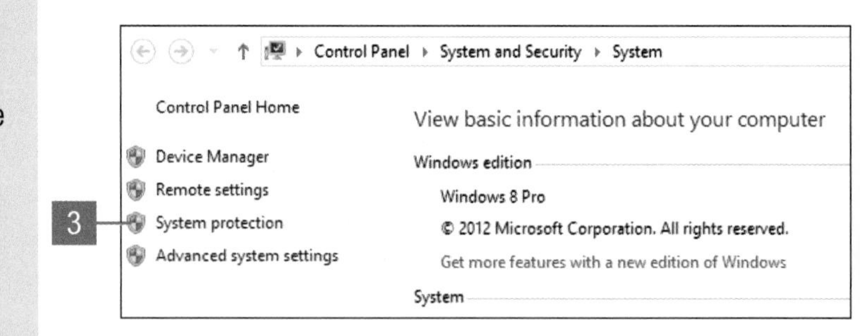


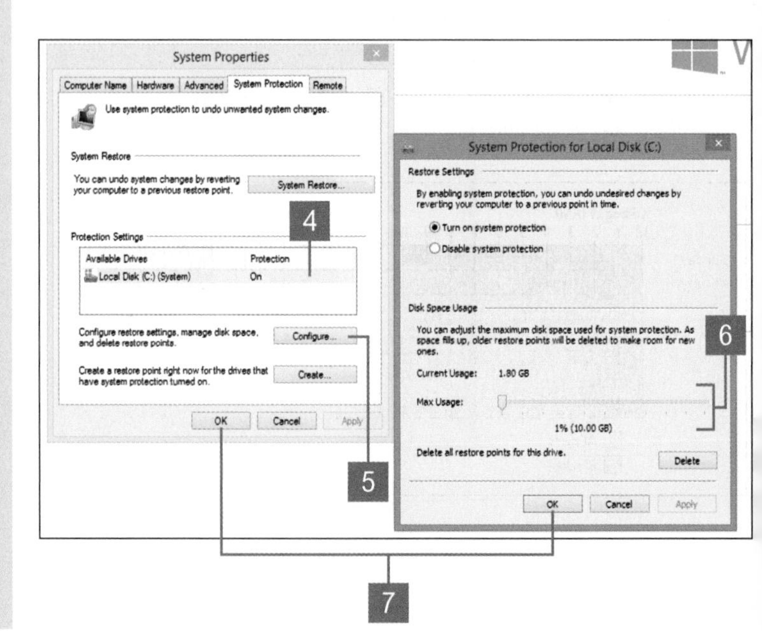

# Consider Family Safety



Family Safety is an option in Control Panel, under User Accounts and Family Safety. You can enable this feature for users who have their own standard account on the computer, such as grandchildren. You may also want to enable Family Safety for spouses or other family members who have very little computer knowledge and who are likely to encounter problems while online or while using the computer. When you enable this feature you can apply various settings, shown here.

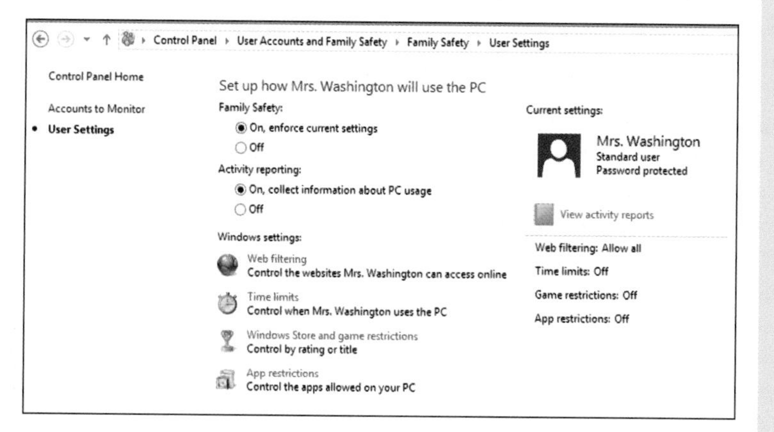


- Web Filtering lets you control which websites a user can visit. You can set a filtering level, or create a specific list of websites the user can visit. You can also block all websites.
- Time Limits lets you control how many hours a user can access the computer per day, or set what time of day the user can access the PC. Blue means the time is blocked; white means it's allowed.

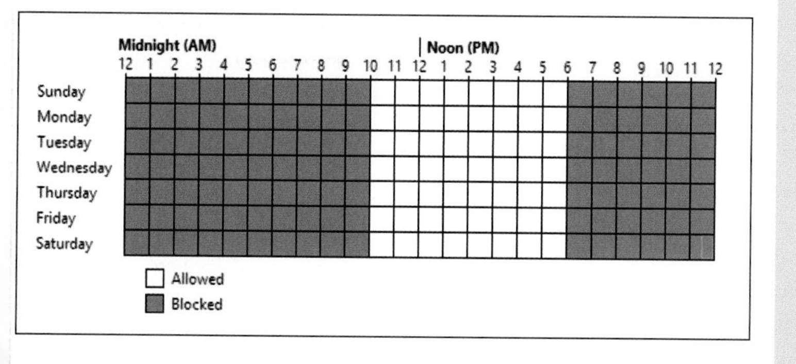

## Consider Family Safety (cont.)

- Windows Store and Game Restrictions help you control what the user can do in the Store and while playing games. You can control this by rating or title, or block all games or specific games.
- App Restrictions let you control what apps the user can access. You may block access to, say, Camera, Maps and News, for instance.
- View Activity Reports lets you see what the user has done during their allotted and allowed computer time.

To get started, open Control Panel, then click Set up Family Safety for Any User. Choose the user to apply limits to and configure them as desired.

## Back up your data

You need to manually back up your data often. One option is to drag and drop data from any library or folder to an external drive or a network drive. Here we're dragging and dropping some folders from the Windows 8 computer's Documents library to a backup drive on another PC on the network. This is quite effective.

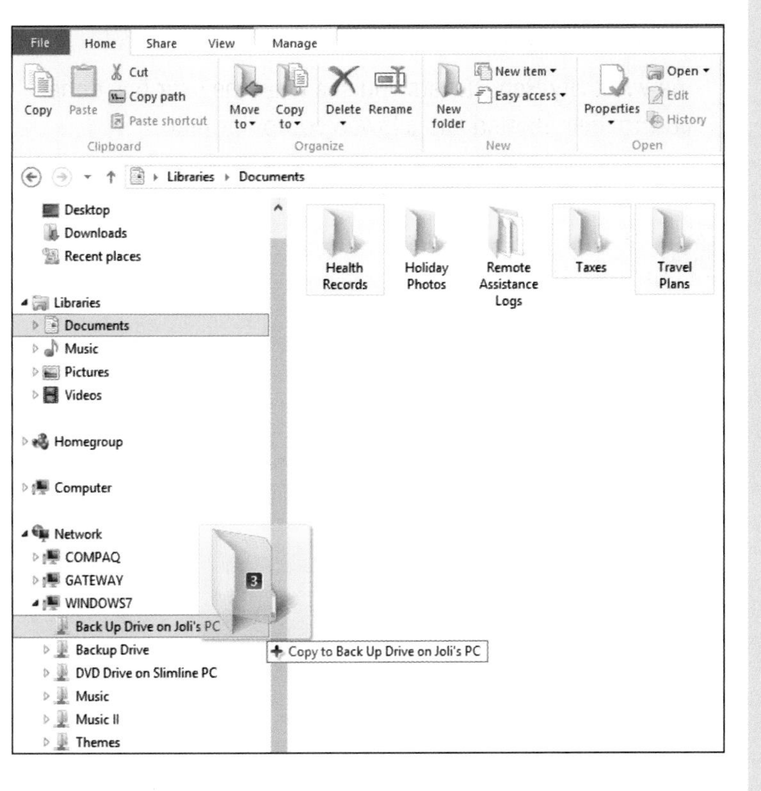


There are other options though:

- Copy data to a USB thumb drive.
- Copy date to a local external drive.
- Purchase, install and use a third-party backup program.
- Burn data to CDs or DVDs.

# Back up your data (cont.)

## Create your first backup

1. Connect an external device you can back up data to.
2. Open the Desktop.
3. Click the folder icon on the Taskbar.
4. Locate and select the data to back up. (Use Ctrl to select multiple non-contiguous files; Shift for contiguous ones.)
5. From the Home tab, click Copy to.
6. Click Choose Location.
7. Locate the desired drive.
8. Click Copy.

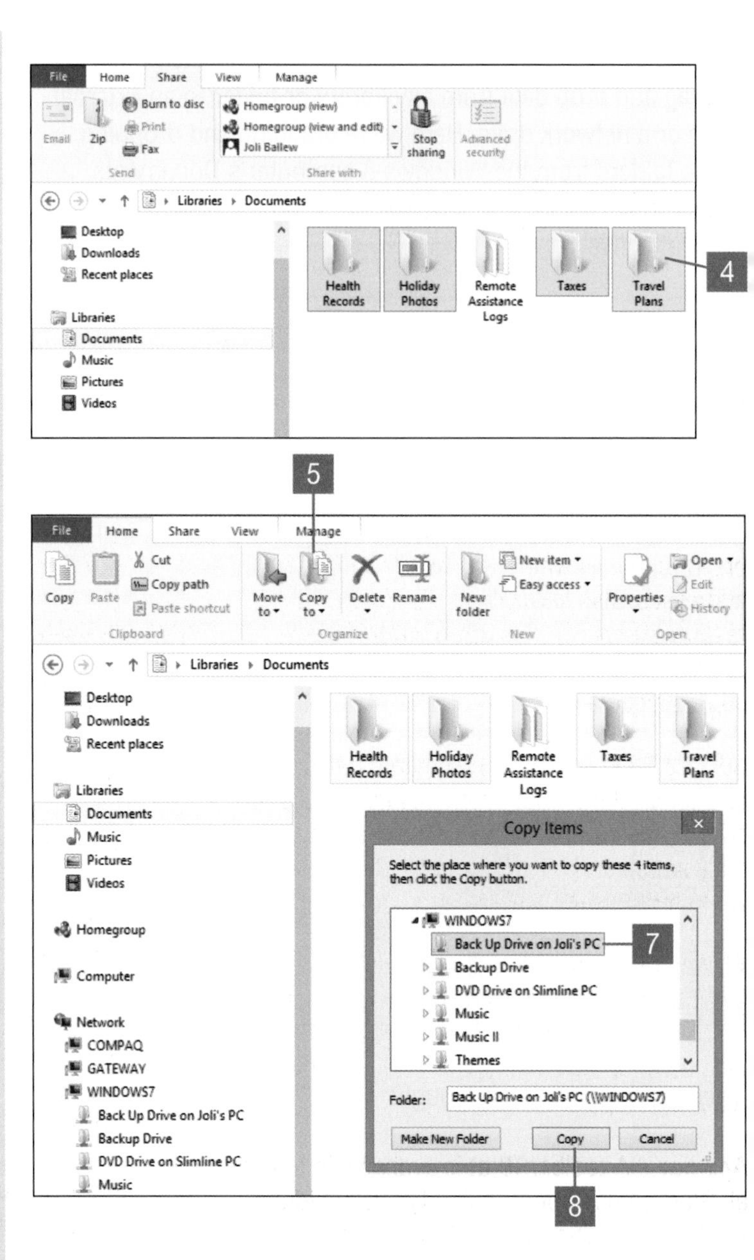

# Jargon buster

**Action Center** – A feature in Windows 8 that allows you to view problems, fix problems and run automated troubleshooters.

**Address bar** – In Internet Explorer or any web browser, this is where you type in Internet addresses, also known as URLs (uniform resource locators). Generally, an Internet address takes the form of http://www.companyname.com.

**Adware** – Internet advertisements (which are also applications) that often include additional code that can be used to track a user's personal information and pass it on to third parties, without the user's authorisation or knowledge.

**All Apps screen** – The All Apps charm becomes available when you right-click an empty area of the Start screen. You have access to all tiles here for apps and applications from the resulting Apps screen.

**App bar** – A toolbar (that is available in almost all Start screen apps) that is typically hidden until needed. The App bar holds commands that may enable the user to configure the app, input a location, add an event, delete an item, view properties, and more.

**Applications** – Software installed on your PC other than the operating system that is not apps. Some applications come pre-installed, like Paint, WordPad, Snipping Tool and Sticky Notes. All applications open on the Desktop and are thus often referred to as Desktop applications. Applications also include third-party software you purchase separately and install yourself, such as Microsoft Office or Photoshop.

**Apps** – In the context of Windows 8, apps are applications, but they are not fully fledged or feature rich. Apps enable you to perform a task quickly and without much distraction from the interface. Apps offer charms you use to configure and personalise the app. App tiles appear on the Start screen and the All Apps screen.

**Attachment** – Something you add to an email, such as a photograph, a short video, a sound recording, document or other data. There are many ways to attach something to an email.

**Bandwidth** – Generally this is used to represent how much data you send and receive on a paid connection, like a smartphone or Internet connection.

**Bcc** – If you want to send an email to someone and you don't want other recipients to know you included them in the email, add them to the Bcc line. Bcc stands for blind carbon copy and is a secret copy.

**Boot up** – When a computer is switched on, it goes through a sequence of tasks before you can access it. This process is called the booting-up process. Computers can be rated by many factors, and one of those factors is how long the booting-up process takes.

**Browse** – Browsing for a file, folder or program is the process of drilling down into the operating system's folder structure to locate the desired item. Browse can also be the process of surfing web pages on the Internet.

**Burn** – A term used to describe the process of copying music from a computer to a CD or DVD. Generally music is burned to a CD, since CDs can be played in cars and generic CD players, and videos are burned to DVDs since they require much more space and can be played on DVD players.

**Cc** – If you want to send an email to someone and you don't need them to respond, you can put them in the Cc line. Cc stands for carbon copy. (Bcc is a blind carbon copy; other recipients cannot see the Bcc field address.)

**Charms** – When in an app, charms enable you to configure the app, set preferences and so on. There are five default charms you can access at any time: Search, Share, Start, Devices and Settings. You can access these by placing your cursor in the bottom right corner of the screen. You can also use the key combination Windows + C.

**Contacts** – People you communicate with. A contact card may include email addresses, pictures, phone numbers, home and business addresses, and more.

**Control Panel** – A place where you can change computer settings related to system and maintenance, user accounts, security, appearance, networks and the Internet, the time, language and region, hardware and sounds, visual displays and accessibility options, programs and additional options.

**Cookies** – Small text files that include data that identifies your preferences when you visit particular websites. Cookies are what allow you to visit, say, www.amazon.com and be greeted with 'Hello <your name>, We have recommendations for you!' Cookies help a site offer you a personalised web experience.

**Copy command** – Copies the data to the Clipboard (a virtual, temporary holding area). The data will not be deleted from its original location even when you 'paste' it somewhere else. Pasting copied data will copy the data, not move it.

**Cut** – Use to remove the selected text, picture or object.

**Cut command** – Copies the data to the Clipboard (a virtual, temporary holding area). The data will be deleted from its original location as soon as you 'paste' it somewhere else. Pasting cut data moves the data from its original location.

**Deleted Items** – This folder holds email you've deleted.

**Desktop application** – See Applications.

**Desktop folder** – Contains links to items on your Desktop.

**Dialogue box** – A place to make changes to default settings in an application. Clicking a photo, clicking the Share tab and then clicking Print, for instance, opens the Print Pictures dialogue box where you can configure the type of paper you're using, select a printer, and more.

**Disk Cleanup** – An application included with Windows 8 that offers a safe and effective way to reduce unnecessary data on your PC. With Disk Cleanup you can remove temporary files, empty the Recycle Bin, remove setup log files and downloaded program files (among other things), all in a single process.

**Disk Defragmenter/Optimize Drives** – An application included with Windows 8 that analyses the data stored on your hard drive and consolidates files that are not stored together. This enhances performance by making data on your hard drive work faster by making it easier to access. Disk Defragmenter runs automatically, once a week, in the middle of the night.

**Domain name** – For our use here, a domain name is synonymous with a website name.

**Downloaded program files** – Files that are downloaded automatically when you view certain web pages. They are stored temporarily in a folder on your hard disk and accessed when and if needed.

**Downloads folder** – Does not contain anything by default. It does offer a place to save items you download from the Internet, such as drivers and third-party programs.

**DPI** – Dots per inch refers to how many dots (or pixels) per inch are on a computer monitor.

**Drafts** – This folder holds email messages you've started and then saved, but not yet completed and sent.

**Driver** – A piece of software (or code) that allows the device to communicate with Windows 8 and vice versa.

**Email address** – A virtual address you use for sending and receiving email. It often takes this form: yourname@yourispname.com.

**Ethernet** – A technology that uses Ethernet cables to transmit data and network computers.

**Ethernet cable** – A cable that is used to connect PCs to routers and cable modems, among other things.

**Family Safety** – If you have children or grandchildren, or even a forgetful or scatterbrained partner who needs imposed computer limitations, you can apply them using Family Safety controls. With these controls you are in charge of the hours a user can access the computer, which games they can play and what programs they can run (among other things).

**Favourite** – A web page for which you've chosen to maintain a shortcut in the Favorites Center.

**Favorites Center** – This folder contains the items in Internet Explorer's Favorites list. It may also include folders created by the computer manufacturer or Microsoft.

**File Explorer** – A window that opens on the Desktop that enables you to view all the data on your computer, work with and group data, delete data and otherwise manage it. You can also print, share, preview and sort data, among other things.

**File History** – A backup feature that saves copies of your files so you can get them back if they are lost or damaged. This feature is not enabled by default and works best if you to have an external location to save the backups.

**Flash drive** – A small, portable device that is used for quick backups of data or ReadyBoost. Flash drives are often referred to as thumb drives and plug into an available USB port.

**Flick** – A gesture that is performed with a single finger by swiping quickly left, right, up or down.

**Flip** – A way to move through open windows graphically instead of clicking the item on the Taskbar.

**Folder** – A data unit (similar to a folder in a filing cabinet) that holds files and subfolders. You use folders to organise data. Some folders come with Windows 8, including but not limited to My Documents, Public Pictures, My Videos, Downloads, Contacts, Favorites and Searches.

**Form data** – In Internet Explorer, information that's been saved using Internet Explorer's autocomplete form data functionality. If you don't want forms to be filled out automatically by you or someone else who has access to your PC and user account, disable this.

**Formatting toolbar** – A toolbar in an application window that often sits just below a standard toolbar and offers drop-down lists for the font, font size and language, as well as options to configure the font (or any selected text) as bold, italic or underlined. There's often a Color option for assigning a colour to a font too, as well as alignment tools for Align Left, Center, Align Right and finally Bullets.

**Gestures** – Techniques you can use to navigate a touch screen. You can flick up and down, tap, double-tap, and tap and hold.

**GHz** – Short for gigahertz, this term describes how fast a processor can work. One GHz equals 1 billion cycles per second, so a 2.4 GHz computer chip will execute calculations at 240 billion cycles per second. It's only important to know that the faster the chip, the faster the PC.

**GPU** – Short for graphics processing unit, it's a processor used specifically for rendering graphics. Having a processor just for graphics frees up the main CPU (central processing unit), allowing it to work faster on other tasks.

**Hardware** – Physical computing devices you connect externally to the computer, and the physical items inside it. Common hardware includes printers, external USB drives, network interface cards, CPUs, RAM, and more.

**History** – In Internet Explorer, this is the list of websites you've visited and any web addresses you've typed. Anyone who has access to your PC and user account can look at your History list to see where you've been.

**Homegroup** – A feature you can enable to share data more easily between other networked Windows 7 and Windows 8 Computers. It's secured with a homegroup password.

**Home page** – The web page that opens when you open IE8. You can set the home page and configure additional pages to open as well.

**Hot corner** – An area of the screen that, when the cursor is placed there, offers information. The bottom right or top right corner of any screen is a hot spot that offers access to the five default charms. The bottom left corner offers access to the Start screen. The top left corner offers access to previously used apps and applications.

**Hot spot** – A Wi-Fi hot spot lets you connect to the Internet without having to be tethered to an Ethernet cable or tied down with a high monthly wireless bill. Most of the time this service is free, provided you have the required wireless hardware.

**Icon** – A visual representation of a file or folder that you can click to open.

**Inbox** – This folder holds email you've received.

**Input device** – A piece of hardware that enables you to type, select, open or otherwise interact with the computer. Common input devices include mice and keyboards. However, your finger can be an input device, and there are several speciality input devices for people with disabilities.

**Instant messaging (IM)** – Text and instant messaging require you to type your message and click a Send button. It's similar to email, but it's instantaneous: the recipient gets the message right after you send it. Instant messaging is the term generally reserved for text communications between two or more computers; text messaging is a term generally reserved for communicating between two mobile phones.

**Interface** – What you see on the screen when working in a window. In Paint's interface, you see the Menu bar, Toolbox and Color box, for instance.

**Internet** – A large web of computers that communicates via land lines, satellite and cable for the purpose of sharing information and data. Also called the World Wide Web.

**Internet server** – A computer that stores data off site. These Internet servers hold email and data so that you do not have to store this on your PC. Internet servers allow you to access information from any computer that can access the internet.

**ISP** – Internet Service Provider. A company that provides Internet access, usually for a fee.

**Junk e-mail** – This folder holds email that your mail program thinks is spam. You should check this folder occasionally, since Mail may put email in there you want to read. It may also be called spam.

**Library** – A virtual data unit that offers access to both the related private and public folders. As an example, the Documents library offers access to the My Documents and Public Documents folders, and the data is grouped together to appear as a unit. You can separate the data if desired.

**Link** – A shortcut to a web page. Links are often offered in an email, document or web page to allow you to access a site without having to actually type in its name. In almost all instances, links are underlined and in a different colour than the text on the rest of the page.

**Links folder** – This folder contains shortcuts to the Desktop, Downloads, Recent Places, and more.

**Load** – A web page must 'load' before you can access it. Some pages load instantly while others take a few seconds.

**Lock screen** – The screen you must bypass when you turn on or wake up your Windows 8 computer. You can select the Lock screen background.

**Magnifier** – A tool in the Ease of Access suite of applications. You use Magnifier to drastically increase the size of the information shown on the screen.

**Mail server** – A computer that your ISP configures to allow you to send and receive email. It often includes a POP3 incoming mail server and an SMTP outgoing mail server, although IMAP is becoming more and more popular. Often the server names look something like pop.yourispnamehere.com and smtp.yourispnamehere.com.

**Malware** – Stands for malicious software. Malware includes viruses, worms, spyware, etc.

**Menu** – A title on the Menu bar (such as File, Edit or View). Clicking a menu name opens a drop-down list with additional choices (Open, Save, Print).

**Menu bar** – A bar that runs across the top of an application that offers menus. Often, these menus include File, Edit, View, Insert, Format and Help. You may be able to show a menu bar by clicking the Alt key on the keyboard.

**Multi-touch gestures** – Gestures that require two (or more) fingers to perform, such as pinching to zoom in and out of the computer screen.

**Narrator** – A basic screen reader included with Windows 8. This application will read text that appears on the screen to you, while you navigate using the keyboard and mouse.

**Navigate** – The process of moving from one web page to another or viewing items on a single web page. Often the term is used as follows: 'Click the link to navigate to the new web page.'

**Network** – A group of computers, printers and other devices that communicates wirelessly or through wired connections.

**Network adapter** – A piece of hardware that lets your computer connect to a network, such as the Internet or a local network.

**Network and Sharing Center** – A collection of features where you can easily access network connections, sharing options, networked computers and devices, and diagnose and repair features.

**Network Discovery** – A state where computers can find other computers on the network. Network Discovery must be on to locate and communicate with network devices.

**Network window** – Offers links to computers on your network and the Network and Sharing Center. You can also add printers and wireless devices here.

**Notification area** – The area of the Taskbar that includes the clock and the volume icons, and also holds icons for applications that are running in the background. You may see icons for your anti-virus software, music players, updates or Windows security alerts.

**Offline web pages** – These are web pages you choose to store on your computer so you can view them without being connected to the Internet. Upon connection, the data is synchronised.

**On-screen keyboard** – A feature that is available as part of Windows 8 that enables you to input text and interact with the computer using a virtual keyboard. On touchscreen-only devices, like tablets, this is the main way to interact.

**Operating system** – In this case, the operating system is Windows 8. This is what allows you to operate your computer's *system*. You will use Windows 8 to find things you have stored on your computer, connect to the Internet, send and receive email, and surf the web, among other things.

**Outbox** – This folder holds email you've written but have not yet sent.

**Page Setup button** – Clicking Page Setup opens the Page Setup dialogue box. Here you can select a paper size, source, and create headers and footers. You can also change orientation and margins, all of which is dependent on which features your printer supports.

**Partition** – A hard drive has a certain amount of space to store data, sometimes 120 GB, 500 GB, 1 TB, or more. Often, people or computer manufacturers separate this space into two or three distinct spaces, called partitions, drives or volumes. One partition may contain system files, one may contain program files and the other may contain data.

**Paste command** – Copies or moves cut or copied data to the new location. If the data was cut, it will be moved. If the data was copied, it will be copied.

**PC Settings** – The app version of Control Panel. This 'hub' offers options you can use to personalise your computer, including adding users, changing the Lock screen picture, changing the design behind the Start screen tiles, creating or joining a homegroup, and more.

**Peek** – To see what's on the Desktop but behind open windows and applications. To use Peek you position your mouse in the bottom right corner. Peek must be enabled to work.

**Permissions** – Rules associated with a shared resource, such as a folder, file or printer, that define who can use a resource and what they can do once they have access to it.

**Phishing** – A technique used by computer hackers to get you to divulge personal information like bank account numbers. In other words, an attempt by an unscrupulous website or hacker to obtain personal data, including but not limited to bank account numbers, National Insurance numbers and email addresses. Phishing filters warn you of potential phishing websites and emails, and are included in Windows 8.

**Picture password** – A new method of logging in to Windows. Instead of typing a password or PIN, you can use a series of touch gestures to a particular part of a photo that you select.

**PIN password** – A new method of logging in to Windows. The PIN, a four-digit numeric password, is similar to what you type in an ATM machine.

**Pixel** – The smallest unit for data displayed on a computer. Resolution is defined by how many pixels you choose to display.

**Playlist** – A group of songs that you can save and then listen to as a group, burn to a CD, copy to a portable music player, and more.

**Podcast** – An online broadcast, like a radio show.

**POP3 server name** – The name of the computer that you will use to get your email from your ISP. Your ISP will give you this information when you subscribe.

**Power plan** – A group of settings that you can configure to tell Windows 8 when and if to turn off the computer monitor or display, and when or if to put the computer to sleep.

**Print button/Print icon** – Clicking Print opens the Print dialogue box where you can configure the page range, select a printer, change page orientation, change print order and choose a paper type. Additional options include print quality, output bins, and more. Of course, the choices offered depend on what your printer offers. If your printer can only print at 300 × 300 dots per inch, you can't configure it to print at a higher quality.

**Print Preview button** – Clicking Print Preview opens a window where you can see before you print what the printout will actually look like. You can switch between portrait and landscape views, access the Page Setup dialogue box, and more.

**Processor** – Short for microprocessor, it's the silicon chip that contains the central processing unit (CPU) inside a computer. Generally, the terms CPU and processor are used interchangeably. A CPU does almost all the computer's calculations and is the most important piece of hardware in a computer system.

**Programs** – See Applications.

**Public folder** – Folders where you can share data. Anyone with an account on the computer can access the data inside these folders. You can also configure the Public folder to share files with people using other computers on your local network.

**RAM** – Short for random access memory, it's the hardware inside your computer that temporarily stores data that is being used by the operating system or programs. Although there are many types of RAM, all you need to know is that the more RAM you have, the faster your computer will (theoretically) run and perform.

**ReadyBoost** – A technology that lets you add more temporary cache to a PC using a USB flash drive or a secure digital memory card (like the one in your digital camera), which works like RAM, if it meets certain requirements.

**Recycle Bin** – Holds deleted files until you decide to empty it. The Recycle Bin serves as a safeguard, allowing you to recover items accidentally deleted or items you thought you no longer wanted but later decide you need. Note that once you empty the Recycle Bin, the items in it are gone for ever.

**Refresh your PC** – A feature you can use to reinstall system files, remove third-party programs, but keep photos, music, videos and personal files. You can refresh your computer when it isn't working properly. Try System Restore first though.

**Remote Desktop Connection** – A Windows 8 program you can use to access your computer from somewhere else, such as an office or hotel room.

**Reset Your PC** – A new service in Windows 8 that returns your PC to its factory settings. It does this by wiping all the data from it and reinstalling Windows. Once complete the computer will appear as it did the first time you turned it on, right out of the box.

**Resolution** – How many pixels are shown on a computer screen. Choosing 800 by 600 pixels means that the Desktop is shown to you with 800 pixels across and 600 pixels down. When you increase the resolution, you increase the number of pixels on the screen.

**Ribbon** – The feature that runs across the top of every File Explorer window that offers tabs such as File, Home, Share, View, Manage and so on.

**Rip** – A term used to describe the process of copying files from a physical CD to your hard drive, and thus your music library.

**Router** – A piece of equipment used to send data from computer to computer on a network. A router 'routes' the data to the correct PC and also rejects data that is harmful or from unknown sources.

**RSS** – A novel way to access information on the Internet. Also called Really Simple Syndication (and occasionally Rich Site Summary), you can use this technology to 'subscribe' to RSS data, and the information or website you subscribe to will be updated automatically on your PC, and will only acquire information you've yet to view.

**Screensaver** – A picture or animation that covers your screen and appears after your computer has been idle for a specific amount of time that you set. You can configure your screensaver to require a password on waking up for extra security.

**Scroll bar** – Appears when what needs to be shown on the screen is more than can be viewed on it. You'll see a scroll bar on the Start screen, on web pages, in long documents, and other places.

**Scroll up and scroll down** – A process of using the scroll bars on a web page or the arrow keys on a keyboard to move up and down the pages of a website or to navigate through open windows.

**Sent Items** – This folder stores copies of e-mal messages you've sent.

**Setup Log files** – Files created by Windows during set-up processes.

**SkyDrive** – A place 'in the cloud' offered by Microsoft, where you can store things. Data you save is saved on Internet servers, enabling you to access the data from an Internet-enabled compatible device.

**SMTP server name** – The name of the computer that you will use to send email using your ISP. Your ISP will give you this information when you subscribe.

**Snap** – The process by which two apps can be displayed side by side in Windows 8.

**Snipping Tool** – A feature in Windows 8 that allows you to drag your cursor around any area on the screen to copy and capture it. Once captured, you can save it, edit it and/or send it to an email recipient.

**Sound Recorder** – A simple tool included with Windows 8 with only three options: Start recording, Stop recording and Resume recording. You can save recorded clips as notes to yourself or insert them into movies or slide shows.

**Spam** – Unwanted email. Compare spam to junk faxes or junk postal mail.

**Speech Recognition** – A program included with Windows 8. This program does a good job of allowing you to control your computer with your voice. From the speech recognition options you can set up your microphone, take a speech tutorial, train your computer to better understand you, and more.

**Standard toolbar** – A toolbar that is often underneath a Menu bar (in an application window) that contains icons, or pictures, of common commands. Common commands include New, Open, Save, Print, Print Preview, Find, Cut, Copy, Paste, Undo and Date/Time.

**Start screen** – The screen that holds the tiles for apps and applications. This is the starting point in Windows 8.

**Status bar** – A toolbar that often appears at the bottom of an application window and offers information about what you are doing at the moment. If you aren't doing anything, it often offers the helpful words 'For Help, press F1', otherwise it offers information regarding the tool you've selected from a toolbar or information about the task you're performing.

**Sticky Keys** – This setting allows you to configure the keyboard so that you never have to press three keys at once (such as when you must press the CTRL, ALT and DELETE keys together to log on to Windows). With Sticky Keys, you can use one key to perform these tasks. You configure the key to use for three-key tasks.

**Subfolder** – A folder inside another folder.

**Sync** – The process of comparing data in one location with the data in another and performing tasks to match it up. If data has been added or deleted from one device, for instance, synching can also add or delete it from the other.

**System Restore** – If enabled, stores 'restore points' on your PC's hard drive. If something goes wrong you can run System Restore, choose one of these points and revert to a pre-problem date. Since System Restore deals only with 'system data', none of your personal data will be affected (not even your last email).

**System Restore Point** – A snapshot of the computer that Windows 8 keeps in case something happens and you need to revert to it, because of a bad installation or hardware driver.

**Tags** – Data about a particular piece of data, such as a photo or a song or album. Tags can be used to group pictures or music in various ways. Some tags are applied automatically when you import pictures from a digital camera, including the date they were uploaded, along with any name you applied to the imported group. You can also create your own tags.

**Taskbar** – The bar that runs horizontally across the bottom of the Windows 8 desktop and offers the Notification area. It also offers a place to view and access open files, folders and applications.

**Temporary files** – Files created and stored by programs for use by the program. Most of these temporary files are deleted when you exit the program, but some remain.

**Temporary Internet files** – Files that contain copies of web pages you've visited on your hard drive, so that you can view the pages more quickly when visiting them again.

**Text messaging** – Text and instant messaging (IM) require you to type your message and click a Send button. It's similar to email, but it's instantaneous: the recipient gets the message right after you send it. Instant messaging is the term generally reserved for text communications between two or more computers; text messaging is a term generally reserved for communicating between two mobile phones.

**Thumbnails** – Small icons of your pictures, videos and documents.

**Tiles** – Squares and rectangles found in the Windows 8 Start screen. Tiles may offer live information, such as the current weather or the number of unread emails.

**Touch gestures** – Techniques you can use to navigate a touch screen. You can flick up and down, tap, double-tap, and tap and hold, among others.

**URL** – Stands for Uniform Resource Locator and denotes a location on a network, either the Internet or a local network.

**USB** – Universal Serial Bus, a standard for transmitting data between an external device and a computer. There are all kinds of USB devices, including mice, keyboards, flash drives, printers, cameras and backup devices. USB devices are plug-and-play and thus easy to install.

**User profile** – The data associated with a user such as the location of their personal files, wallpaper and screensaver, preferences, password, and so on.

**Video format** – The video file type, such as AVI or WMA.

**Video messaging** – A form of instant messaging where one or both users also offer live video of themselves during the conversation.

**Virus** – A self-replicating program that infects computers with intent to do harm. Viruses often come in the form of an attachment in an email.

**Web browser** – Windows 8 comes with Internet Explorer, an application you can use to explore the Internet. Internet Explorer lets you 'surf the web', and it has everything you need, including a pop-up blocker, zoom settings and accessibility options, as well as tools you can use to save your favourite web pages and set home pages. There are two versions, the Internet Explorer app and the Internet Explorer desktop app.

**Webcam** – A camera that can send live images over the Internet.

**Website** – A group of web pages that contains related information. Microsoft's website contains information about Microsoft products, for instance.

**Window** – When you open a program, document, folder or picture, it opens in a 'window'. Window, as it's used in this context, is synonymous with an open program, file or folder and has nothing to do with the word Windows, used with Windows 8.

**Windows Defender** – You don't have to do much to Windows Defender except understand that it offers protection against Internet threats. It's enabled by default and it runs in the background. However, if you ever think your computer has been attacked by an Internet threat (virus, worm, malware, etc.) you can run a manual scan here.

**Windows Firewall** – If enabled and configured properly, the firewall will help prevent hackers (people whose job it is to get into your computer and do harm to it) from accessing your PC and data. The firewall blocks most programs from communicating outside the network (or outside your PC). If you want to allow a program to communicate outside your safety zone you can 'allow' a program by adding it to an 'exceptions' list. This is all very easy to do.

**Windows Media Center** – An application that allows you to watch, pause and record live television, locate, download and/or listen to music and radio, view, edit and share photos and videos, and play DVDs (among other things). It is not included with Windows 8 but you can purchase it as an add-on.

**Windows Mobility Center** – An application that lets you adjust your mobile PC, tablet PC or laptop computer settings quickly, including things like volume, power and brightness.

**Windows Update** – If enabled and configured properly, when you are online, Windows 8 will check for security updates automatically and install them. You don't have to do anything, and your PC is always updated with the latest security patches and features.

**Worm** – A program that infects computers with intent to do harm. However, unlike a virus, it does not need to attach itself to a running program.

# Troubleshooting guide

## 1. Get to Know Windows 8



## 2. Use apps



## 3. Use Desktop applications



## 4. Manage open apps and applications, and Windows



## 5. Personalising your computer

## 6. Manage files, folders and libraries



## 7. Configure and use Mail



## 8. Surf the web with Internet Explorer



## 9. Play and manage media



## 10. Configure and manage a network

## 11. Secure and troubleshoot Windows 8